LITERARY DORSET

RODNEY LEGG INCLUDES HARDY, BARNES AND POWYSES. BUT THIS LITERARY GUIDE OFFERS MUCH MORE. IT IS AN ENCYCLOPÆDIA OF DORSET AUTHORS — PRESENTED AS AN ABC OF PLACES AND THEIR SPECIAL PEOPLE WHO MADE AN IMPACT UPON THE MIND OF MAN.

LITERARY DORSET

RODNEY LEGG

Dorset Publishing Company dpc
at the WINCANTON PRESS
National School, North Street, Wincanton, Somerset BA9 9AT

To old friends **William Hoade**
(from Wimborne to Woolley and Wallis)
and **Peter Shaw** (Sherborne to publishing Punch)
without whom I would have empty shelves.

Copyright Rodney Legg © 1990

First published 1990,
by the Dorset Publishing Company,
at the Wincanton Press,
National School, North Street,
Wincanton, Somerset BA9 9AT

Typesetting input by Reg Ward,
at Holwell, Dorset, and output
by Wordstream Limited,
St Aldhelm's Road, Poole, Dorset

Printed in Great Britain
by Dotesios Printers Limited
at Kennet Way, Trowbridge, Wiltshire

International standard book number [ISBN] 0 948699 09 4

Note on the layout of entries — encyclopaedic, as an **ABC** of
town and parish placenames and their special associations.
Cross-referencing of the names of authors acts as an integral
index, and there is also listing of secondary placenames
that are covered by other entries.

The text evolved as part of the author's 'Dorset Encyclopaedic Guide'
until the literary entries expanded into their present format and
outgrew the original work. That will still have a strong literary
component, but recast as a potted Dorset 'Who's Who' and merged
with similar alphabetic entries for places, buildings, wildlife and events.

Also by Rodney Legg

Editor *Dorset — the county magazine* [issues 1 to 114, 1968-87]
Purbeck Island [two editions: 1972, 1989]
A Guide to Dorset Ghosts
Ghosts of Dorset, Devon and Somerset
with Mary Collier, Tom Perrott
Afterword, *Coker's Survey of Dorsetshire* [for the
1980 second edition of the 1732 work]
Editor *Steep Holm — a case history in the study of ecology*
Annotator *Monumenta Britannica* with John Fowles [first
edition as two volumes 1980, 1982: volume one re-issued
as an expanded first American edition, 1981]
Exploring Ancient Wiltshire with George Osborn
Old Portland with Jean M. Edwards
Romans in Britain
Purbeck Walks [three editions: 1983, 1985, 1988]
Old Swanage
The Dorset Walk with Ron Dacombe, Colin Graham
Stonehenge Antiquaries
Guide to Purbeck Coast and Shipwreck
Hardy Country Walks
The Steep Holm Guide
Lulworth and Tyneham Revisited
Walks in West Dorset
The Blandford Forum Guide
Cerne's Giant and Village Guide
Dorset's War 1939-45
East Dorset Country Walks
Blackmore Vale and Cranborne Chase Walks
Exploring the Heartland of Purbeck
Brownsea — Dorset's Fantasy Island
Purbeck's Heath — nature, claypits and the oilfield
Wincanton's Directory [annually 1987-90]
Mysterious Dorset
Walks in Dorset's Hardy Country
National Trust Dorset with Colin Graham
Lawrence of Arabia in Dorset
Steep Holm Wildlife with Tony Parsons
Dorset Encyclopaedic Guide
Dorset at War — Diary of WW2

Kenneth Allsop [1920-73] at his Milton Mill home,
in the deep-cut valley west of Powerstock.
'I am happiest here in the intricate and moody
countryside of South Wessex,' he wrote in his
last book, 'In the Country'. See page 131

OPPOSITE
Came Rectory, beside the Wareham road a mile out of
Dorchester, was the last home of Dorset poet William
Barnes. He was the rector of Winterborne Came for
twenty-four contemplative years. Among his visitors
was the curate and diarist Francis Kilvert [1840-79],
seeking out 'the great idyllic Poet of England'.
See pages 184-189

Barnes's Orchard was on the east side of the droveway
across Bagber Common, north-west of Sturminster Newton.
Here is the site of the suitably humble cottage birthplace
of Dorset poet, philologist, schoolmaster, scholar and
rector William Barnes [1801-86]. His old home was pulled
down circa 1850. See page 152

'Barnes Poems' says the title on the spine of the book
in the hands of master scholar William Barnes, patriarch
of learned Dorset, painted by G. Stuckey. Barnes's formative
years were at Sturminster Newton and his Academy
was in Dorchester. See pages 89-90 and 152-153

The Celtic cross above the grave of Dorset poet William
Barnes beside his church at Winterborne Came, south-east
of Dorchester: 'For 24 years Rector of this Parish.'
See page 185

The literary landscape of Sturminster Newton. The ridge
at the western side of the town overlooks the River Stour,
crossed by Colber Bridge which carries the footpath from
William Barnes's home-hamlet of Bagber Common. On the
hill itself, dialect songster Robert Young [1811-1908] lived
in The Hive (centre) and in 1877 Thomas Hardy wrote
'The Return of the Native' in Riverside Villas (sitting
in the visible upper window of the house on the right).
See pages 152-155

OPPOSITE
William Barnes, standing beside the porch of St Peter's
church in High West Street, Dorchester. The life-size
bronze statue was unveiled in 1889.
Some young person has given him a bobble-hat (likewise
Thomas Hardy, at Top-o'-Town, never looks more natural
than when reading 'The Sun'). See page 90

CHRESTOLEROS.

Seuen bookes of

Epigrames written by T B.

Hunc nouere modum noſtri ſeruare libelli,
Parcere perſonis: dicere de vitiis.

Imprinted at London by Richard
Bradocke for I. B. and are to be ſold at
her ſhop in Paules Church-yarde at the
ſigne of the Bible. 1 5 9 8.

Title-page to the epigrams of Blandford-born
Thomas Bastard [1566-1618]. 'Much guilty of
the vices belonging to the poets' he went from
Oxford to the Church and became vicar of Bere
Regis in 1593. There he became deranged, bemoaning an
intolerable marriage and was thrown into Dorchester
prison, dying 'obscurely and in a mean condition'.
See page 54

OPPOSITE
Robert Boyle [1627-91] of Stalbridge Park constantly
broke new ground in a succession of titles that
established several of the basic rules of science.
'Boyle's Law' was the discovery that the volume of a
gas varies inversely as its pressure. See pages 141-143

The Hon:ble: Robert Boyle.

London Printed for Tho: Cockerill at ye 3 Legas in ye Poultry.

The key diagram in Robert Boyle's 'New Experiments and Observations Touching Cold' which was published in the Plague year of 1665 and contains the first description of a graduated thermometer. Boyle termed it a thermoscope. He knew that cold prevented the decomposition of animal tissues and therefore was a means of preserving meat. **See page 142**

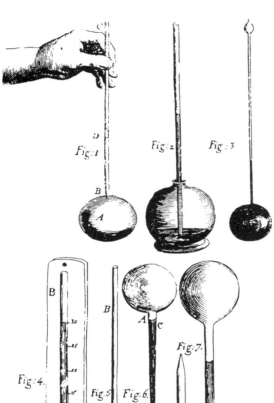

Figure 1. *Page* 9, 10, 11, & 98.
A the Ball or Egg.
B C the Stem.
D the little Aqueous Cylinder.

Figure 2. the open Weather-glaſs mentioned *pag*. 24, & 43.

Figure 3. the ſeal'd Weather-glaſs or Thermoſcope mentioned *pag*. 24, 55, 56.

Figure 4. the Barometer or Mercurial Standard placed in a Frame B B mentioned *pag*. 25.

Figure 5. an Inſtrument mentioned *pag*. 93.
A the Vial.
B C the Pipe cemented into the neck of the Vial, open at C and ſeal'd at B.

Figure 6. *pag*. 97.
A the Bolt-head.
B the ſmall Stem,
B C the Cylinder of water encloſ'd.

Figure 7. *pag*. 101.

RODNEY LEGG COLLECTION

Cumberland Clark [died 1941] wrote his own exit line:
'Down in our Air-Raid Shelter
we'll be cosy, you and I.'
He was killed when the Luftwaffe bombed Bournemouth
Square. Clark was a superlatively bad poet whose
output was monumental. See page 66

Ego, non sum Ego.

GENEROSI ÆTATIS Suæ 25 VERA ET VIUA EFFIGIES IOHANIS CLAUEL

That I may neither beare anothers blame
Through wronge suspicions nor yet act ye same
At any time hereafter, but prove true
Loe to be knowne yow haue my face at viewe

GERALD NORRIS

Gentleman poet John Clavell [1603-42] was a highwayman.
The nephew of Sir William Clavell of Kimmeridge, he was
sentenced to hang, but wrote his way out of trouble
with verses that won a royal pardon from Charles I.
See page 107

OPPOSITE
Baron Corvo was the name given to himself by Frederick
Rolfe [1860-1913], before he claimed to be a reincarnated
mediaeval Pope. His masterpiece, 'Hadrian the Seventh'
portrayed him in that role. He had been befriended at
Christchurch by Gleeson White, who would be the first
to recognise the talent of Aubrey Beardsley. See pages 82-83

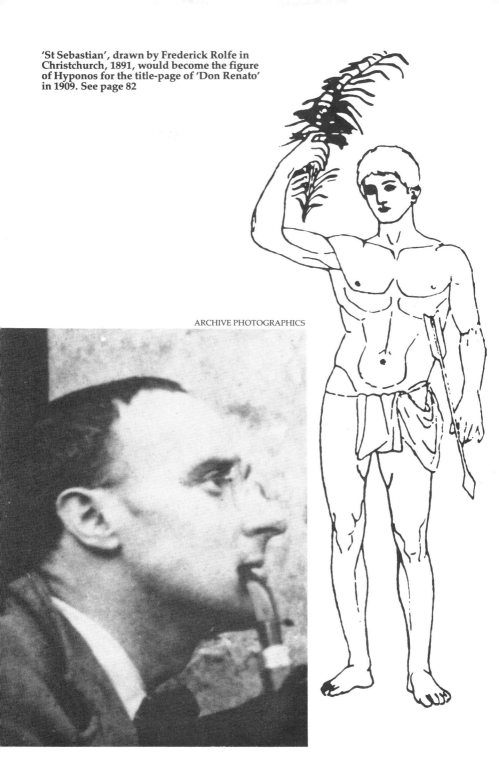

'St Sebastian', drawn by Frederick Rolfe in Christchurch, 1891, would become the figure of Hyponos for the title-page of 'Don Renato' in 1909. See page 82

ARCHIVE PHOTOGRAPHICS

Charles Dickens [1812-70] came to Sherborne to
read from his novel 'A Christmas Carol' in 1846.
His closest friend, top character actor William
Macready [1793-1873], lived at Sherborne House,
in Newland, which became Lord Digby's School in 1931.
See pages 137-139

Continued on page 3

'Wulf the Briton' was the creation of the comic
strip artist Ron Embleton [1930-87] of Bournemouth,
whose output ranged from cowboys to Biggles and went
on into outer space and the permissive society, with
'Wicked Wanda' — his sex-satire for Penthouse. See page 67

Henry Fielding [1705-54], the father of the English
novel, wrote 'Tom Jones, or the History of a
Foundling' at East Stour. Others have claimed it
was written at Twerton, near Bath, but Fielding
describes it as the 'labour of some years of my life'
which puts it firmly into his Dorset period. Copies
were delivered to the shops at breakfast-time and sold
out by teatime. It was the hottest literary product
in Europe, with translators producing editions from
Madrid to Moscow. See pages 96-97

OPPOSITE

John Fowles [born 1926] at Belmont House, Lyme Regis,
with a smuggler's weight. He advanced the literary
arts with 'The French Lieutenant's Woman', which is
Hardyesque in itself and has the distinction of being
the first Dorset novel to upstage the works of Thomas
Hardy, by extending the story-telling craft. See page 116

Francis Glisson [1597-1677] of Rampisham was the
first person in Britain to observe and describe
the symptoms of rickets and scurvy. His book
about these diseases is regarded as Britain's
first medical textbook. See page 133

OPPOSITE
Title-page of the English edition of Francis Glisson's
'Treatise of the Rickets' which appeared in 1651 and
was the first study of a disease to be published
in Britain. He had observed the bow-legged county
children of west Dorset and pointed to 'some errors
in the point of the diet' as the cause of the disorders.
See page 133

A Treatise of the
RICKETS:
Being a Diseas common
to CHILDREN.

Wherein (among many other things) is
shewed,

1. *The Essence*
2. *The Causes*
3. *The Signs* } *of the Diseas.*
4. *The Remedies*

Published
in Latin by } *Francis Glisson,*
George, Bate,
And
Ahasuerus Regemorter;

Doctors in Physick, and Fellows of the
Colledg of Physitians at *London.*

Translated into English by *Phil. Armin.*

LONDON:
Printed by *Peter Cole*, at the sign of the
Printing-Press, in Cornhil, near the
Royal Exchange. 1651.

Lady Charlotte Guest [1812-95] of Canford Manor
translated the Welsh 'Mabigonion' and provided
her friend Alfred Tennyson with the Arthurian
legends for his 'Idylls of the King'. Her
lasting contribution to English culture was to
have free newspapers delivered daily to London
taxi-drivers, with the result that every cabbie
is a philosopher. See page 123

Thomas Hardy

RODNEY LEGG

Built by Thomas Hardy's grandfather in 1801, Hardy's Cottage is at the end of Cherry Lane, Higher Bockhampton. It was the birthplace of the novelist and poet Thomas Hardy [1840-1928] and is preserved in his memory by the National Trust. See page 145

HARDY'S BIRTHPLACE

is a National Trust property, with its tenants acting as custodians [telephone appointments: Dorchester (0305) 62366] but the Trust asks us to point out that it is a home rather than a museum and there cannot be public access to all rooms. This plan, compiled with help from Anna Winchcombe, shows the cottage as it was in the novelist's youth. Most of the changes have been at the south end (this half of the page). North is at the *bottom*, where the brick wall stands beside the lane.

GROUND FLOOR

© Rodney Legg
1984, with
widths of walls
and windows
corrected
against Roger
W. Evans's
plan of 1964

UPPER FLOOR

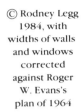

Gran's Room

ladder

Hardy's Room
where
Under the Greenwood Tree
was written

window seat
with view
to the
Admiral
Hardy
Monument

Parents' Room
where Hardy
was conceived
and born

stairs

The Girls' Room

RODNEY LEGG

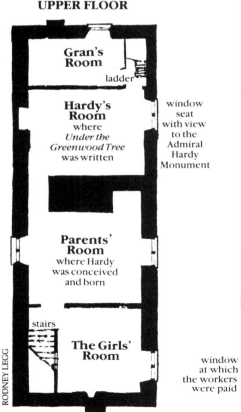

Wash Room

the copper

pump

letter box

Back Porch

Lobby

Larder

ladder

Kitchen

bread-oven

Porch

ingle-nook fireplace

squint window
where Grand-
father Hardy is
said to have
watched for
Excisemen
coming to
search for
smuggled
spirits

Living Room

window
at which
the workers
were paid

stairs

Father's Office

Scale: $1^3/_{16}$ inch = 10 fe
(The cottage is 62 feet lon

north
↓

Hardy's Cottage, Higher Bockhampton, Stinsford:
the middle bedroom upstairs in which Hardy was born
[2 June 1840]. His parents' room is furnished
from Kingston Lacy House. See page 145

Hardy's Cottage, Higher Bockhampton: Thomas Hardy's
bedroom, where 'Under the Greenwood Tree' was
written, is the southern upstairs room. Its present
furniture is from Kingston Lacy House. See page 145

RODNEY LEGG COLLECTION

Thomas Hardy at twenty-one [1861].

OPPOSITE
Last lines of Thomas Hardy's letter of 5 July 1897 to William Isbister, publisher of the magazine Good Words. He had sold the first serial rights of 'The Trumpet Major' for £400, and requested the services of a skilful artist 'not above accepting from me rough sketches of any unusual objects that come into the tale'. The closing words are about the summer weather. 'Hail and hurricanes are the rule here, & we are thinking of beginning fires again.' See page 90

North Cottage, Riverside Villas, Sturminster Newton (left) was the first home of Thomas Hardy and his first wife Emma [1876-78] and the house where 'The Return of the Native' was written. North Cottage was their home − not the adjoining South Cottage (right) which was provided with the Hardy plaque thanks to Olive Knott's misinformation. See pages 153-154

COLIN GRAHAM

I trust that there will be a few days at least of summer weather before you return. Hail & hurricanes are the rule here, & we are thinking of beginning fires again. Believe me

Yours very truly

Thomas Hardy.

Thomas Hardy at thirty-two [1872].

OPPOSITE
Hardy's inscription in his presentation copy of 'Wessex Poems'
to Algernon Charles Swinburne [1837-1909] at Christmas 1898.
They regarded themselves, in Hardy's words, as 'the two most
abused of living writers' — Swinburne for 'Poems and Ballads'
and Hardy for 'Jude the Obscure'. See page 92

Thomas Hardy at forty [1880].

To
   Algernon Charles Swinburne.
whose genius has for more than thirty years
         been the charm of
                  Thomas Hardy.

Dec. 1898.

OPPOSITE
'Hay-trussing — ?' said the turnip hoer, who
had already begun shaking his head. "O no".'
This drawing by Robert Barnes fronted the
serialisation of 'The Mayor of Casterbridge'
by Thomas Hardy in the Graphic magazine on
2 January 1866. See pages 91-93 and 143-144

ANGLO-AMALGAMATED FILM DISTRIBUTORS

Julie Christie as Bathsheba Everdene and Terence
Stamp as Sergeant Troy on Weymouth sands in 1966
for John Schlesinger's film of Thomas Hardy's
novel 'Far from the Madding Crowd'. See page 177

OPPOSITE
John Collier illustrated Thomas Hardy's novel
'The Trumpet Major' for the magazine Good Words [1880].
Here the heroine, Anne Garland, finds that the
'quadrangle of the ancient pile was a bed of mud
and manure'. See page 90

One of John Collier's full-page illustrations
for the serialisation of 'The Trumpet Major' in
Good Words [1880]. King George III and his court
are in Weymouth for the waters. Festus Derriman leans
out of a window as Anne Garland approaches: 'Before her
she saw a flower lying — a crimson sweet-william — fresh
and uninjured.' See page 90.

Foreword

"Is it so important if Thomas Hardy had something to do with a place?" The question was put to me by Timothy Eden, at eleven, as we walked through a beech avenue at Tarrant Gunville on a windy summer's day. I don't know why it had occurred to him to ask. There was no compelling Hardy association to hand.

Had there been, it would not have added to the visual landscape values; yet for somewhere to have once been the workshop of a major novelist of the English-speaking world does add that extra sparkle to one's perceptions and expectations.

Twentieth century Dorset is the Hardy Country though the only hoardings that demarcated the Wessex of my youth, beside the pre-motorway arterial roads, told us "You are entering the Strong Country" and were erected for a brewery rather than an author.

London on the other hand was obviously a mind factory, with blue plaques everywhere, including Hardy's at 16 Westbourne Park Villas, but then it was always in the business of creating great people. With time, and some surprise, I came to realise that my home town of Bournemouth was also saturated with literary associations, many of which are still a closed book to me, excepting Robert Louis Stevenson who was not only *Treasure Island* but *Kidnapped,* a comic-strip version of which I still half-know by heart. I have tried here to search them out, expanding my reading list by finding that Phyllis Bottome fancied the St Peter's curates, as indeed had Paul Verlaine. Unlike Radclyffe Hall, who would have shown no interest whatever.

There is something sleazy in seeking the spirits of people who lived in towns. There are always too many eyes and it is usually depressingly physical, down to the mess on the pavements. It is in the open countryside that book people can have their freedom. Purbeck's quarrylands are Eric Benfield, Lulworth Cove is John Keats almost at peace for his last hours in England. East Chaldon is Beth Car for T.F. Powys, the Sailor's Return for David Garnett, and the churchyard for Sylvia Townsend Warner together for ever with Valentine Ackland and 1066 scholar Hope Muntz.

Things are even more confusing as one nears Dorchester. Came Rectory and all within walking distance is William Barnes. Dorchester Prison is Richard Carlile. Hardy is spread everywhere, but congeals in the County Town from an omnipotent presence into a physical reality so formidable that the Dorchester branch of Barclay's Bank is Michael Henchard's house with a blue plaque to prove it. I try here to tie the great man down to a representative selection of locales but I shall inevitably fail to find everyone's special spot that is Hardy.

There are other more transient greats. Racedown, above Lyme Regis, is Wordsworth, though to others he is daffodils — to me he is the moody waters of the Shambles off Portland Bill which claimed his brother, John Wordsworth, commanding the *Abergavenny* in 1805, which being the year of Nelson's victorious death led to William commemorating the pair in his *Happy Warrior.*

Blandford Camp is Rupert Brooke for the words that are those of all Englishmen who fulfilled their vow to king and country in another land. Latter-day heroes include one from whom I learnt about the late war in Europe. Sydling St Nicholas is George Millar.

Here and there I can claim a personal friend. West Milton and Eggardon

Hill are Kenneth Allsop. Belmont House is John Fowles though he has to share Lyme's literary gloss with Jane Austen.

I find it easier to come to terms with those whose writings were for science. Robert Boyle is Stalbridge and Boyle's Law. Broadstone cemetery is a fossil tree-trunk to Alfred Russel Wallace who so nearly eclipsed Darwin. The latter did manage a Bournemouth holiday; Bournemouth International Centre is on its site.

I delight in many of those who have been introduced to me by the Dorset connection, but it is untenable, unfortunately, to claim that magnificent landscapes produce great writers — human experience rather than environment is necessary to put depth into words. Repression and confinement heighten their quality, as Picasso observed when he noted that Russians write at their best when they are in prison.

What Dorset produces, unrepresented here, is a steady summertime flow of quasi-religious thanksgiving poetry that celebrates scenic exhilaration. All Dorset editors reject it by the day, though some finds ultimate expression through vanity publishing, and the sad weakness of this output is that thank you letters to our maker have as much to do with literature as the mushy verses from Christmas cards are able to stand comparison with the ringing words of the King James Bible.

I make no excuse for including Thomas J. Clarke as a Portlander — albeit compulsorily — whose name in print may have done little for literature but who was to literally lay his life on the line and tear the island of Ireland apart cartographically, politically and in blood. Nearby, Portland Museum was Marie Stopes's gift to the Dorset island she loved but there on my first visit, at fourteen, I found nothing to tell us that she had given the world birth control. Likewise at school I was given a Dorset history book that had no mention of the Tolpuddle Martyrs.

None of which has answered Timothy's question. If knowing of Hardy contributes anything it is to add a strand to English culture, as Sir Edward Elgar's music does to the concept of the countryside around the Malvern Hills. It is an attempt to ingrain an appreciation of people who led the nation's thought processes from the front — with the opprobrium that this so often entails — into our perceptions of the face of Britain. The process is educational, in the best possible way, if we come to understand something of what participants from our own communities have done to shape the mind of man.

R.L.

DORSET GENERAL

Dorset folksong: *The Noble Pirate.*

A county's literary heritage is bound to be dominated by the literati. It will be here, but to offset some of the diversions into higher learning I have chosen a folksong, heard in west Dorset, which brings a ripple of past nautical perils down into the late twentieth century, as an example of the people's words, before moving on to the men of letters.

It has been reassembled from two fragmentary versions. The Barbary Coast was the term given to Barbarossa's string of pirate states along the seaboard of North Africa — from Casablanca to Benghazi — which sprang up around 1518. I record it here out of the excitement I had in realising I was listening to words that had been passed down in these valleys for four hundred and fifty years beyond the time when "New Barbary" had meaning for its audience. Moments like this are one's roots.

> *It was of two noble ships, from England did set sail*
> *One's name was* Prince of Lewis, *and tother* Prince of Wales
> *Blow high, blow low, and so sailed we*
> *Cruising down the coast of New Barbary.*
>
> *"Look ahead, look astarn, look a-weather, look a-lee"*
> *Blow high, blow low, and so sailed we*
> *O weather look-out man, "A lofty sail" said he*
> *Cruising down the coast of New Barbary.*
>
> *"O hail her, O hail her," our noble captain cried*
> *Blow high, blow low, and so sailed we*
> *"Are you a man o' war or a privateer you be"*
> *Cruising down the coast of New Barbary.*
>
> *"I am no man o' war, nor a privateer I be"*
> *Blow high, blow low, and so sailed we*
> *"But I am a noble pirate a cruising on the sea"*
> *Cruising down the coast of New Barbary.*
>
> *"Then it's quarters for quarters," our noble captain cried*
> *Blow high, blow low, and so sailed we*
> *And the quarters that we showed to them, we sank them in the sea*
> *Cruising down the coast of New Barbary.*
>
> *So now this noble pirate is coming to an end*
> *Blow high, blow low, and so sailed we*
> *With the ship she was their coffin, their grave it was the sea*
> *Sunk down on the coast of New Barbary.*

DORSET GENERAL and particularly STINSFORD and DORCHESTER

Hardy placenames: a Checklist.

Before embarking on cataloguing the literary associations of individual Dorset parishes it seems sensible to attempt a glossary of the placenames in the works of Thomas Hardy, given that these spread not only across Dorset but beyond. It is the thing to which some readers of the book are likely to refer many times. Some are my own discoveries, like finding Wherry Cottage at Winterbourne Abbas, to clinch the identification of "Wherryborne", and coming across the Devil's Den cromlech in the middle of a Wiltshire valley, and with many others I offer variations on conventional wisdom after combining the scanning of post code directories with renewed bouts of country walking. All I can promise is that it differs from the lists others have compiled, and for me, at least, is much more convincing.

Given their geographical spread, I have put county names throughout — even for Dorset locations — and in line with the general format of this book I have ensured that the penultimate Dorset placename (for example, Stinsford) is the name of the parish concerned. I'll even give the postcodes of some of the Dorset buildings; they add a whole new dimension to the game. It is one where readers, particularly those who walk in the Dorset countryside, can frequently outwit the scholars — but beware, they will squeal to the defence of the most untenable book-theories and stick with implausibility to the end!

Abbey, north of Blackmore = Sherborne Abbey, Dorset.
Abbey, south of Blackmore = Milton Abbey, Milton Abbas, Dorset.
Abbot's Cernel = Cerne Abbas, Dorset.
Abbotsea = Abbotsbury, Dorset
Aldbrickham = Reading, Berkshire.
Alderworth = Alderley, Briantspuddle, in Affpuddle parish, Dorset DT2 7HR.
Alfredston = Wantage, Berkshire.
Ancient West Highway = Roman road west of Winterbourne Abbas, Dorset (north of the present A35) to Eggardon Hill and from there on an uncertain course towards Exeter, Devon.
Anglebury = Wareham, Dorset.
Anglebury Heath = Northport Heath, now southern part of Wareham Forest, and Great Ovens Hill, Wareham St Martin parish, Dorset.
Arrowthorne Lodge = Minstead Lodge, New Forest, Hampshire (the "arrow" connection being that King William II was assassinated a mile and a half to the north-west, at what became Rufus Stone, between Minstead and Blackthorn Copse).
Aquae Sulis = itself, being the Roman name for Bath, Avon.
Athelhall = Athelhampton Hall, Athelhampton, Dorset DT2 7LG.
Badger's Clump = possibly near Chydyok Farm, a mile south of East Chaldon, Chaldon Herring, Dorset, on a coastal smuggling route.
Bank Walk = itself, westward, beside the north arm of the river, from Lower Bockhampton bridge to Stinsford, Dorset.
Barnes's Lane = itself, now a bridleway on the parish boundary of Buckland Newton with Alton Pancras, Dorset (nearly two miles long, north of Holcombe Dairy).
Barrow Beacon = composite of Beacon Hill, Puddletown, with the Rainbarrows, Duddle Heath, Puddletown, Dorset.
Barwith Strand = Trebarwith Strand, near Tintagel, Cornwall.
Batten Castle = Lulworth Castle, East Lulworth, Dorset.
Beal Lantern = Portland Bill Lighthouse, Dorset, but the one that is now the Bird Observatory rather than the 1905-built present tower. "The Beell" is the name of the island's southern tip on the 1710 map in John Hutchins's County History.
Bede's Inn = Clement's Inn, London WC2.
Beersheba = Jericho district of inner-city Oxford.
Belvidere Hotel = itself, Belvidere Private Hotel, now known as the Sands

Hotel, 117-118 Esplanade, Weymouth, Dorset DT4 7EL.

Benvill Lane = itself, Benville Lane, Corscombe, Dorset DT2 0NW and DT2 0NN.

Biblioll College = Balliol College, Oxford.

Birthplace = Hardy's Cottage, Cherry Lane (formerly Veterans' Alley), Higher Bockhampton, Stinsford, Dorset DT2 8QJ.

Black Bull Hotel = Bull Hotel, 34 East Street, Bridport, Dorset DT6 3LF.

Blackmoor = itself, though it is now spelt Blackmore Vale, Dorset.

Black'on = itself, Black Down, Portesham, Dorset (on which stands Admiral Hardy's Monument).

Blooms-End = Bhompston Farm, between Lower Bockhampton and Norris Mill, Stinsford, Dorset DT2 8QN.

Bramshurst Manor = Moyles Court, Ellingham, Ringwood, Hampshire.

Bredy Knap = itself, on the A35 above Long Bredy, Dorset.

Broad Sidlinch = Sydling St Nicholas, Dorset.

Brown House = Red House, between Fawley and Wantage, Oxfordshire.

Bubb-Down Hill = itself, Bubb Down Hill, Melbury Bubb, Dorset.

Buckbury Fitzpiers = Okeford Fitzpaine, Dorset (renamed *Oakbury Fitzpiers* for the later novels).

Budmouth = Weymouth, Dorset.

Budmouth Regis = Melcombe Regis, Weymouth, Dorset.

Bulbarrow = itself, Bulbarrow Hill, above Stoke Wake and Woolland, Dorset.

Bull Stake Square = itself, though it has since become known as the North Square, Dorchester, Dorset.

Camelton = Camelford, Cornwall.

Cardinal College = Christ Church College, Oxford.

Cardinal Street = St Aldate's Street, Oxford.

Carriford = West Stafford, Dorset.

Carriford Road = Crossways, at the junction of the parishes of Owermoigne, Woodsford and Moreton, Dorset.

Carriford Road Station = Moreton Station, Dorset (I do not go along with Hermann Lea's dismissal of the "Carriford" placenames as "imaginary creations" because in 1964 I was directed to "the Crossways Road Station" from West Stafford, and it happens to be the only railway station in these parts that was built to serve a road rather than a community).

Casterbridge = Dorchester, Dorset.

Castle Boterel = Boscastle, Cornwall.

Castle Inn = itself, 7 Middle Street, Yeovil, Somerset (demolished in the 1920s).

Castle Royal = Windsor Castle, Berkshire.

Catknoll Street = Chetnole, Dorset.

Chalk Newton = Maiden Newton, Dorset.

Chalk Walk = Colliton Walk, Top o' Town, Dorchester, Dorset.

Charmley = Charminster, Dorset.

Chaseborough = Cranborne, Dorset.

Chasetown = alternative for Cranborne, Dorset.

Chateau Ringdale = house at Allington, Bridport, relocated to Harbour Road, West Bay, Bridport, Dorset.

Chene Manor = Canford Manor, Poole, Dorset (so named because Lady Wimborne's Drive led from Canford Manor, Canford Magna, down to Branksome Dene Chine on the coast at Westbourne).

Chief Street = High Street, Oxford.

Chillington Wood = Killerton Gardens, the grounds of Killerton House, Broadclyst, near Exeter, Devon (where Fred Pitfield has found the summer house, specimen trees and a whole setting that Hardy detailed). I think Hardy borrowed the name from the real Chillington Wood, on the slopes leading up to Windwhistle Inn between Crewkerne and Chard, Somerset (which Hardy certainly knew as he has a footnote to "A Tramp-Woman's Tragedy" saying that when he asked for tea at the Windwhistle Inn he was told he would have to walk back down the hill to fetch the water).

Christminster = Oxford.

Church "with the Italian porch" = St Mary the Virgin, Oxford.

Cirque of the Gladiators= Maumbury Rings, Dorchester, Dorset.

Clammers Gate = itself, being the gate at the south end of Melbury Osmond, Dorset, leading into Melbury Park.

Classical Mansion = Wilton House, Wiltshire.

Clavinium = the "Clavino" of the Ravenna Cosmography, a placename of Roman west Dorset, which Hardy applied to the probable Roman temple found on Jordan Hill, Weymouth.

Clyffe-Hill Clump= Pallington Clump, above Clyffe House, Tincleton, Dorset (but in Affpuddle parish at Ordnance Survey map reference SY 787 922, growing on a Bronze Age burial mound).

Cloton = in the Dorset-Somerset borderlands westwards of Corscombe; perhaps Chedington or Clapton.

Cliff Martin= Combe Martin, Devon.

Cliff "without a name" = Beeny Cliff, Boscastle, Cornwall.

Coomb-Barn = barn south of Puddletown, Dorset.

Coomb-Ewelease = sheep pasture on White Hill, Puddletown, Dorset.

Corvsgate = Corfe Castle village, Dorset, using one of the names from the Middle Ages for this gap in the Purbeck Hills.

Corvsgate Castle = Corfe Castle itself, Dorset.

Cresscombe = Letcombe Bassett, near Wantage, Oxfordshire.

Creston = Preston, Dorset.

Crimmercrock Lane = Cromlech Crock Lane, as it then was on the Ordnance Survey map, sheet XVIII, running up out of Maiden Newton and across Rampisham Down, Dorset (now A356).

Crossy Hand = Cross and Hand (roadside stone), Batcombe, Dorset.

Crozier College = Oriel College, Oxford.

Crozier Hotel = Mitre Hotel, Oxford.

Cuckoo Lane = itself, being the lane northward past Higher Bockhampton from Stinsford Cross, Dorset.

Deadman's Bay = Lyme Bay, Dorset, and in particular the inner curve at Chesil Cove, Portland, which was notorious for shipwrecks.

Deansleigh Park = Broadlands, Romsey, Hampshire.

Devil's Bellows = Culpepper's Dish, Affpuddle, Dorset (though I have seen it identified as "a knoll" on Egdon Heath; Hardy's etymological knowledge was such that he would have used bellows for a "bag" in the landscape).

Devil's Door = Devil's Den, Clatford Bottom, Fyfield, near Marlborough, Wiltshire (described by Hardy as a trilithon on the Marlborough Downs, as it was depicted by William Stukeley in 1723, though the capstone of the burial chamber is in fact supported by four sarsen base stones and one of these now has a concrete buttress, dated 1921).

Devil's Kitchen = itself, half a mile north-west of Dogbury Gate, Minterne Magna, Dorset, in the trees at the foot of High Stoy.

Dole Hill = itself, Dole's Hill, Piddlehinton, Dorset.

Dorchester 43 = Thomas Hardy's telephone number at Max Gate, which he started to give his friends in 1920 at the age of eighty and thoroughly enjoyed their calls (the instrument had been in the house for years but he had refused to use it).

Downstaple = Barnstaple, Devon.

Duke's Arms = Grosvenor Arms, Shaftesbury, Dorset (Grosvenor being the family name of the Duke of Westminster).

Dundagel = Tintagel, Cornwall.

Durnover = Fordington, Dorchester, Dorset.

Durnover Great Field = Fordington Field, Dorchester, Dorset.

Durnover Green = Fordington Green, Dorchester, Dorset.

Durnover Hill = Fordington Hill, Dorchester, Dorset.

Durnover Hole = weir-pool on the River Frome downstream from Grey's Bridge, Fordington, Dorchester, Dorset.

Durnover Lea = water-meadows beside the River Frome at Fordington, Dorchester, Dorset.

Durnover Mill = East Mills, Mill Street, Fordington, Dorchester, Dorset.

Durnover Moor = the broader expanse of water-meadows beyond the north bank of the River Frome, opposite Fordington, Dorchester, Dorset, but actually in the parish of Stinsford.

Earl of Wessex = Digby Tap, Cooks Lane, Sherborne, Dorset DT9 3NS (though the Digbys were actually the Earls of Bristol).

East Egdon = Affpuddle parish, Dorset (which includes the hamlets of Briantspuddle and Throop, though the present "model" village at Briantspuddle dates from the 1920s).

East Endelstow = Lesnewth, near Boscastle, Cornwall.

East Mellstock = Lower Bockhampton, Stinsford, Dorset.

East Quarriers = Grove Cliff group of quarries on Portland, Dorset (namely France, High Headlands, Broadcroft, Yeolands and Silklake Quarries).

Eastern village = Easton, Portland, Dorset.

Egdon Heath = the south Dorset heath stretching from Hardy's birthplace to Poole (in particular the part from Stinsford to Turners Puddle).

Eggar = Eggardon Hill, Askerswell, Dorset.

Elm Cranlynch = Corfe Mullen, Dorset. In the Middle ages the manor was owned by the Phelips family of Montacute House, near Yeovil, with which Elm Cranlynch has been misidentified. Fred Pitfield, in *Hardy's Wessex Locations*, points out that the novelist describes what can only be the Jacobean Court House in the Stour valley which, with Pamphill on the other side of the river, used to have the tallest elms in Dorset.

Elsenford = Ilsington, Puddletown, Dorset DT2 8QW (on the Tincleton boundary and not to be confused with Ilsington House in Puddletown village, DT2 8TQ).

Emminster = Beaminster, Dorset.

Endelstow = St Juliot, near Boscastle, Cornwall.

Endelstow House = house in the valley of the River Valency, near Boscastle, Cornwall.

Endelstow Vicarage = St Juliot Rectory, near Boscastle, Cornwall.

Enkworth Court = Encombe House, west of Worth Matravers on the Purbeck coast, Dorset.

Evershead = Evershot, Dorset.

Exonbury = Exeter, Devon.

Falcon Hotel = White Hart Hotel, Launceston, Cornwall.

Falls Park = Mells Park, near Frome, Somerset.

Fane, The = Temple-style summer house beside the lake, Kingston Maurward, Stinsford, Dorset.

Farnfield = Farnborough, Hampshire.

Fensworth = a village near Fawley, Berkshire.

Fernell Hall = Embley House (Embley Park School) near Romsey, Hampshire.

Field of the tombs = Cemetery, Weymouth Avenue, Dorchester, Dorset.

Flintcomb Ash = Barcombe Farm, Alton Pancras, Dorset DT2 7RT (there is also an actual Flintcomb at Alton Pancras; DT2 7RS).

Flower-de-Luce Inn = Fleur-de-Lis public house, Cranborne, Dorset.

Flychett = Lytchett Minster, Dorset.

Forest of the White Hart = King Stag, Lydlinch, Dorset (the hamlet of King Stag now has a White Hart Close).

Forum = Blandford Forum, Dorset.

Fountall = Wells, Somerset.

Fourways = Carfax, Oxford (itself a corruption of the French for crossroads).

Froom Everard = Stafford House, West Stafford, Dorset DT2 8AA.

Froom River = River Frome, Dorset (it being pronounced as Hardy wrote it).

Froom Side Vale = valley of the River Frome, Dorset.

Gaymead = Shinfield, near Reading, Berkshire.

Giant's Town = Hugh Town, St Mary's, Isles of Scilly.

Glaston = itself, being the milestone contraction for Glastonbury, Somerset.

Gloucester Lodge = Gloucester Hotel, Gloucester Row, 85 The Esplanade, Weymouth, Dorset DT4 7AU.

Great Forest = New Forest, Hampshire.

Great Grey Plain = Salisbury Plain, Wiltshire.

Great Hintock = Minterne Magna, Dorset.

Great Hintock House = Minterne House, Minterne Magna, Dorset DT2 7AU.

Great Mid-Wessex Plain = Salisbury Plain, Wiltshire.

Great Plain = ditto, Salisbury Plain, Wiltshire.

Great Pool = weir on the River Frome, Woodsford, Dorset.

Greenhill = Woodbury Hill, Bere Regis, Dorset.

Greenhill Fair = Woodbury Hill Fair, Bere Regis, Dorset.

Grey's Bridge = itself, Grey's Bridge being "the second bridge of stone" over the main-stream of the River Frome on the turnpike road east of Dorchester, Dorset

Grey's Wood = itself, Grey's Wood, Higher Kingston, Stinsford, Dorset.

Haggardon Hill = Eggardon Hill, Askerswell, Dorset.

Hangman's cottage = itself, Hangman's Cottage, Glydepath Road, Dorchester, Dorset DT1 1XE.

Havenpool = Poole, Dorset.

Heedless William's Pond = itself, on the south side of Duddle Heath at the parish boundary of Stinsford with Puddletown, Dorset.

Henry the Eighth's Castle = Sandsfoot Castle, Weymouth, Dorset.

High Place Hall = Colliton House, Glyde Path Road, Dorchester, Dorset.

Higher Crowstairs = Waterston Ridge, which is the lip of the downs between the Frome and Piddle valleys at the northern extremity of Stinsford parish (Ordnance Survey map reference SY 717 943).

Hintock House = Turnworth House, Turnworth, Dorset (demolished about 1960).

Hintocks = countryside around Minterne Magna, Melbury Osmond and Hermitage on the northern lip of the Dorset Downs (since being given reality by the Post Office/British Telecom adopting "Hintock" as the name for a telephone exchange).

Hocbridge = amalgam of Hoccum and Stourbridge, to convey a town in the

West Midlands.

Holway or *Holloway Lane* = itself, from Cattistock north to Evershot, Dorset.

Holmstoke = amalgam of East Stoke and East Holme, Dorset (they are adjoining parishes beside the River Frome upstream of Wareham).

Hope Church = St Andrew's church, Church Ope Cove, Portland, Dorset (now a ruin).

Icen Way = the Roman road across Puddletown Heath, Puddletown, Dorset.

Icenway House = Hackwood House, Winslade, Basingstoke, Hampshire.

Idmouth = Sidmouth, Devon.

Ikling Way = Ackling Dyke Roman road, Badbury Rings, Shapwick, Dorset, to Salisbury and London.

Isle of Slingers = Portland, Dorset.

Ivel or *Ivell* = Yeovil, Somerset.

Ivelchester = Ilchester, Somerset.

Ivel Way = Long Ash Lane, now the A37 road from Dorchester and Stratton, Dorset, to Yeovil, Somerset.

Jordon Grove = itself, the Jordan valley south of Preston, near Weymouth.

Kennetbridge = Newbury, Berkshire (on the River Kennet).

Kingsbere = Bere Regis, Dorset.

Kingsbere Hill = Black Hill, Bere Regis, Dorset.

Kingsbere-sub-Greenhill = ditto, the allusion being Bere Regis village beneath the slopes of Woodbury Hill.

King's Hintock = Melbury Osmond, Dorset.

King's Hintock Court = Melbury House, Melbury Sampford, Dorset (seat of the Earls of Ilchester).

Knapwater House = Kingston Maurward House, Stinsford, Dorset DT2 8PY (being named for its position beside a lake).

Knollingwood Hall = Wimborne St Giles House, Wimborne St Giles, Dorset (which is on a rise among the trees south of Cranborne; the seat of the Earls of Shaftesbury).

Knollsea = Swanage, Dorset.

Leddenton = Gillingham, Dorset (the River Lodden flows east of the town).

Lewgate = identified by Fred Pitfield as another name for the vicinity of Hardy's Cottage birthplace at Stinsford, but it has been associated with Lewesdon Hill, Stoke Abbott, Dorset, and even Leweston near Sherborne (Stevens Cox gives "Lewstock" as the actual placename, but that has me more puzzled; it sounds like a Hardyesque fusion of Lewesdon and Burstock, near Broadwindsor).

Little Enkworth = Kingston hamlet, south of Corfe Castle, Dorset.

Little Hintock = Stockwood and Melbury Bubb, Dorset, or alternatively Hermitage, Dorset.

Little Weatherbury Farm = Druce Farm, half a mile north-west of Puddletown, Dorset DT2 7SU.

Little Welland = Winterborne Zelstone, Dorset.

Long Ash Lane = itself, the Roman road along the four miles of the western boundary of Sydling St Nicholas parish, Dorset (now the A37).

Longpuddle = Piddletrenthide ("Upper Longpuddle") and Piddlehinton ("Lower Longpuddle"), Dorset.

Longpuddle church = All Saints church, Piddletrenthide, Dorset.

Lornton Inn = Horton Inn, a mile north-west of Horton, Dorset BH21 5AD.

Lower Longpuddle = Piddlehinton, Dorset.

Lower Mellstock = Lower Bockhampton, Stinsford, Dorset.

Lower Wessex = Devon.

Lulstead = West Lulworth, Dorset.

Lulwind Cove = Lulworth Cove, West Lulworth, Dorset.

Lumsdon = Cumnor, near Oxford.

Maidon = Maiden Castle, Winterborne St Martin, Dorset.

Mai Dun Castle = ditto, Maiden Castle, Winterborne St Martin, Dorset.

Manor Court = Rushmore House, Tollard Royal, Wiltshire (the seat of the Pitt-Rivers family).

Markton = Dunster, Somerset.

Marlbury Downs = Marlborough Downs, Wiltshire.

Martlott = Marnhull, Dorset.

Marshall's Elm = itself, on the Polden Hills a mile south of Street, Somerset.

Marshwood = Middlemarsh, Minterne Magna, Dorset (in damp and densely wooded countryside).

Martock Moor = transferred to the flat-lands at Martock on the edge of the Somerset Levels but Hardy had in mind his "Durnover Moor" at Fordington, Dorchester, Dorset.

Marygreen = Fawley, Berkshire.

Max Gate = itself, Max Gate, Alington Avenue, Dorchester, Dorset DT1 2AA (Hardy adopted the name of the old turnpike barrier and toll house, Mack's Gate, which stood opposite his new home).

Melchester = Salisbury, Wiltshire.

Melchester Cathedral = Salisbury Cathedral, Wiltshire.

Mellstock = the parish of Stinsford, Dorset (in which Hardy was born).

Mellstock Cross = Stinsford Cross, Stinsford, Dorset (between the hamlets of Lower Bockhampton and Higher Bockhampton).

Mellstock churchyard = St Michael's church, Stinsford (in which Hardy's heart would lie; his body, against his wishes, was incinerated at Woking for a state funeral in Poet's Corner, Westminster Abbey).

Mellstock Lane = lane from the main road at Stinsford Hill, east to Stinsford Cross, then continuing to Tincleton, Dorset.

Mellstock Leaze = meadow lands (the Saxon word) south of Church Lane, Stinsford, Dorset.

Mellstock Rise = Stinsford Hill, Stinsford, Dorset (which is only a gentle rise, half a mile north-east of Grey's Bridge, on the old course of the A35 with the milestone "Blandford 15. Dorchester 1").

Middleton = Milton Abbas, Dorset (the actual name of its demolished mediaeval town).

Middleton Abbey = Milton Abbey, Milton Abbas, Dorset.

Mid Wessex = Wiltshire.

Millpond St Jude's = Milborne St Andrew, Dorset.

Milton Wood = woods around Delcombe Bottom, Milton Abbas, Dorset.

Mistover = scattering of cob and thatch cottages on Puddletown Heath, Dorset.

Mistover Knap = house (demolished) on Puddletown Heath, Puddletown, Dorset.

Mixen Lane = Mill Street, Fordington, Dorchester, Dorset.

Moreford = Moreton, Dorset.

Moreford Rise = Broomhill, Winfrith Newburgh, Dorset.

Mount Lodge = Killerton House, Broadclyst, near Exeter, Devon (another of Fred Pitfield's identifications in *Hardy's Wessex Locations*).

Narrobourne = West Coker, near Yeovil, Somerset.

Nest Cottage = Chine Hill Cottage, Druce, Puddletown, Dorset DT2 7ST (Fred Pitfield tells me it has been demolished).

Nether Moynton = Owermoigne, Dorset.

New Castle = Pennsylvania Castle Hotel, Wakeham, Portland, Dorset DT5 1HZ (to distinguish this early nineteenth century castellated house from the genuine mediaeval ruin, Rufus Castle, alias "the Red King's Castle" on the adjacent clifftop).

Newland Buckton = Buckland Newton, Dorset.

Nicholas's Cottage = possibly St Nicholas Cottage, East Chaldon, Chaldon Herring, Dorset DT2 8DN.

Norcombe = Burnt Bottom and Westcombe Coppice, Hooke, Dorset (the first element has been transferred from Norwood Farm, Corscombe).

Norcombe Hill = Winyard's Gap, Chedington, Dorset (after Toller Down and Corscombe Down where the highway, Cromlech Crock Lane, plunges into a deep cutting).

North Wessex = Berkshire, particularly the part given to Oxfordshire in 1974.

Nuttlebury = Hazelbury Bryan, Dorset.

Nuzzlebury = ditto, Hazlebury Bryan, Dorset.

Oakbury Fitzpiers = Okeford Fitzpaine, Dorset (called "Buckbury Fitzpiers" in the earlier Hardy's novels).

Octagonal Chamber = Cupola, Sheldonian Theatre, Oxford.

Old Melchester = Old Sarum, near Salisbury, Wiltshire.

Old Rooms Inn = itself, the Old Rooms, Trinity Street, Weymouth, Dorset DT4 8TW.

Old Time Street = Oriel Lane, Oxford.

Oldgate College = New College, Oxford.

Oozewood = Ringwood, Hampshire.

Oriel Window = the former building where the Buzz Inn now stands, in High West Street, Dorchester, Dorset.

Outer Wessex = Somerset.

Overcombe = Sutton Poyntz, near Weymouth, Dorset.

Oxwell Hall = Poxwell House, Poxwell, Dorset DT2 8ND.

Peakhill Cottage = Manor Gardens Cottage, Lower Bockhampton, Stinsford, Dorset DT2 8PZ

Pen-Zephyr = Penzance, Cornwall.

Peter's Finger = King's Head, Mill Street Fordington, Dorchester, Dorset (the county's actual St Peter's Finger being at Lytchett Minster, west of Poole).

Phoenix Inn = itself, now Phoenix Court, High East Street, Dorchester, Dorset DT1 1NB.

Port Bredy = Bridport, Dorset.

Pos'ham = itself, being how the locals pronounce Portesham, Dorset.

Puddle-sub-Mixen = a lesser parish of Dorset's Piddle valley, downstream of a mill, with Affpuddle being the prime contender.

Pummery = Poundbury Camp hill-fort, Dorchester, Dorset.

Pummery-Tout = ditto.

Pure Drop Inn = The Crown, Marnhull, Dorset DT10 1LN (actual Pure Drop inns being at Glanvilles Wootton and in West Street, Wareham, Dorset; since closed).

Quartershot = Aldershot, Hampshire (suggested by the quarters there for the troops).

Pydel Vale = valley of the River Piddle upstream of Puddletown, Dorset.

Quiet Woman Inn = former Wild Duck Inn, at Duck Dairy House, Duddle Heath, Puddletown, Dorset (Dorset's actual Quiet Woman Hotel being at Halstock, and the similarly inspired, beheaded, Silent Woman at Coldharbour, in the parish of Wareham St Martin).

Red King's Castle = Rufus Castle, Church Ope Cove, Portland, Dorset (William II was nicknamed Rufus on account of his red hair).

Revellers' Inn = former Revel's Inn, Cosmore, Buckland Newton, Dorset DT2 7TW.

Rimsmoor Pond = itself, Rimsmoor Pond, Bryants Puddle Heath, Affpuddle, Dorset.

Rings Hill Speer = Weatherby Castle Obelisk, Milborne St Andrew, Dorset.

Rollivers Inn = Blackmore Vale Inn, Burton Street, Marnhull, Dorset DT10 1JJ.

Rookington House = Hurn Court, Hurn, Dorset (though it has been known as Heron Court since becoming an independent boys' school in 1952).

Rookington Park = Hurn Park, Hurn, Dorset (the thirty acres around Heron Court School were formerly the seat of the Earl of Malmesbury).

Roy-town = Troy Town, Puddletown, Dorset (the hamlet below Yellowham Hill; its real name usually means slums, but there may be a purer derivation in this case, from a mediaeval maze on the chalky hill to the north).

Rubdon Hill = Bubb Down Hill, Melbury Bubb, Dorset.

Rubric College = Brasenose College, Oxford.

Rushy Pond = itself, Rushy Pond, Duddle Heath, Puddletown, Dorset.

St Launce's = Launceston, Cornwall.

St Maria's = St Mary's, Isles of Scilly.

St Peter's Finger = King's Head, Mill Street, Fordington, near Poole (the actual St Peter's Finger being at Lytchett Minster, near Poole).

St Silas = St Barnabas church, Oxford (designed by Hardy's architectural associate Sir Arthur Blomfield [1829-99] who specialised in ecclesiastical buildings, including Church House, Westminster).

Sandbourne = Bournemouth, Dorset.

Sandbourne Moor = Bourne Bottom, Poole, Dorset.

Sarcophagus College = Corpus Christi College, Oxford (the name meaning "body of Christ" and hence sarcophagus; I can see no sense in Hermann Lea suggesting New College as an alternative).

Scrimpton = Frampton, Dorset.

Shadwater = Woodsford, Dorset.

Shadwater Weir = weir at Woodsford Farm, Woodsford, Dorset.

Shakeforest Towers = probably Clatford House, near Fyfield, on the Marlborough Downs, Wiltshire.

Shaston = itself, being the milestone contraction for Shaftesbury, Dorset.

Sherton Abbas = Sherborne, Dorset.

Sherton Castle = Sherborne Castle, Sherborne, Dorset.

Sherton Turnpike = Turnpike Toll House (now West Hill Cottage) at the northern extremity of Longburton parish, on the hill above Sherborne, Dorset.

Shottsford = Blandford, Dorset.

Shottsford Forum = ditto, the formal name for Blandford Forum, Dorset.

Sidlinch = Sydling St Nicholas, Dorset.

Silverthorne Dairy = farm at Up Exe on the River Exe, beside its former branch railway, between Silverton and Thorverton, Devon.

Sleeping Green = village green in the area of Carhampton and Withycombe, between Minehead and Williton, Somerset.

Slopeway Well = Fortuneswell, Portland, Dorset (which is indeed built upon a slope).

Slyer's Lane = itself, Slyer's Lane, Coker's Frome, Stinsford, Dorset DT2 7SD.

Snail-creep = track from Hardy's cottage birthplace north to Grey's Wood,

Higher Kingston, Stinsford, Dorset.

Solentsea = Southsea, Hampshire (though the waters off Southsea are known as Spithead, the Solent starting to the west).

Southerton = Stoborough, Dorset (to distinguish this part of "Anglebury", as Hardy called Wareham, from its Northport suburb which clusters around the railway station on the other side of the Piddle meadows).

South Wessex = Dorset.

Sow and Acorn = itself, almost, being the Acorn Inn, Evershot, Dorset.

Springham = Warmwell, Dorset (the wet bit of the parish being a mile north of the village on Empool Heath).

Stagfoot Lane = Hartfoot Lane, Bingham's Melcombe, in the parish of Melcombe Horsey, Dorset DT2 7PF (where there is now also a Stagfoot Cottage).

Stancy Castle = Dunster Castle, Dunster, Somerset.

Standfast Bridge = bridge at East Mills, Mill Lane, Fordington, Dorchester, Dorset.

Stapleford = Stalbridge, Dorset.

Stapleford Park = Stalbridge Park, Stalbridge, Dorset.

Stoke-Barehills = Basingstoke, Hampshire (Hardy was not alone among English writers in showing a prejudice against Basingstoke).

Stoke Lane = itself, between Mappowder and Stoke Wake, Dorset.

Stourcastle = Sturminster Newton, Dorset (which does have a castle, the ruin of a fortified manor house with a view over the River Stour).

Street of Wells = High Street, Fortuneswell, Portland, Dorset.

Sylvania Castle = Pennsylvania Castle Hotel, Wakeham, Portland, Dorset DT5 1HZ.

Talbothays = Lower Lewell Farm, West Knighton, Dorset DT2 8AP (Denys Kay-Robinson having shown that Hermann Lea's claim that "the dairy house is drawn from no particular building" is itself fiction, this three-storey farmhouse with an eighteenth century thatched barn being not only identifiable but having in the novels the give-away Hardy character Bill Lewell working there).

Talbothays Lodge = itself, Talbothay[e]s, West Stafford, Dorset DT2 8AL (built by Hardy for his sister, Kate, and only half a mile from Lower Lewell farm, on the same road, giving its fictional name a physical reality).

Targan Bay = Pentargon Bay, near Boscastle, Cornwall (the modern spelling ends in "on", not "an", as given by Stevens Cox and others).

Ten Hatches = Coker's Frome Weir, Stinsford, Dorset.

Ten Hatches Hole = pool below Coker's Frome Weir, Stinsford, Dorset.

Tess's Cottage = two claimants have since adopted her name: Tess Cottage, Walton Elm, Marnhull, Dorset DT10 1NH, and Tess Cottage, just west of the church at Evershot, Dorset.

The Hintocks = countryside around Minterne Magna, Melbury Osmond and Hermitage below the downland escarpment west of Bulbarrow, Stoke Wake, Dorset.

The Fane = Temple-style summer house beside the lake, Kingston Maurward, Stinsford, Dorset (Fred Pitfield points out that "fane" means "temple").

The Island = Isle of Wight.

The Ring = Maumbury Rings, Dorchester, Dorset.

The Slopes = foothills of Cranborne Chase, Dorset.

The Union = itself, the Union Workhouse, otherwise known as the Poor Law Institution, Damer's Road, Dorchester, Dorset (facing the junction with Maud Road).

Theatre of Wren = Sheldonian Theatre, Oxford.

Thorncombe Wood = itself, Thorncombe Wood, Higher Bockhampton, Stinsford, Dorset (the deciduous wood beside Hardy's Cottage birthplace, on its south side).

Three Mariners' Inn = former King of Prussia tavern, High East Street, Dorchester, Dorset (it stood on the north side of the street, east of Friary Lane).

Three Tranters' Inn = probably the Wise Man Inn, West Stafford, Dorset DT2 8AG.

Tintinhull = itself, Tintinhull, near Montacute, Somerset.

Tintinhull valley = itself, beside Wellhams Brook below Stoke sub Hamdon, near Montacute, Somerset.

Tolchurch = Tolpuddle, Dorset.

Toneborough = Taunton, Somerset (which is on the River Tone).

Toneborough Deane= Vale of Taunton Deane, Somerset.

Tor-upon-Sea = Torquay, Devon.

Trantridge = Pentridge, Dorset.

Trufal = itself, Trufal, Cornwall.

Tudor College = Brazenose College, Oxford.

Union, The = itself, the Union Workhouse, otherwise known as the Poor Law Institution, Damer's Road, Dorchester (facing the junction with Maud Road).

Uplandtowers = St Giles House, Wimborne St Giles, Dorset BH21 5NA.

Upper Longpuddle = Piddletrenthide, Dorset.

Upper Mellstock = Higher Bockhampton, Stinsford (the hamlet of Hardy's birth).

Upper Wessex = Hampshire.

Vagg Hollow = itself, the cutting below Vagg Farm through which the lane which was the Roman road from Dorchester to Ilchester descends from the hills on the north-west side of Yeovil, Somerset (James Stevens Cox, in *Hardy's Wessex*, misplaces Vagg Hollow "on the Fosseway" — the Fosse is on the other side of Tintinhull; Vagg Hollow is at Ordnance Survey map reference ST 532 187).

Valley of the Great Dairies = Valley of the River Frome, south Dorset.

Valley of the Little Dairies = Blackmore Vale, north Dorset.

Vindilia = Portland, Dorset.

Vindogladia = Woodyates, Pentridge, Dorset (though its earthworks date from the end of the Roman period, and archaeologists now apply the "White Ditches" placename to Badbury Rings).

Warborne = Wimborne, Dorset (though the "War" element is hardly obvious in relation to the town, unless it is a reference to the Minster's association with Saint Walburga, one of its nuns who left to join Boniface and founded a German monastery, and Hardy avoided "Wal" so as not to imply Wareham-type town walls).

Warm'll Cross = Warmwell Cross, Warmwell, Dorset (now a roundabout).

Waterstone Ridge = itself, Waterston Ridge is half a mile south of Lacock Dairy Farm, Puddletown, Dorset.

Weatherbury = Puddletown, Dorset (called Piddletown in Hardy's time). "Weatherbury" is a transferred real name, from Weatherby Castle hill-fort, Milborne St Andrew, Dorset.

Weatherbury Farm = Waterston Manor, a mile and a half up the Piddle from Puddletown, Dorset DT2 7SP (neither spelt nor pronounced "Waterson" as Stevens Cox gives it).

Welcome Home Inn = Ship Inn, Boscastle, Cornwall.

Welland House = Charborough House, Morden, Dorset BH20 7EW.

Wellbridge = Wool Bridge, Wool, Dorset.

Wellbridge Abbey = Bindon Abbey, Wool, Dorset.
Wellbridge House = Woolbridge Manor Cottages, Wool, Dorset.
Wellbridge Manor = Woolbridge Manor, Wool, Dorset BH20 6HQ.
Wessex Heights = escarpments of the Dorset Downs and the whole chalk mass eastwards around the edge of the Hampshire Basin to Ingpen Beacon.
West Endelstow = St Julietta's church, St Juliot, near Boscastle, Cornwall.
West Mellstock = Stinsford, Dorset (the part around the parish church).
Weydon Fair = Weyhill Fair, near Andover, Hampshire.
Weydon Priors = Weyhill, near Andover, Hampshire.
Wherryborne = Winterborne Came, Dorset.
Wherryborne Wood = Big Wood, Longlands, Winterbourne Abbas, Dorset (Hardy forgot its location, but Wherry Pit and Wherry Cottage, DT2 9LW, are to the west of the Nine Stones, Winterbourne Abbas, at the A35 end of the mile-long drive from Lodge Wood and through the Big Wood).
Whit' Sheet Hill = itself, White Sheet Hill, where Cromlech Crock Lane (the A356 westwards from Maiden Newton) ascends the downs north of Toller Fratrum, Dorset.
Windy Beak = Cambeak, St Gennys, near Bude, Cornwall.
Wintoncester = Winchester, Hampshire ("Winton" being its Latin name and the signature of the bishop).
Wolfeton House = itself, Wolfeton House, Charminster, Dorset DT2 9QN.
Wyll's Neck = in the Quantock Hills, Somerset.
Wyndway House = Upton House, Poole, Dorset.
Yalbury Bottom = coombe on the west side of Yellowham Wood, Stinsford, Dorset.
Yalbury Hill = Yellowham Hill, Puddletown, Dorset.
Yalbury Wood = Yellowham Wood, Stinsford and Puddletown parishes, Dorset.
Yellowham Bottom = itself, the coombe on the west side of Yellowham Wood, Stinsford, Dorset.
Yewsholt Lodge = Farr's House, Cowgrove, Pamphill, Dorset BH21 4EL.

Others can come to their own conclusions. That the list has had a couple of dozen embarrassing howlers filtered out is thanks to Bere Regis historian and architect Fred Pitfield who was working on his own much more exhaustive *Hardy's Wessex Locations*. This gives snippets from the novels and short stories and compares the literary glosses with a potted description of reality. In this Fred Pitfield, as a working architect, has the advantage of a shared profession with the early Thomas Hardy. He also has the benefit of knowing the Hardy country from birth, and having explored its recesses with clutches of book extracts in his arms.

GREETINGS - - - from
Mr. and Mrs. THOMAS HARDY

Max Gate.
Dorchester.

Xmas. 1923

'Greetings from Mr and Mrs Thomas Hardy' at Christmas, 1923.
Guarding the Max Gate porch is Wessex. He was his master's
principal solace as life advanced — through the eighties
for one and into double figures for the other. In the event it would
be Wessex who died a year before Hardy, to receive the major monument
in the Max Gate pets' cemetery: 'The famous dog Wessex. Aug 1913-
27 Dec 1926. Faithful, Unflinching.' See page 177

ABBOTSBURY and SHERBORNE

Ashes of John Cowper Powys.

Though born at Shirley in Derbyshire, and having died in the Land of his Fathers — he traced his descent to the Welsh princes — John Cowper Powys [1872-1964] wanted his ashes cast upon the Dorset sea. That was done, from the Chesil Beach at Abbotsbury — because he had used the treacherous shingle bank for the shipwreck scene in his novel *Weymouth Sands* [1934]. There, Angus Wilson considered, he wrote "not of heroes or even of men, but of men beside nature".

Of *Wolf Solent* the Sunday Times had written in 1929: "Its background is Dorset, and it is a Dorset which has rarely been painted more graciously, even by Hardy himself."

The country of *Wolf Solent* is from the Powys schooldays, public at Sherborne, westwards across the pasture and former pond of Lenthay Common to Bradford Abbas, and to the big cities of this world — Yeovil, Dorchester and Weymouth.

It was a case of absence making the mind pound faster as he travelled the United States — missing only two in its pre-Hawaii and Alaska boundaries — and his was a more hedonistic philosophy than that of his author brothers, with masturbation at its summit. Among his other novels are *Wood and Stone* and the period-piece *The Brazen Head*. Poetry included *Wolfsbane, Mandragora* and *Samphire*, and the deeper thoughts are in *The Religion of a Sceptic* and *In Defence of Sensuality*. His literary criticism, on which he lectured in the States, ranged from *Visions and Revisions* and *The Meaning of Culture* [1930] to his 1934 autobiography, *Morwyn* [1937] and *The Pleasures of Literature* [1938].

ABBOTSBURY (EAST BEXINGTON)

Old Coastguards Cottages: *Gallion's Reach.*

The literary journalist and novelist Henry Major Tomlinson [1873-1958] bought the Essex-style weather-boarded Old Coastguards Cottages when the service disposed of them in 1926. These are the last buildings in Abbotsbury parish, a lawn being all that separates them from the Chesil Beach, at East Bexington (Ordnance Survey map reference SY 543 857). They are reached by the beach track, a mile after the Sub-Tropical Gardens.

Tomlinson loved the sea. He wrote *The Sea and the Jungle* [1912], *Old Junk* [1918], *London River* [1921], *Tidemarks* [1924] and *Gallion's Reach* — which he was proof-reading at the time of the move to Abbotsbury. It was published in 1927.

Beside the Chesil Beach he became more reflective. *Between the Lines* was published in 1928 and *All Our Yesterdays* in 1930. In the early 1930s he built his own house, which had to be called Gallion's Reach, on a plot sold-off by the nearby Labour-in-Vain Farm.

Books still flowed — *Mars His Idiot* [1935], *All Hands* [1937] and *The Day Before* [1939].

Ackland — for VALENTINE ACKLAND [1906-69]
see CHALDON HERRING (EAST CHALDON)

Adam — for ADAM of BARKING [early 13th century]
see SHERBORNE

Adams — for DOUGLAS ADAMS [20th century]
see STALBRIDGE

Aelfric — for AELFRIC [10th century], known as GRAMMATICUS,
see CERNE ABBAS

ALDERNEY — see POOLE (ALDERNEY)

Aldhelm — for SAINT ALDHELM [?640-709]
see SHERBORNE

Allsop — for KENNETH ALLSOP [1920-73]
see POWERSTOCK (WEST MILTON)

Ashley — for SIR ANTHONY ASHLEY [1551-1628]
see WIMBORNE ST GILES

Aubrey — for JOHN AUBREY [1626-97]
see BLANDFORD

Austen — for JANE AUSTEN [1775-1817]
see LYME REGIS for Jane Austen: *Persuasion*; and separate item on
the Jane Austen Garden

Bailey — for ALBERT CHARLES BAILEY [early 20th century]
see WEYMOUTH [SUTTON POYNTZ]

Baldwin — for BALDWIN, ARCHBISHOP OF CANTERBURY [died
1190] see THORNCOMBE (FORDE)

Bankes — for HENRY BANKES [1757-1834]
see PAMPHILL (KINGSTON LACY)

Barnes — for WILLIAM BARNES [1801-86] see STURMINSTER
NEWTON (BAGBER) for William Barnes: born at Bagber Common.
STURMINSTER NEWTON for Penny Street: Barnes as schoolboy and
clerk. DORCHESTER for 40 South Street: Barnes the schoolmaster.
DORCHESTER for St Peter's church: statue of Barnes. DORCHESTER
for Leader Scott: Barnes's daughter. WINTERBORNE CAME for
William Barnes: much more than a folksy poet; Barnes on class;
Francis Kilvert's visit.

Bastard — for THOMAS BASTARD [1566-1618]
see BERE REGIS

BEAMINSTER
Dean Sprat: born at Parnham.

"Maxime semper valuit authoriatate" is the inscription on the memorial to
Thomas Sprat [1635-1713] in St Nicholas chapel at Westminster Abbey.

He was their Dean and would be remembered as a poet but his great
contemporary power was in the sharp delivery of cutting words. These
poured out and were often stunning and highly charged, merging politics
and religion as he defended the divine right of kings. He also combined
church work with the emergent study of the sciences and in 1667 published
the *History of the Royal Society of London*.

Sprat was born at Beaminster, at Parnham House. His father, the minister
in Beaminster, had married one of the Strode daughters. As the Dean, Sprat

delivered *A Sermon Preach'd to the Natives of the County of Dorset* to the "anniversary feast" of Dorsetmen in London on 8 December 1692. He had survived months of troubles caused by Robert Young, who hatched London's conspiracy theory of the year — his accomplice Stephen Blackhead planted a forged letter at the Bishop's Palace, Bromley, which purported to be a scheme by Sprat and others to achieve the restoration of the exiled monarch James II.

That close shave caused Sprat to moderate his public utterances for the last years of his life. He had principles but was also careful of his comforts, Lord Ailesbury pointed out, and "loved hospitality beyond his purse".

BEAMINSTER
Samuel Hearne: *Journey from Hudson's Bay.*

Samuel Hearne [1745-92] lived as a youth in Beaminster. Many there recalled him in 1770 when news came back to Britain that he had spent two years in finding the passage through the icy waters along the north-western edge of America. He had forced the North West Passage for the Hudson's Bay Company.

Hearne's book of the experiences, *Journey from Hudson's Bay to the Northern Ocean*, would be published posthumously in 1795.

BEAMINSTER
Conan Doyle: woken by Parnham's hound.

The most famous hound in English literature is said to have had its first howl in the Parnham night when Sir Arthur Conan Doyle [1859-1930] was staying at the house. Dates I have seen quoted for this are in the 1920s, when the house was some kind of exclusive country club, but if so then the story is a fabrication — for Doyle had published *The Hound of the Baskervilles* in 1902.

Wherever the occurrence, he moved the setting westwards to Dartmoor, though that is acceptable literary licence as the west Dorset countryside is a little short on moor and mire, though it does have a sufficiency of hill-fog. After 1902, the legend went with the man, and the baying of a dog would have been inevitable cause for comment.

BEAMINSTER — see POWERSTOCK for Thomas Russell: young poet

Beaufoy — for MARK BEAUFOY [1764-1827]
see IWERNE MINSTER

Beckford — for PETER BECKFORD [1740-1811]
see IWERNE STEPLETON

Bell — for ANDREW BELL [1753-1832]
see SWANAGE

Bell — for THOMAS BELL [1792-1880]
see POOLE

Benfield — for ERIC BENFIELD [20th century]
see WORTH MATRAVERS

Benson — for WILLIAM BENSON [1682-1754]
see STUDLAND (BROWNSEA ISLAND)

Bentham — for JEREMY BENTHAM [1748-1832] see THORNCOMBE (FORDE)

BERE REGIS, BLANDFORD and DORCHESTER

Chrestoleros: the crazed vicar.

Thomas Bastard [1566-1618] was born in Blandford. His literary abilities emerged at Oxford with a contribution to a memorial volume in tribute to Sir Philip Sydney. He was "much guilty of the vices belonging to the poets" and was forced by his "libelling" to abandon his fellowship in 1591.

He had, however, friends in high places. Through the efforts of Thomas Howard, Earl of Suffolk and Lord Treasurer of England, he was found a little country living. That was Bere Regis where he was instituted as vicar on 27 January 1593.

"He was clearly a genial, not to say jovial parson, after the type of Robert Herrick," says the *Dictionary of National Biography*. There he became the satirical priest, and *Chrestoleros: Seven Bookes of Epigrames* was published in 1598. Much of it is bitter but he had a gentler side, angling in the Bere stream, as he told fellow poet Sir Henry Wotton:

> *Wotton, my little Bere dwells on a hill,*
> *Under whose foot the silver Trout doth swim*
> *The Trout silver without and gold within.*

Bastard claimed he had a miserable family life, with a wife who was "no great help-meet", and according to the journal Athenae he became "towards his latter end crazed" and was put into prison "in Allhallows (All Saints) parish in Dorchester, where, dying very obscurely and in a mean condition, he was buried in the churchyard belonging to that parish on 19 April 1618, leaving behind him many memorials to his wit and drollery".

BERE REGIS – see WAREHAM for Orme Angus: Bere's whirlwind

BETTISCOMBE – see LYME REGIS for James Strong: *Femine valour*

Bickersteth – for HENRY BICKERSTETH, Bishop of Exeter [1825-1906] see HINTON MARTELL

BINDON – see THORNCOMBE (FORDE) for John of Forde: *Song of Songs*

BINGHAM'S MELCOMBE – see MELCOMBE HORSEY

BLANDFORD

John Aubrey: schooled at Blandford.

Wiltshire boy John Aubrey [1626-97] was sent to Blandford Grammar School in 1638. "Here I recovered my health, and got my Latin and Greek," he recalled, though he had a low opinion of his master. William Sutton BD "was ill-natured".

It had "in Mr William Gardner's time" been "the most eminent school for the education of gentlemen in the West of England". As for the town, Aubrey remembered in Blandford "as much roguery as at Newgate".

It is to Aubrey that the seventeenth century owes much of its continuing life. He collected people, with jottings that encompass the best of London and country house gossip on whose mothers were whores, and whose sons inclined the same way. This is mixed with general tittle-tattle. It is from Aubrey that we learn that when as a butcher's son Shakespeare "killed a calf he would do it in a high style, and make a speech".

Often the sexual revelations come in some of the most beautifully precise words that have ever been penned in English. Take this passage from *Brief Lives*:

"Sir William Petty had a boy that whistled incomparably well. He after waited on a Lady, a widow, of good fortune. Every night this boy was to whistle this Lady asleep. At last she could hold out no longer, but bids her chamber-maid withdraw; bids him come to bed, sets him to work, and marries him the next day. That is certain true."

Aubrey became the father of antiquarian studies. His magnum opus was *Monumenta Britannica*, which is a listing of all the archaeological sites he could find in the British Isles. Dorset features well — with hill-forts, barrows and stone circles. To his disappointment it was unprinted at his death, and would remain confined to the Bodleian Library at Oxford for nearly three centuries until William Hoade and I began work in 1978 upon its publication through Dorset Publishing Company. This was brought to fruition in two volumes, 1980-82, with the novelist John Fowles, in Lyme Regis, as the overall editor.

Fowles credits Aubrey with the most pleasing single sentence in the English language: "I did see Mr Christopher Love beheaded on Tower Hill in a delicate clear day."   No one but Aubrey would have included the word "delicate"; that also sums up his genius for conveying the best of indelicacies.

BLANDFORD and SHERBORNE

Thomas Creech: a classic exit.

Thomas Creech [1659-1700] was born at Blandford and sent to Sherborne School. His father, also Thomas, outlived him, and his mother, Jane Creech, died in 1693. They both stayed in Blandford and were proud of a son who became one of Britain's most accomplished translators of the classics from the Greek and Roman world.

His Lucretius was a best seller. "Incomparable", it was called. Creech became headmaster of Sherborne School in 1694-96, but then fell in love with Miss Philadelphia Playdell of Oxford, whose parents would not approve of a marriage.

Creech's last months were a manic depression and their end is recorded by John Hobson: "He had prepared a razor and a rope, and with the razor he had nicked his throat a little, which hurt him so much that he desisted; then he took the cord and tied himself up so low that he kneeled on his knees while he was dead."

His sister, Bridget, was married to Thomas Bastard, the town architect at Blandford. They and the Playdells found themselves the centre of attention as catch-penny scandal-sheets were printed about the suicide: *A Step to Oxford, or a Mad Essay on the Reverend Mr Thos Creech's hanging himself (as 'tis said) for love. With the Character of his Mistress.*

BLANDFORD and PIMPERNE

Christopher Pitt: translated Virgil.

Christopher Pitt [1699-1748] was born in Blandford and died in Pimperne, where he was rector from 1772, suffering from and succumbing to the family disease of the great Pitts, which was gout. He is buried in the parish church at Blandford and has an inscription to his "candour and primitive simplicity of manners" which goes on to state that he "lived and died beloved".

He was a minor poet, whose main claim to fame lay with his essay on

Virgil's *Aeneid* which by 1738 had extended to a translation in two volumes of the whole poem. In it he followed John Dryden's footsteps, with much greater faithfulness to the original, but Dr Samuel Johnson considered that a doubtful improvement: "Dryden's faults are forgotten in the hurry of delight, and Pitt's beauties are neglected in the languor of a cold and listless perusal; Pitt pleases the critics, and Dryden the people; Pitt is quoted, and Dryden read."

BLANDFORD

Joseph Sherer: rejected the National Anthem.

On 4 October 1801, in celebration of peace with France, the organist incorporated the tune of *God Save the King* as he played to a packed Sunday congregation in Blandford parish church. His rector, Rev Joseph Godfrey Sherer, was furious and ordered the organist to stop.

The rector defended his intervention by publishing a twelve-page discourse, *Remarks on the Effects of Church-Music occasioned by the Introduction of a well-known tune.* In it he argues that *God Save the King* is "A song expressive of loyalty to the king and attachment to the state ... and as such it operates on the feeling of every faithful subject with a fascination, influence and ... with a degree of enthusiasm bordering upon devotion, and for that reason if for no other is unfit to be introduced into the worship of God 'whose jealousy burneth like fire for ever'. 'Render unto Caesar the things which are Caesar's, and unto God the things which are God's.'"

BLANDFORD

Legion House: where Richard Pulteney adopted Linnaeus.

The British Legion headquarters in Church Lane occupies the town's "largest and most splendidly decorated house of the post-fire period", to quote the Royal Commission on Historical Monuments, who add that it is notable in being the only one embellished with Portland stone dressings to its brick facade. They call it Coupar House, which was the name given to it by Francis James Stuart, sixteenth Earl of Moray [1842-1909], after his estate in Scotland.

The imposing frontage, which bears comparison with the style of the Town Pump and is almost certainly a creation of the Bastards, lies behind curving brick walls and two carved stone urns. It is the sort of place that always had important owners, the first probably being Port wine importer Robert Lewen, who died in 1752 and was succeeded by Sir George Glyn, the son of a former Lord Mayor of London.

The most eminent of them was Dr Richard Pulteney FRS, MD [1730-1801], who was the leading British exponent of the ideas of Carl von Linné, who pioneered the Linnaean system of scientific biological classification. Thomas Beach painted Pulteney's portrait for an engraving that was included with a biography of the Blandford naturalist in the 1805 edition of his work *General View of the Writings of Linnaeus*.

Pulteney himself was a first-rate botanist whose *Catalogues of the Birds, Shells and Rare Plants of Dorsetshire* was acclaimed as "one of the most valuable provincial catalogues connected with natural history that has hitherto been published in England". This is incorporated in the exceedingly rare second edition of John Hutchins's Dorset *County History*; the editors chucked it out of the Victorian third edition.

BLANDFORD

Harcourt's speech: decided Gladstone's successor.

Sir William Harcourt [1827-1904], Chancellor of the Exchequer in Gladstone's last government, used a speech to a Liberal rally at Blandford on 24 September 1885 to scupper Joseph Chamberlain's chances of becoming the next Prime Minister. It decided the succession in favour of Lord Rosebery.

A decade later, in his late sixties, Harcourt followed Rosebery as the leader of the Liberals in opposition. That position he lost in 1898; his credibility tarnished by an attempt at pushing through Parliament a Local Veto Bill which would have enabled municipalities to ban the sale of alcohol in their areas. Temperance was going out of favour as the new century approached.

BLANDFORD − see BERE REGIS for *Chrestoleros*: the crazed vicar

BLANDFORD ST MARY

Browne Willis: topographical mediaevalist.

Browne Willis [1689-1760] was born at Blandford St Mary. He had a Westminster School education and devoted his life to topographical antiquarianism, becoming one of the first mediaevalists. He inherited Buckinghamshire and Herefordshire properties.

His major three-volume work was *Notitia Parliamentaria; or an History of the Counties, Cities and Boroughs of England and Wales* [1715]. He also acted as a benefactor, informant, and general encourager to a number of researchers working on their own local histories − notably, for Dorset, John Hutchins of Wareham.

Less academically, he printed anonymously his *Reflecting Sermons Consider'd on discourses in Bletchley Church*, and in 1717, *The Whole Duty of Man, abridged for the benefit of the Poorer Sort*. It is at Bletchley, Buckinghamshire, that he is buried.

BLOXWORTH

Octavius Pickard-Cambridge: spider man.

Rev Octavius Pickard-Cambridge [1828-1917] was the first great expert on British spiders. He was rector of Bloxworth, where St Andrew's church had its own extensive spider fauna until rebuilding in 1870 disturbed the habitat, and the two volumes of *The Spiders of Dorset* [1897-81] are a milestone in entomological research.

Pickard-Cambridge was one of England's last naturalist parsons. Ignoring any conflict between Darwinism and Christianity he devoted much of his life to studying spiders. Indeed he became the first real expert in his subject and was elected to the Royal Society in 1877.

He doubled as paternalistic squire, having been born in the Jacobean mansion Bloxworth House − which in 1967 came to the cinema as Bathsheba Everdine's house in the film of Thomas Hardy's novel *Far from the Madding Crowd*. Bloxworth is just north of the A35 three miles east of Bere Regis (Ordnance Survey map reference SY 881 947). The Pickards were a musical family. Octavius and all fourteen of his brothers and sisters could sing.

BLOXWORTH

Sir Arthur Pickard-Cambridge: Greek studies.

Professor Arthur Wallace Pickard-Cambridge [1873-1952] became Sir Arthur Pickard-Cambridge in 1950. He had an eminent career in Greek studies, at several universities, and published numerous works on his chosen subject, from *Select Greek Comic Fragments* [1900] to *The Theatre of Dionysus at Athens* [1946].

Though he had his father's touch for spiders, and the love of music that came to all who passed into the world through Bloxworth Rectory, he developed into a committee man. He was on the executive councils of several quasi-governmental and cultural institutions including the Public Schools' Governing Bodies Association, the British Council, the British Academy and the wartime London Tribunal for Conscientious Objectors.

BLOXWORTH and POOLE (BROADSTONE)

W.A. Pickard-Cambridge: *Dorset Carols.*

The best old-style English country carols, and the tradition of singing them each Christmas in St Andrew's church at Bloxworth, have survived thanks to the efforts of William Adair Pickard-Cambridge [1879-1957], the rector's son. Eight local carols had been recorded at Bloxworth by John Skinner, the parish clerk from 1817-79, and were set out, with their music and other Dorset versions which were sung in the main to the "Old Methodist" type of tune, in *A Collection of Dorset Carols* [1926].

W.A. Pickard-Cambridge also translated Aristotle, the *Topica* and *Sophistici Elenchi*, for Oxford University Press [1928]. He was a classics lecturer and an organist. On retirement to Brimlands, in Water Tower Road at Broadstone, he became conductor of the Madrigal Group of Bournemouth Chamber Music Society [1950-54] and produced many original songs and motets.

Blyton — for ENID BLYTON [died 1968]
see SWANAGE

BOCKHAMPTON — see STINSFORD (HIGHER BOCKHAMPTON)

BOSCOMBE — see BOURNEMOUTH (BOSCOMBE) entries

Bosworth Smith — for REGINALD BOSWORTH SMITH [19th century] see MELCOMBE HORSEY

Bottome — for PHYLLIS BOTTOME [1884-1963]
see BOURNEMOUTH

BOURNEMOUTH

Frankenstein's author plus Mary Wollstonecraft Godwin, and anarchist husband William Godwin; buried with poet Shelley's heart in St Peter's churchyard.

An horizontal gravestone on the wooded rise above the south-east corner of St Peter's church, opposite Beales in Hinton Road, is used by the squirrels for chomping fircones. Beneath, in a vault, lie the remains of four literatis who in life had no connection whatever with the virtually non-existent hamlet of Bournemouth.

Mary Wollstonecraft Shelley died in London on 1 February 1851 and her son, Sir Percy Florence Shelley of Boscombe Manor, had the body brought to the new vault in St Peter's churchyard. Mary Wollstonecraft Shelley [1797-1851] was the widow of the famous poet, whom she married in 1816, but something she created is better known than either of them. Her novel *Frankenstein* [1818] would be turned by the twentieth century cinema into a cult. Frankenstein, incidentally, was the mad professor – not his monster. In 1826 she wrote another novel on a theme that still haunts humanity; *The Last Man* is the story of the annihilation of the human race by an epidemic.

On 5 February 1851, Sir Percy obtained faculty permission to exhume Mary's mother, Mary Wollstonecraft Godwin [1759-97], from St Pancras churchyard, London, along with the remains of her husband, William Godwin [1756-1836] and put them into the St Peter's churchyard vault. Mary Wollstonecraft Godwin was also forward thinking, advocating and practising free love before her marriage and founding the feminist movement with her *Vindication of the Rights of Women* [1792].

William Godwin was likewise intellectually advanced, renouncing his preacher's pulpit for atheism and anarchism. His *Enquiry Concerning Political Justice* [1793] still wins the acclaim of a minority though a wider audience has appreciated his children's books and novels, including the *Adventures of Caleb Williams* [1794] which would be televised in the 1980s. The fourth and last second-hand literary connection to go into this Bournemouth vault was the heart of the poet Shelley.

That burial, however, had to be postponed for the lifetime of Sir Percy Florence Shelley who kept the shrivelled heart of his father, Percy Bysshe Shelley [1792-1822] in its own shrine at Boscombe Manor [see its entry]. The heart has a macabre story; it was removed from the funeral pyre of the drowned poet on a beach beside the Gulf of Spezia in 1822 for the practical reason that it would not burn. At Boscombe Manor it was in a casket in the drawing room, set in an alcove behind silk curtains, in front of which a red lamp was continuously burning.

When Sir Percy died in 1889 the heart is said to have been secretly placed in his coffin which is also in this family vault. What St Peter's does not possess is the magnificent sculpture by Henry Weekes which shows the drowned body of the poet in the arms of his widow. It was carved in 1854 but the vicar, Rev Alexander Morden Bennett, refused to have it in his church on the grounds that it might attract notoriety. Sir Percy thereupon gave the carving to Christchurch Priory [see its entry].

BOURNEMOUTH (BOSCOMBE)

Boscombe Manor: Shelley's son.

In 1844, on the death of Sir Timothy Shelley, the baronetcy passed to the only surviving son of the poet Percy Bysshe Shelley, to Percy Florence Shelley [1819-89], "this most gentle and lovable man" the *Dictionary of National Biography* calls him, "the inheritor of most of his father's fine qualities and many of his tastes". He was given his middle name because that was where he was born.

His mother was Mary Wollstonecraft Shelley [1797-1851], the daughter of William Godwin [1756-1836] and Mary Wollstonecraft Godwin [1759-97]. Her first love child with the poet, named William, was born in Rome in 1816, before the suicide of Shelley's first wife, Harriet Shelley. Two weeks after that, the poet married Mary at Christmas 1816.

In 1849, two years before Mary Shelley died, Sir Percy Shelley built Boscombe Manor which has since expanded into a collection of municipal buildings but would regain the Shelley connection in the 1970s with the transfer of the Shelley Museum from Italy. There had been something shrine-like about Sir Percy's original home and his self-effacing personality meant that he would always be regarded as the poet's son rather than someone in his own right.

Above the entrance to the Shelley Museum is a cast-iron plaque: "Borough of Bournemouth. Sir Percy Florence Shelley, son of the poet Percy Bysshe Shelley, lived here from 1849 to 1889 and erected a private theatre in the building, Boscombe Manor."

BOURNEMOUTH

Sir Hubert Parry: baptised at St Peter's.

Hubert Parry was born in Bournemouth on 27 February 1848, the son of Thomas Gambier Parry, but for his mother the strain of a second child was too much and she died a fortnight later. Charles Hubert Hastings Parry [1848-1919] was christened at St Peter's church, Hinton Road, on 20 March 1848, two days after his mother had been buried there, and he was then removed to Highnam Court, Gloucestershire. His name appears on the first page of St Peter's register of baptism, and there is a memorial to him in the Winter Gardens: "Born in this town February 27, 1848. A great musician whose influence on British music will always be remembered."

We hear him most often in what became an alternative national anthem, his *Jerusalem*. A setting of words from William Blake's *Milton*, it was written for children's unison voices, and performed as a choral song with orchestra at the Leeds Festival in 1922, three years after his death, in a setting by Elgar. His masterpiece *Blest Pair of Sirens*, with words from Milton, is one of a series of major choral works which were regularly performed and greatly admired in his time. The Piano Concerto was an early success, in a large output of music which included songs, chamber music, church music and five symphonies. At the other extremity of the national musical heritage, it was a folk arrangement, the *Londonderry Air*, that provided what he considered "the most beautiful tune in the world".

As a senior statesman and administrator of English music, teacher and writer, Parry's influence was considerable. He was Professor of Music at Oxford University and Director of the Royal College of Music in London. For his services to music, he was knighted in 1898, and raised to a baronet in 1903, but had no son to inherit the title.

He contributed poems to Macmillan's Magazine in 1875, articles for the first edition of *Grove's Dictionary of Music and Musicians* [1878], and wrote books including *Studies of Great Composers* [1886], *The Evolution of the Art of Music* [1896], *Johann Sebastian Bach, the Study of a Great Personality* [1909], and the masterly *Style in Musical Art* [1911].

BOURNEMOUTH

Sir Henry Taylor: at Hinton Road.

Sir Henry Taylor [1801-86] the author of the historical novel and play *Philip van Artevelde*, which was published in 1834, moved to Bournemouth to spend the summers from 1861 onwards. Then with his wife he set up their permanent home at Rawden, which was then called The Roost, in Hinton

Road. They were friends of Tennyson, Garibaldi and R.L. Stevenson, and occasionally crossed to Freshwater in the Isle of Wight to stay with Charles Hay and Julia Margaret Cameron.

"The place is beautiful beyond any sea-side place I have ever seen except the Riviera," he wrote on arrival in Bournemouth, "and the air is dry and pure, unacquainted with anything but sea, the pine woods, which reach for miles inland, and the sandy soil in which they grow." The population comprised "two clergymen, two doctors, three widows, and six old maids. Of these the doctors and two of the widows have families. The clergymen and the old maids have none." Sir Henry is buried in St Peter's churchyard.

BOURNEMOUTH
Bournemouth International Centre: where Darwin revisited Patagonia.

On the west side of Bournemouth International Centre, a short distance from the cliff-edge at South Cliff Road, stood the Cliff Cottage. It was a picturesque thatched cottage lodge owned by the Drax family of Charborough.

Charles Darwin [1809-82] was its notable visitor, staying there in September 1862, with his wife who was suffering at the time from scarlet fever. He was unimpressed by the lowland heath about which so many twentieth century naturalists enthuse.

It was a wild expanse of landscape that included most of what is now the Bournemouth conurbation but even in quantity it left Darwin unmoved. "It is a nice but barren country, and I can find nothing to look at. Even the brooks and ponds produce nothing. The country is like Patagonia." The cottage was demolished in 1876 and a century later its environs were selected for the redevelopment that became Bournemouth International Centre in 1982-84.

BOURNEMOUTH
John Keble: died at Brookside.

John Keble, the divine and poet, died on 29 March 1866. He was less than a month from his seventy-fourth birthday, and had been ill for only a week. This shy and unassuming cleric wrote *The Christian Year* which was published anonymously in 1827. Its hymns were printed as a result of the urgings of his father and friends, and by the time of his death it had passed through ninety-four editions.

He died at Brookside, a house overlooking the gardens and stream near the Pier Approach, which is now attached to the White Hermitage Hotel, Exeter Road. Keble moved there in 1865, for the benefit of his wife's health, after thirty years as vicar of Hursley, near Winchester. He is commemorated in Bournemouth by the Keble Chapel in St Peter's church, close to the seat in the south transept where he had been coming to pray each day. The couple are buried at Hursley.

BOURNEMOUTH (SOUTHBOURNE)
Henry Reeve: unofficial diplomat.

"Rode to Hengistbury Head and saw for the first time the Southbourne Estate," political man of letters Henry Reeve [1813-95] wrote in 1872. "I have taken a great fancy to the spot and should be very well contented to end my days there, gazing on that magnificent view of the coast and sea." That home, in 1874, was Foxholes House, which became St Cuthbert's School.

Reeve was the editor of the Greville memoirs and, for forty years, the influential Edinburgh Review. He mediated in top-level European diplomacy and as a result received Sylvia, a collie, from M. Sylvain van de Weyer, the Belgian ambassador; her brother was presented to Queen Victoria and became her favourite dog. The day of Sylvia's death there appeared in The Times a note that Her Majesty was mourning the loss of the other collie. Henry Reeve is buried at Brookwood cemetery, Woking.

BOURNEMOUTH (BOSCOMBE)

Chine Hotel: Sir Henry Drummond Wolff formed the Primrose League.

The five-storey Boscombe Spa Hotel, since enlarged into the Chine Hotel, 25 Boscombe Chine Road, was built by Sir Henry Drummond Wolff [1830-1908] on the east side of the clifftop at Boscombe Chine in 1874. Sir Henry had an international reputation as a diplomat, and a local one as the "Great Improver".

He was the leading speculative property developer who transformed Bournemouth's eastern seaboard into a playground for the nouveau riche. Politically, his impact was through the series of mini-conferences he hosted, at which the Primrose League was founded. The primrose was wrongly assumed to be Disraeli's favourite flower, due to a misunderstanding of the message on his wreath from Queen Victoria.

Sir Henry was a clerk by training, and settled into a literary retirement, producing *A Life of Napoleon at Elba, Letters on the Suez Canal*, and *Some Notes of the Past* [1892].

BOURNEMOUTH

Paul Verlaine and his scandal: 24 Surrey Road.

The French poet Paul Verlaine [1844-96] came to live and teach at a private school on the corner of Surrey Road and Queens Road (now number 24 Surrey Road) in 1876-77. His *Romances sans paroles* were published in 1875 and he left France following a homosexual scandal, which began in 1871 when he walked out on his wife after only eighteen months of marriage and set-up home with the sixteen-year-old poet, Arthur Rimbaud. In July 1874, Verlaine shot Rimbaud in the wrist, during a lovers' tiff, and was imprisoned for two years.

Verlaine went into exile after leaving prison, teaching French and the classics at Saint Aloysius College, and whilst in Bournemouth he wrote poems named for the town and "Le Mer de Bournemouth". Rimbaud, on the other hand, turned his attentions southward and proceeded to make a fortune as a North African trader.

BOURNEMOUTH

John Nelson Darby: 'The Exclusive Brethren'.

There is none so revered as he who creates a sect within his own cult. John Nelson Darby [1800-82] did that for the Plymouth Brethren which he had founded in 1830, and his supporters' club became known as the Darbyites.

He took the cause to Switzerland and proselytised on a monumental scale. Thirty-three volumes of his miscellaneous writings and lectures would eventually be collected.

Meanwhile, he attempted a return to the heartland of his brand of religion, to Plymouth in 1845, but moved to Bristol after a series of deep rows. By 1859 he felt he was losing support in Britain and embarked upon an ambitious world tour that would take in Canada, Germany, the United States of America, New Zealand and the West Indies.

The Darbyites continued to sub-divide until the last pure group, still faithful to the founder, was dubbed the Exclusive Brethren. Their leader died in Bournemouth on 29 April 1882, and is buried at the Cemetery Junction, Wimborne Road.

BOURNEMOUTH (WESTBOURNE)

Skerryvore: R.L. Stevenson's 61 Alum Chine Road.

In February 1884, the Scottish engineer Thomas Stevenson gave his son Robert Louis Stevenson [1850-94], the invalid author of *Treasure Island*, a house at (61) Alum Chine Road, Westbourne, that was previously known as Sea View.

They renamed it Skerryvore, after the famous lighthouse designed by the author's uncle, Alan Stevenson. From Bournemouth, during 1884, R.L. Stevenson saw *Kidnapped* and *The Strange Case of Dr Jekyll and Mr Hyde* into print though the final proofs of the latter had to be read at the Royal National Sanatorium in Bourne Avenue, where the writer was undergoing fresh-air treatment for the alleviation of tuberculosis.

On 17 August 1887 his family, including his mother, sailed for New York. The decision to leave Bournemouth had followed the death in May 1887 of the author's father.

Stevenson was off on his great adventure, that was to bring some relief to his health and take him right across the Pacific, to Honolulu, the Gilbert Islands, Samoa and Sydney. His last home was in a South Sea paradise, at Vailima, in the island of Apia, Samoa, where he died of a brain haemorrhage at the age of forty-four in 1894.

The Westbourne house was damaged by a German bomb on 15 November 1940. No one troubled to repair it, and in 1954, after the site had been cleared, Bournemouth Corporation turned it into a memorial garden. The layout of the house footings can be seen and there is a miniature Skerryvore lighthouse.

BOURNEMOUTH

Radclyffe Hall: spokesperson for lesbianism.

Marguerite Radclyffe Hall [1886-1943] was born at 6 Durley Road, on the south side of Poole Hill.

Writing as Radclyffe Hall, with *Poems of the Past and Present* and verse on *The Forgotten Island* she made an instant literary mark. This was underscored with novels that were a triumph. They came thick and fast with *The Unlit Lamp* [1924], *Adam's Breed* [1926] — taking the James Tait-Black Prize — then *The Well of Loneliness* [1928], which was a study in lesbianism. It was too hot for the English and publication took place in the United States. Marguerite lies in Marx-land, at Highgate.

BOURNEMOUTH (BOSCOMBE)
Rob Roy's final mile: to Wharncliffe Road.

One of the literati who came to Bournemouth to die was John Macgregor [1825-92] who did so at 21 Wharncliffe Road, off Boscombe Spa Road. He was Rob Roy to his public, using as his pseudonym the nickname of the Scottish rustler Robert Macgregor, having first applied it to the lightweight canoe he designed in 1865.

In 1886 he published *A Thousand Miles in the Rob Roy Canoe* and the sequel was *The Rob Roy in the Baltic*.

BOURNEMOUTH (WESTBOURNE)
Alum Chine: Churchill's most dangerous moment, falling from the bridge.

The closest shave of his life for future prolific author and national hero Winston Spencer Churchill [1874-1965] took place in the Chines area of Bournemouth. Here he was staying at his aunt's seaside villa in the summer of 1892. Lady Wimborne owned Branksome Dene and some forty acres of pinewoods in Alum Chine Road (now Alumhurst Road).

The inland end of the deep-cut Alum Chine was then spanned by a rustic wooden bridge and Churchill ran across it whilst trying to hide from his brother and cousin. This old footbridge has been replaced by a pedestrian suspension bridge. At the time the nearest villa was Alumhurst, to the west, and the track from it (now Beaulieu Road) continued on the other side of the Chine, a straight sandy road across empty heath to the nearest houses in the east, which were at the top of Poole Hill.

Churchill's misadventure was to fail in a leap from the bridge on to a pine tree and he fell twenty-nine feet on to the hard surface of the trackway below. His companions thought him dead but the resilient body regained consciousness three days later, though it was three months before he could leave bed.

All this came back to him, with due irony, when he drove by the spot on 17 July 1940 in the company of General Alan Brooke, the chief of Southern Command, as they inspected and carried out token bricklaying on the shore defences that were being hastily completed at nearby Canford Cliffs and Sandbanks to meet Operation Sealion, Hitler's planned cross-Channel invasion. Outwardly they both tried to keep spirits high, but to themselves they admitted that the countermeasures were pathetic. To their relief, and that of the country, Hitler was going to give them time to recover.

BOURNEMOUTH
Phyllis Bottome: admiring the St Peter's curates.

Phyllis Bottome [1884-1963], the novelist, began her teens with a year in Bournemouth. She was the English-born daughter of an American clergyman, Rev W.M. Bottome, who had come across the Atlantic to work as a country parson. He deputised as the senior curate of St Peter's, Hinton Road, where, wrote Phyllis, he "preached the curates and even the vicar off their legs".

The Bottome family lived in The Quadrant, opposite the church. Phyllis compared the three curates with "the flowers and fruit of California; so large, so luscious, so bright and vivid were the prosperous and pleasant young men! Everyone wanted the Bournemouth curates."

Phyllis would enter the literary world in 1905 with *Raw Material* and later through relief work in Vienna after the Great War she gathered the experiences that became *Old Wine*. Her other books include *Private Worlds* [1934], *Level Crossing* [1936], *Danger Signal* [1939], *Mortal Storm* [1940] and *London Pride* [1941].

BOURNEMOUTH (BOSCOMBE)

Grand Theatre and Russell-Cotes Museum: echoes of Sir Henry Irving.

England's greatest actor, Sir Henry Irving [1838-1905], included Boscombe's Grand Theatre on his farewell spring tour of 1905. On Thursday 2 February he was *Becket*, and on Friday he performed in *The Lyons Mail*, whilst on Saturday a matinee of *The Merchant of Venice* was followed by evening roles as Corporal Gregory Brewster at *Waterloo* and Mathias in *The Bells*.

The final words of the martyred Becket would eight months later become Irving's exit line, as he finished his performance at the Theatre Royal, Bradford: "Into Thy hands, O Lord! Into Thine hands." Upon leaving the theatre, and walking into the Midland Hotel, he collapsed and died.

There is a room with Irving memorabilia in the Russell-Cotes Art Gallery and Museum on Bournemouth's East Cliff. The Grand is no longer a theatre.

BOURNEMOUTH

Rupert Brooke: 'decrepit invalids'.

The famous words of Rupert Brooke [1887-1915] about dying for England were to be penned at Blandford Camp. Before the European cataclysm he had holidayed in Bournemouth with his grandfather, Rev Richard England Brooke, at Grantchester Dene in Littledown Road. The house still stands but has been attached to Dean Park Road since the inner relief-road sliced through its neighbours.

"Here Rupert Brooke 1887-1915 Discovered Poetry" the plaque says. Hardly – he was in an academic environment from birth. His father was a master at Rugby. Rupert graduated at Cambridge and travelled far beyond his grandfather's sedate coast, to America and New Zealand. He found Bournemouth unexciting. It was full of "moaning pines" and derelict humanity: "With decrepit and grey-haired invalids I drift wanly along the cliffs".

Before the war his *Poems* [1911] had shown the talent to come. He would pass through Blandford Camp when he was commissioned in the Royal Naval Division and from that period came *1914 and Other Poems*. His corner of that foreign field is on Skyros in the Aegean; he was put there by sunstroke and blood poisoning rather than war.

The great truth behind his lines is that England has, with the exception of 1940 from the air, had no major clash of arms on its soil since 1685. That, fortunately, was his great prediction and it would hold true for the remainder of the twentieth century.

What are now "Grantchester Dene Holiday Flats" in Dean Park Road have an oval plaque beside the right-hand downstairs bay windows.

BOURNEMOUTH (TALBOT WOODS)

Percival Christopher Wren: *Beau Geste.*

Percival Christopher Wren [1885-1941], world traveller, ex-British cavalryman and sometime trooper with the French Foreign Legion, took advantage of the comparative peace of his home in Talbot Woods, Bournemouth, to complete the most famous of his novels, *Beau Geste*, in 1924.

BOURNEMOUTH

Cumberland Clark: war with words.

Cumberland Clark was a magnificently bad poet. Though his sixty-seven books ranged from Shakespearean and Dickensian themes to the achievements of the British Empire, and are logical enough chunks of prose, interspersed are such delights as *The Ferndown Girl Guides' Song Book* and *War Songs of the Allies*. He lived in St Stephen's Road, off Richmond Hill, and penned some memorable lines on Bournemouth girls:

> Girls who right throughout their lives
> have followed Nature's path
> Girls though born in Bournemouth
> have never had a bath.

Other lines are a travelogue, as with this advice about Christchurch:

> In the distance there looms a fine priory
> Make a note of the fact in your diary.

Or, regarding another Dorset town:

> Take this good advice of mine:
> Visit Poole, it's very fine.

As a splendid old gentleman, distinguished by walrus moustache and white hair, he produced the uplifting *War Songs of the Allies* which ironically contained his own exit line:

> Let the bombs bounce round above us,
> And the shells come whizzing by,
> Down in our Air-Raid Shelter
> We'll be cosy, you and I.

That was tempting fate. At midnight on 10 April 1941 a single raider came over Bournemouth Square and dropped a bomb that destroyed his flat and killed the sleeping poet. The same bomber was also responsible for the incendiary device that burnt out Woolworths.

BOURNEMOUTH

Tolkein: a Bournemouth connection?

J.R.R. Tolkein [1892-1973] is said to have retired to Bournemouth but as yet I have not discovered an address or the dates. He published *The Hobbit* in 1937 and its three volume sequel *The Lord of the Rings* in 1954-55. These are lands of mystery with magical inhabitants and legends and language to match.

Whatever the Bournemouth connection, it was in Oxford that his mind-children were created and discussed over drinks at meetings of "The Inklings" in the back bar of the Eagle and Child in St Giles. His cronies included C.S. Lewis [1898-1963] and the poet and novelist Charles Williams [1886-1945]. Theirs was an elitist but productive literary clique.

BOURNEMOUTH

Rupert Croft-Cooke: longest autobiography in the language.

Rupert Croft-Cooke [1903-78] spent much of his life writing about himself and his twenty-four volumes on this subject comprise the longest autobiography in the English language. He lived at Amira Court in Bourne Avenue, in the centre of Bournemouth, after making a typical expatriate's return in 1973 — from just about everywhere — to an England of pop festivals, football violence, mugging, incompetent policing, poverty for the rich, a failing health service, pot, women's lib and inflation.

Croft-Cooke was a novelist, playwright, biographer and a writer on food and other pleasures of *The Sensual World*, as he called his autobiographical series. The thinking is simple and logical rather than deep; even in food his desires were plebeian rather than exotic. Grey squirrels delighted him on his bench between the pines and he was disgusted to see beaming park keepers displaying armfuls of them as dead trophies in a Bournemouth Echo photograph.

Socially he saw "men of homosexual mind" as "the best levellers, the least class conscious of all the minorities of the world" and pointed to this as the cause of "the enmities from which they suffer".

His own confrontation with society resulted from taking home two sailors. The motive was asssumed: why else, the high-minded prosecutors asked, would a man educated at public school and acknowledged as a reputable writer, would such a man invite home a couple of matelots?

In the terms of his contemporary Lord Bradwell it all sounds eminently respectable and classically clean: "Youth always inspires me."

BOURNEMOUTH (SOUTHBOURNE)

Ron Embleton: brought Biggles to life.

"Ron" was the signature of the most famous comic strip artist of the twentieth century. Cartoonist Ronald S. Embleton [1930-87] lived at 50 Carbery Avenue, Southbourne, Bournemouth. He had created adventure strips for the *Big* series of comics published by Scion and his first complete book appeared in 1948.

By the 1950s his output was prodigious, in *Buffalo Bill, Gallant Adventure, Gallant Detective, Gallant Science, Gallant Western, Five Star Western, Star Rocket* and serials for *Comic Cuts* and *The Wonder*. He brought "Johnny Wonder" to *Reveille* and "The Life of Ben Hogan" to Beaverbrook newspapers.

In 1957 he was painting a colour page for the front of the *Express Weekly* comic, with the saga of "Wulf the Briton", and drew Biggles for the inside pages. Then he turned to science fiction for the 1970s, with characters based on the puppets "Stingray" and "Captain Scarlet and the Mysterons" in *TV Century 21*.

Keeping up with popular taste he followed his maturing clientele from the golden age of comics to the flowering of the permissive society. His special talent had always been the drawing of pretty girls and from 1972 these could strip everything in "Wicked Wanda" — the sex-satire strip of the glossy adult magazine Penthouse. His skill was in coupling this vitality with an instinctive precision that never seemed to be compromised by the fact that all his editors wanted the work delivered yesterday.

BOURNEMOUTH (WESTBOURNE)
Max Bygraves: *Wanna Tell You a Story.*

Viewport House in Sandbourne Road on the cliffs at the east side of Alum Chine (Ordnance Survey map reference SZ 074 903) is the home of one of the best known cabaret singers in the English-speaking world. Max Bygraves is his real name — he was the son of Henry and Lilian Bygraves of Rotherhithe. He was born in 1922 and became an entertainer after five years as a wartime RAF fitter. Annual "Royal Command" performances would follow.

His literary debut was in 1976 with his autobiography *I Wanna Tell You a Story* which was followed by a novel, *The Milkman's on his Way.*

Boyle — for Robert Boyle [1627-91]
see STALBRIDGE

BRADFORD ABBAS
Sidney Savory Buckman: showed how to date the rocks.

Sidney Savory Buckman [1860-1929] of Coombe House, Bradford Abbas, took over his father's investigations of the local fossils and showed how ammonites from the now disused limestone quarries around Halfway House (Ordnance Survey map reference ST 602 164) could be used to date the rock beds from which they had been taken.

Professor James Buckman [1816-84] had introduced his eldest son to the Chapel Quarry and Rock Cottage Quarry where exists the lower and upper Inferior Oolite outcrop beside the A30 on what is now the middle section of the Sherborne to Yeovil dual-carriageway. There he studied the Bajocian ammonites and brachiopods of deposits described by Dr Hugh Torrens to late twentieth century geologists as "one of the most fossiliferous in the world".

The studies of the younger Buckman will endure as the best mollusc fauna in the British Jurassic. He retained a deep attachment for the Dorset countryside and his ashes were scattered from Golden Cap on to the exposed geology of the undercliff beside Lyme Bay.

BRADFORD PEVERELL — see WAREHAM for John Hutchins:
County Historian

BRADPOLE
William Forster: Elementary Education Act.

Forsters, at the east end of the village of Bradpole (Ordnance Survey map reference SY 483 943), was the birthplace on 11 July 1818 of William Forster. His Quaker parents soon moved on and William became Bradford's Liberal Member of Parliament from 1861 until his death in 1886.

It was a career with two milestones. In 1880-81, Forster was one step away from the political graveyard as Gladstone's Secretary of State for Ireland; indeed he was lucky to come through an exhausting couple of years with his life. He had been the prime target for Dublin's Phoenix Park assassins but

Forster resigned and two days later they stabbed a couple of his replacements instead.

If we now remember Forster it is for a far different cause that only feels as if it had been around for as long as the Irish question. In 1870 William Forster saw his Elementary Education Act through Parliament and established the basis for state schooling – not that he succeeded in making it compulsory.

BRADPOLE and BRIDPORT

Brennan on the Moor: **ballad with local colour.**

> *It's of a famous highwayman, a story I will tell,*
> *His name was Willie Brennan, and in Bradpole he did dwell.*
> *And on the Bridport mountains he commenced his wild career,*
> *Where many a wealthy gentleman before him shook with fear.*
> *Brennan on the Moor, Brennan on the Moor,*
> *A brave undaunted robber was bold Brennan on the Moor! . . .*

. . . the start of the west Dorset version of the famous story of an eighteenth century Irish Robin Hood – with the Kilworth mountains of County Cork becoming the somewhat less credible "Bridport mountains". Further on in the song there is a guest appearance by the (Dorset) town mayor:

> *. . . One day upon the highway, as Willie he went down,*
> *He met the Mayor of Bridport a mile outside the town.*
> *The Mayor he knew those features: "I think young man", said he,*
> *"Your name is Willie Brennan, you must come along with me!"*

These local versions were discovered by Maureen Jolliffe and published in 1969. As she points out, the story of Willie's exploits travelled much further than his person: he never came across the water. Willie Brennan's grave is in Kilcrumper churchyard, outside his home town of Fermoy, County Cork.

BRANKSOME PARK – see POOLE (BRANKSOME PARK)

BRIDPORT

Tom Sharpe: *Blott on the Landscape.*

Thomas Ridley Sharpe [born 1928] moved to 170 St Andrew's Road at Bridport, from Cambridge, in 1978. In Dorset a massive acre and a half of garden and a variety of house repairs were to provide something of a distraction from writing for novelist Tom Sharpe.

His first farce, *Riotous Assembly*, had been based on the very different experiences of his middle life when he left Britain for South Africa, which had been his mother's home. Her father, who had been born in Stalbridge in 1838, had begun the building of Johannesburg. When Tom Sharpe realised there would be problems ahead in a society that could ban *Black Beauty* under the misconception that it was about a girl rather than a horse, he returned to England and lectured in history at Cambridge from 1963 until 1971. He then became a full-time writer.

The books that followed were among the most successful of the decade – *Indecent Exposure* [1973], *Porterhouse Blue* [1974], *Blott on the Landscape* [1975], *Wilt* [1976], *The Great Pursuit* [1977], *The Throwback* [1978], and *The Wilt Alternative* [1979].

Ancestral Vices was to follow, from Bridport, but in 1986 there was a story that Tom and Nancy Sharpe were considering leaving the town as its own blot on the landscape – in pre-planning stage when it provided him with a plot in 1975 – was being gouged in their direction. They were destined to have a close encounter with the Bridport by-pass. The irony was not lost on the press, or the author, particularly as the television adaptation of *Blott* was fresh in the national mind.

BRIDPORT – see BRADPOLE for *Brennan on the Moor*: ballad with local colour

BROADSTONE – see POOLE (BROADSTONE)

BROADWINDSOR

Thomas Fuller: 'Worthy' with a brain.

"Thomas Fuller was of middle stature, strong set, curled hair; a very working head, in so much that, walking and meditating before dinner, he would eat-up a penny loaf, not knowing that he did it. His natural memory was very great, to which he added the art of memory: he would repeat you forwards and backwards all the signs from Ludgate to Charing Cross."

That can only be John Aubrey writing, and the subject, the Rev Thomas Fuller [1608-61] who was vicar of Broadwindsor from 1635. There were other Tom Fullers, but this one was very much in the Aubrey mould. Fuller was a wordsmith; he calls "Fair Rosamond" – Henry III's favourite – "the mistress-piece of beauty of the age". He collected people and places and assembled them for a marvel of seventeenth century topography, *The History of the Worthies of England*, which is as exquisite a single (bulky) volume travelogue as the country would ever have. In the introduction, he writes that "hitherto no stationer hath lost by me" but in the event it would be seen into print by his son in the year following his death, at which he had been crying out "for his pen and ink to the last".

Those other works the stationers sold so well were a variety of religious tracts, sermons, poems and monographs. In 1660, first anonymously as "a lover of his native country" and then from the third edition under his own name, he published a pamphlet demanding a free Parliament. Despite the Civil War ousting of clergymen, Dorset landowner John Pinney was so impressed with Fuller's preaching that he had relaxed the rules and allowed him to stay at Broadwindsor, apparently as a curate.

"God bless thee, dear old man!" was Coleridge's less than adequate phrase that has unfortunately stuck to his memory. It diminishes a brain that enabled him, it was said, to recite five hundred strange names after only two or three hearings. None who have found it quaint to refer to "Old Tom Fuller" have been capable of anything approaching that.

His old Vicarage at Broadwindsor survives, though its original form has mushroomed into a substantial yellow-stone building of school-like shape and proportions.

BROADWINDSOR (RACEDOWN)

Racedown: where Wordsworth wrote *The Borderers.*

William Wordsworth [1770-1850], the poet, lived in the western hills of Dorset for two of his most productive years, from 1795 to 1797. With his sister, Dorothy, he was given the use of the Pinney family residence at Racedown, a country house on the west side of the B3165 Lyme Regis to Crewkerne road, a mile north of Birdsmoor Gate (Ordnance Survey map reference ST 394 017).

There he wrote *Guilt and Sorrow* and *The Borderers*. Dorothy enthused over the undulating and varied scenery and wrote in her journals: "We have hills, which, seen from a distance, almost take on the character of mountains, some cultivated nearly to their summits, others in their wild state, covered with furze and broom. These delight me the most as they remind me of our native wilds."

Racedown saw the beginning of the close relationship between the Wordsworths and Samuel Taylor Coleridge [1772-1834] that developed into a fusion of minds that left a mark on English literature. "We are three people," Coleridge wrote, "but only one soul".

Brooke — for SUB LIEUTENANT RUPERT BROOKE [1887-1915]
see BOURNEMOUTH for Rupert Brooke: 'decrepit invalids'.
TARRANT MONKTON (BLANDFORD CAMP) for Rupert Brooke: 'Some corner' where he wrote *The Soldier*; TARRANT HINTON for Great War huts: echoes of Rupert Brooke.

Browning — for ROBERT BROWNING [1812-89]
see PENTRIDGE (WOODYATES)

BROWNSEA ISLAND — see STUDLAND (BROWNSEA ISLAND), as the south-east part of Poole Harbour is in Studland parish

Bubb Dodington — for GEORGE BUBB DODINGTON [1691-1762]
see TARRANT GUNVILLE (EASTBURY)

Buckingham — for JAMES SILK BUCKINGHAM [1786-1855]
see WEYMOUTH

Buckman — for SIDNEY SAVORY BUCKMAN [1860-1929]
see BRADFORD ABBAS

BURTON

Robert Southey: a poet's year.

Burton lies beside and to the east of the B3347 a mile north of Christchurch and was transferred from Hampshire to Dorset in the boundary changes of 1 April 1974. It was a small and pastoral community in 1799 when the poet and travel writer Robert Southey [1774-1843] moved into Burton Cottage, north of the village green and second building beyond Westwood Road, and settled into a spell of hard writing.

He produced many of his ballads, completed the *English Eclogues*, prepared a *History of Portugal*, edited the *Annual Anthology* and wrote a preface for an edition of the works of the brilliant boy-poet Thomas Chatterton.

The work may not have caused, but could hardly have helped prevent, the return of poor health that would force Southey to leave Burton in April 1800. With his wife, Edith, he went to Portugal until the following spring and on coming back to the British Isles they lived at Keswick, Dublin and Bristol before settling permanently in Greta Hall, Keswick, in 1803.

BURTON BRADSTOCK

Adela Curtis: *The New Mysticism.*

Adela Curtis [1864-1960], the Japanese-born author of *Janardana* [1905] and *The New Mysticism*, put her ideas into practice in 1912 with the Order of Silence, a religious community she founded at Coldash, Berkshire. More converts were won over by *Creative Silence: a Manual of Meditation for Beginners in the Practice of Transmutation of the Body* [1920].

In the 1920s, Miss Curtis brought her celibate and contemplative vegetarian Christian commune, who were exclusively female, to the Dorset coast. They were to work the land around the newly built St Bride's Farm, east of Burton Bradstock (Ordnance Survey map reference SY 496 886); the "white ladies" the villagers called them because of their creamy veils and robes.

A large chapel was built beside the farm and opened in 1938. They had become the Christian Contemplatives' Community and evolved a strict set of rules. Papists and Christian Scientists were excluded from membership. Piped water and electricity were banned. Sewage was to be collected for use on the fields as the natural basis for the organic growth of produce. The day would have seven periods of contemplation, starting at five a.m.

Adela Curtis urged others to adopt the power of prayer as a wartime weapon against Adolf Hitler. These prayers were personalised against the target and rendered as a repetitive chant; they were answered, perhaps, by Hitler's suicidal decision to invade Russia instead of Britain.

Miss Curtis never quite reached her century. She died on 17 September 1960 and has her memorial in the chapel: "I have loved thee with an everlasting love."

Her end would have caused disappointment in two ways. Cremation, at Weymouth, offended against her beliefs as she disapproved of the use of gas. Secondly she had wished, as she had urged, for all natural wastes to be returned to the soil.

The Othona Community took over St Bride's Farm and brought a more relaxed regime.

CASTLETON (SHERBORNE CASTLE)

Elizabeth's favourite poet sea-dog: Sir Walter Raleigh.

"The Procession of Queen Elizabeth" hangs in the Red Drawing Room at Sherborne Castle. It is a huge canvas and an appropriate treasure, for the castle owes its existence to her gift of Sherborne lands to her favourite mariner, Sir Walter Raleigh [?1552-1618]. Broadwindsor's seventeenth century historian Thomas Fuller has in his *Worthies of England* a nice little story — almost certainly untrue but still nonetheless worth telling — that Raleigh had scratched with a diamond on a palace window:

Fain would I climb, yet fear to fall. To which Elizabeth is said to have added:
If the heart fails thee, climb not at all.

Raleigh in his twenties dressed up to the nines in the most magnificent high fashion. His visual presence and style were coupled with the verbal dexterity of a "bold and plausible tongue".

In 1584 Raleigh was knighted and the following year Elizabeth prevented him from leaving on the expedition that he had inspired and organised, the attempt at founding a colony to which the queen had personally given the name Virginia, somewhere on the east coast of North America. Raleigh never did see America and therefore his fame rests upon proxies, particularly his servant Thomas Harriot who brought back to England sacks of potatoes and tobacco and wrote in 1588 a *Brief and True Report of Virginia* which describes how the natives used them. Some of the potatoes found their way into Raleigh's garden at Youghal and thereon rooted themselves as the mainstay of the Irish diet. The tobacco became high fashion because Raleigh adopted it to enhance his flamboyant persona and encouraged fellow-courtiers to copy his example.

In 1588, Elizabeth found a new favourite, Robert Devereux, second Earl of Essex, and Raleigh fell from grace when the queen discovered he was having an affair with one of her maids, Elizabeth Throgmorton. The pair spent a few weeks in the Tower of London and he was then released conditionally, as what he called the "Queen of England's poor captive", to sort out the distribution of the £150,000 prize-money — the bulk of it going to the queen — when the great carrack the *Madre de Dios* was brought into Dartmouth. It was sufficient service for the queen to give Raleigh his freedom but he was to be banished from the royal court for four years.

Raleigh married Elizabeth Throgmorton and in January 1592 he bought a ninety-nine year lease on the Old Castle and its park at Sherborne. He put his efforts into repairing the castle, but tired of persistent mould on his clothes, books and other possessions. It was the impossibility of beating the damp that caused him to abandon the improvements to the Old Castle in 1594 and to set about building a modern four-storey home where the early Tudor hunting lodge stood — on the rise a quarter of a mile to the south of the Old Castle (Ordnance Survey map reference ST 649 165).

Dressed stone for the four towers and Dutch-style curves to the top of the facade came from Ham Hill and the curtain wall of the Old Castle was used for the main rubble of the walls. Their general roughness caused the need for plastering, which was then an exceedingly uncommon building technique. Indeed it is one of the earliest plastered houses in the land. It was also an unusually light house, having leaded-glass windows that took up a large proportion of the available wall-space, though most of these were considerably reduced or totally blocked during the subsequent expansion of the house.

Sherborne Lodge it was called, perpetuating the name of the hunting lodge it had replaced, but gradually it became known as Sherborne Castle (or Sherborne New Castle to try and avoid the inevitable confusion with the Old Castle) though it is not a castle at all and would have been impossible to defend with so many ground floor windows. The Keep of the Old Castle was retained as state rooms for entertaining; the one thing for which it was perfectly suited was mediaeval banquets and in it the guests could be given free rein. Adrian Gilbert, his half-brother, was installed there as the bailiff.

Some rooms of the New Castle had austere plastering but others were panelled in oak, and tapestries were hung in the first floor salon which has a superb fireplace and an ornate moulded plaster ceiling which features the Raleighs' coat of arms.

Tree planting was carried out extensively and the last of the great cedars are as old as any in England, having been brought back for Raleigh by his captains from the North American expeditions. Raleigh's Grove survives and below it he had elaborate water-gardens, neat hanging terraces, a bowling green, and fruit orchards.

Thomas Herriot, who had brought Europe its tobacco and potatoes, was given a home. He was a mathematician and a deist, disbelieving that the divine being had manifested himself in Christ. Their unorthodox friends included Christopher Marlowe [1564-93], credited with *The Atheist's Tragedy*. The beautiful lines for which Marlowe is best remembered were dedicated to Walter Raleigh:

> *Come live with me and be my love,*
> *And we will all the pleasures prove.*

They were perceived as a personal invitation to Raleigh and a skit on his imagined responses was produced by Izaac Walton [1593-1683] as *The Nymph's Reply* "made by Sir Walter Raleigh in his younger days". Marlowe was stabbed with a death-thrust into his eye, during a drunken brawl at Deptford. A warrant was out for his arrest on charges of disseminating irreligious tracts.

On 21 March 1594 Thomas Howard, third Viscount Bindon, was ordered by the Ecclesiastical Commissioners to hold an inquiry at Cerne Abbey into allegations that Raleigh had attended an atheistic lecture delivered by Marlowe. There is no surviving documentation of the outcome of this and a series of similar accusations. A Catholic pamphleteer of 1592 had denounced "Sir Walter Rawley's School of Atheism" and claimed its scholars were "taught among other things to spell God backwards".

Raleigh meanwhile turned his energies to the search for Eldorado. The first expedition, on his behalf, brought back nothing so on 9 February 1595 he personally led a fleet of five ships out of Plymouth to the South American coast of Guiana. They did find some gold-stained quartz but no fabulous city. The mahogany they brought back was the first to be seen in England.

In 1596 Raleigh was back at Sherborne and in June he commanded the *Warspite* at the head of the English fleet that carried out the storming of Cadiz, in which he narrowly survived severe wounds. Despite various personal animosities, Raleigh was back in public acceptance if not full favour. He was the member of Parliament for Dorset in 1597 and for Cornwall in 1601 and encouraged West Country boatmen to begin their lucrative trade with the Newfoundland fisheries.

Politics turned against Raleigh on the death of Queen Elizabeth in 1603. James I came to London from Scotland with the belief that Raleigh would oppose him, and though that proved unfounded he was prepared to believe that Raleigh was involved in a "plot to surprise the king's person". The evidence against him was feeble, amounting to the fact that he had borrowed a book that refuted James's title to the throne. That he denied, but then had to admit; and he was known to be on friendly terms with the alleged plotters. It was enough for conspiracy convictions at the time, and Raleigh was convicted and sentenced to death on 11 December 1603.

Instead of execution he was sent to the Tower of London. Legal arguments followed over the forfeiture of the Sherborne estate which from 1608-12 was bestowed upon Robert Carr, Earl of Somerset, but was then bought back by the crown. Raleigh was able to live in the Tower with his wife and son, and to write his *Historie of the World*. His elegant Elizabethan prose twists into a masterly protest against the Stuart "divine-right" absolutism that was to claim his head. Meanwhile he was allowed to set up a laboratory in which he desalinated Thames water by distillation.

In March 1616 he was released from the Tower and allowed to prepare another expedition to the Orinoco, in search of gold, on condition that he did nothing to harass the Spanish. Fourteen ships sailed from Plymouth on 12 June 1617.

They immediately hit trouble. Storm force winds caused one to sink and the rest were scattered. Most eventually staggered into Cork for repairs.

They sailed again on 19 August. This time they would languish for forty days in the doldrums, running short of water and with deaths from fevers and scurvy bringing the crews to the point of mutiny. Worse followed their arrival on the Venezuela coast. Lawrence Kemys was sent ahead to find the gold mine, and instructed to avoid a confrontation with the Spaniards, but on finding the town of San Tomas in the way, he attacked it and Raleigh's son, Walter Raleigh, was killed in the process. Raleigh was so distraught at the outcome that Kemys killed himself. The expedition then fell apart, with some of the ships, Raleigh's included, departing for home via Newfoundland.

He returned with fish rather than gold. Even with the latter he would have been in trouble, however, as James had promised the Spaniards that there would be retribution for the unauthorised attack on their settlement. James ordered Raleigh's trial but it was pointed out that this was a legal impossibility as he was already under sentence of death for treason. That was carried out with an axe on the scaffold in Old Palace Yard on the morning of 28 October 1618.

It was with a brave face that Raleigh made his exit. Someone complained that his head should face towards the east as it lay on the block. "What matter how the head lie," he answered, "so the heart be right?"

CASTLETON (SHERBORNE CASTLE) and SHERBORNE

Alexander Pope: seat and words.

Opposite Raleigh's Seat, on the other side of the cascade in Sherborne Park, stands Alexander Pope's Seat. The poet [1688-1744] was a friend of William Digby, the fifth Baron Digby [1661-1752]. The house fascinated Pope who reflected in 1722 that it was "so peculiar and in its position of so uncommon kind, that it merits a more particular description".

Sherborne Abbey also has its Alexander Pope associations, literally carved in stone, on the graves of two of Digby's children. These poetical inscriptions are in memory of Robert Digby, the fifth Baron's second son, and Mary Digby, his eldest daughter.

CASTLETON (OBORNE) and SHERBORNE

Robert Goadby's memorial: just an empty space.

The iron-railed grave of free-press pioneer Robert Goadby [1721-78] stood beneath a tall elm in the field south of Oborne chapel (Ordnance Survey map reference ST 653 178) until the bicentenary of his death. Then with a cruel twist of fate the tree was dead with Dutch elm disease and its fellers made such a mess of its removal that Goadby's memorial was completely smashed.

A further irony was that the destruction was completely ignored by the Western Gazette — the organ which Goadby had founded, via his Western Flying Post of 1743 — and it was left to me to print the story in issue 70 of Dorset County Magazine. Goadby merged his paper with the Sherborne Mercury and had offices in Long Street, Sherborne. It was Sherborne Printing House and its ideals were inscribed above the door: "The liberty of the Press, and the liberty of the People fall together. May heaven avert it."

The Oborne grave, placed in the field between the chapel and the later railway line, was originally planted with a pine tree. It was a railed rectangle about ten feet by seven feet, and the stone was a celebration of the beauty of nature rather than the power of the printed word:

IN MEMORY
OF MR ROBERT GOADBY
LATE OF SHERBORNE, PRINTER, WHO
DEPARTED THIS LIFE AUGUST 11th
1788 AGE 57

Death is a path that must be trod
If man would ever come to God
The fir tree aspires to the sky
And is enclosed with everlasting verdure
Emblem of the good and of that everlasting life
Which God will bestow on them
Since death is the gate to life
The grave should be crowned with flowers.
Here also lies Rachel, his wife
Who died March 10th 1798.

CASTLETON — see LONG BURTON
for William Sharpe: *Treatise upon Coal Mines*

CERNE ABBAS

Aelfric *Grammaticus*: eleven monastic books.

Eleven influential homilies and treatises by Aelfric, the first Abbot of Cerne at its refounding in 987, have survived in print. He vigorously opposed the doctrine of transubstantiation — the idea of the bread and wine in the Eucharist becoming the body and blood of Jesus Christ — and was therefore reprinted through the centuries as theologians resurrected him in their support whenever the argument broke out again.

The question arises of whether they were written at Cerne. Certainly they are unlikely to pre-date that time as he writes that he was previously " a monk and a mass-priest" at Winchester. His next posting was years later, in

1006, when he became the first Abbot of the newly completed Ensham Abbey.

Aelfric's rising influence was probably contemporaneous with his literary output, which was substantial, and he seems to have been a thinking-king's chaplain at Canute's court. That, however, post-dates Aelfric's Cerne period as Canute fled to Denmark in 1014 and did not seize the English throne until 1016. Some of his benefactions went to Cerne Abbey as recompense for having raided it in his piratical days. Aelfric had by this time written the first essential school-book in the land, a Latin glossary and grammar, and was henceforth known as Grammaticus.

Sadly, there is nothing to prove a Cerne connection with any of the books, nor link any of the surviving architecture with its first Abbot. Most of what remains, which is quaint rather than impressive, dates from the closing phase of mediaeval monasticism some four centuries later.

CERNE ABBAS

Richard Pococke: discovered the Cerne Giant.

To Dr Richard Pococke [1704-65], the traveller across the Alps and up the Nile, goes the distinction of being the earliest person — so far as is known — to note the existence of the chalk-cut representation of a naked man at Cerne Abbas. That was in 1754, a decade after the explorations of *A Description of the East*.

He noticed the figure of the Cerne Giant carved on a hillside in what he describes as "a gentell posture". The words, perhaps, are less than adequate, but Pococke would be the Bishop of Meath towards the end of his life, which must somewhat restrict one's vocabulary.

Chafin — for WILLIAM CHAFIN [died 1818]
see CHETTLE

CHALDON HERRING (EAST CHALDON)

Beth Car: where T.F. Powys wrote
Mr Weston's Good Wine.

First it was the terraced Lilac Cottage in the village and then Beth Car, the red-brick villa set back from the south side of the lane at the west end of East Chaldon, that were the homes of the novelist Theodore Powys [1875-1953] from summer 1908 to 1940. The latter looks across his "Madder Hill" and provided the solitude which he found vital for his work.

Here in 1925 he wrote *Mr Weston's Good Wine*, which has now made it into paperback as a modern classic. It tells how God visited East Chaldon, or Folly Down as it is called, in the person of Mr Weston, a travelling wine merchant, who came in an old Ford van.

Rosemary Manning, who stimulated the revival of interest in Powys in the mid-1970s, called it "one of the few perfect novels in the English language".

Powys moved from Beth Car (Ordnance Survey map reference SY 788 831) to the mid-Dorset village of Mappowder because of the influx of troops to the coast as the country prepared for invasion.

Theodore Powys may not have "degraded the rich comedy of which he was capable to an almost bestial farce", as The Times obituary writer believed, but he had penned delightful allegories on the inherent contradiction between an ever-present God and nature's obsession with procreation. "Queer, blind, half-dumb, earthy folk, lusting and fumbling in the endless preoccupation of sex." These, as a critic wrote, were the fellow inhabitants of T.F. Powys's village of life.

CHALDON HERRING

Llewelyn Powys: isolated home and clifftop grave.

"Llewelyn Powys, 13 August 1884. 2 December 1939. The living, the living, he shall praise thee." The inscription is on a block of Portland stone above the ashes of the Dorset writer, put there by Elizabeth Muntz [1894-1977] on 3 October 1947 at the edge of a field between the cliffside navigation beacons to the south of Chaldon Herring (Ordnance Survey map reference SY 783 811).

It is beside the more inland of the two coastal footpaths that run between White Nothe, the headland which he insisted was correctly called White Nose, and the car-park at Lulworth Cove.

He was usually in such poor health, suffering tuberculosis, that he felt compelled to live for the moment: "To be alive, only to be alive, may I never forget the privilege of that."

He is remembered as a fine essayist through his collections of *Thirteen Worthies*, on his literary roots, *Earth Memories, Somerset and Dorset Essays, The Glory of Life* — written here "in a cornfield on the Dorset Downs under a cloudless sky" — and *A Baker's Dozen* in which he took final refuge in childhood memories. These are complemented by the autobiographies of *Skin for Skin*, about the search for a cure, *Black Laughter*, on his four years in East Africa, and *The Verdict of Bridlegoose* which describes his next overseas period in the United States from 1920-25.

There on 30 September 1924, he married the writer Alyse Gregory and when the Dorchester-born author returned to his homeland it was to make their home near White Nose and then from 1931-37 in a dry chalkland coombe, with a view opening inland towards the Frome Valley, a mile south of East Chaldon.

The slate-roofed nineteenth century house (Ordnance Survey map reference SY 793 817) has walls of banded flint and brick. It is beside a rough flinty track that leads to the white cliffs at Bat's Head. The building is called Chydyok (previously Chideock, but not to be confused with Chideock the village).

Llewelyn Powys was the eighth of the eleven children born to Rev Charles Francis Powys and his wife Mary Cowper Johnson. He is third in their literary stakes in terms of current acclaim, behind brothers John and Theodore, but for me Llewelyn has the distinction of having been able to express that bond which so many of us feel with the landscape of Dorset.

CHALDON HERRING (EAST CHALDON)

Sailor's Return: David Garnett's book.

The characterful cob-walled nineteenth century public house at East Chaldon is the Sailor's Return, the Folly Down Inn of Theodore Powys, which under its real name provided the title for a novel by David Garnett [1892-1981]. That was, in 1928, ahead of its time in having a black hero.

Garnett's output was wide-ranging and highly acclaimed, springing from the Hawthornden and Tait-Black prizes in 1923. These were his publications: *The Kitchen Garden and its Management, Lady into Fox, A Man in the Zoo* [1923]; *The Sailor's Return, Go She Must, The Old Dovecot* [1928]; *No Love* [1929]; *The Grasshoppers Come* [1931]; *A Rabbit in the Air* [1932]; *Pocahontas* [1933]; *Beany-Eye* [1935]; *War in the Air* [1941]; *The Golden Echo* [1953]; *Flowers of the Forest, Aspects of Love* [1955]; *A Shot in the Dark* [1958]; *A Net for Venus* [1959]; *The Familiar Faces* [1962]; *Two by Two* [1963]; *The Ulterior Motives* [1966]; *A Clean Slate* [1971]; *The Sons of the Falcon* [1973]; *Purl and Plain, Plough over the Bones* [1973]; *The Master Cat* [1974]; *Up She Rises* [1977] and *Great Friends* [1979]. He also edited several collections of letters, including those of his friend T.E. Lawrence in 1938.

The last part of his life was spent in Montcuq, France, but his body was brought home to East Chaldon to consummate his lasting love affair with this coastal corner of literary Dorset.

CHALDON HERRING (EAST CHALDON)
Sylvia and Valentine: lesbian authors.

Authors Sylvia Townsend Warner [1893-1978] and Valentine Ackland [1906-69] were lesbian lovers and they share a headstone at East Chaldon churchyard. It was the village where, in the magic and footsteps of T.F. Powys, they had sought seclusion through a series of short-term cottage rentings. They worked together on *Whether a Dove or Seagull* in 1934.

Sylvia Townsend Warner's books include *The Espalier* [1925]; *Lolly Willowes* [1926]; *Mr Fortune's Maggot* [1927]; *Time Importuned* [1928]; *The True Heart* [1929]; *Opus 7* [1931]; *The Salutation* [1932]; *Summer Will Show* [1936]; *After the Death of Don Juan* [1938]; *A Garland of Straw* [1943]; *The Museum of Cheats* [1947]; *The Corner That Held Them* [1948]; *The Flint Anchor* [1954]; *Winter in the Air* [1956]; *Boxwood* [1960]; *The Cat's Cradle Book* [1960]; *A Spirit Rises* [1960]; *A Stranger with a Bag* [1966] and *The Innocent and the Guilty* [1971].

Her biography, *Sylvia, an honest account*, was written by Valentine. In it she admits there was something beyond her own poetry that had stimulated Sylvia's interest: "I had shown her some poems of mine; very weakly and bad ones, and she had seen good in them, or perhaps good in me, and become friendly to me."

They had met in Dorset in 1926. Valentine was ahead of her time, in Dorset at least, in wearing trousers and propounding the virtues of the Communist Party. The pair would play a part in the Republican propaganda machine during the Spanish Civil War.

As years became decades, Sylvia would have fame and growing spirituality, and Valentine her drink and other lovers.

CHALDON HERRING (EAST CHALDON)
Hope Muntz: *The Golden Warrior.*

The mediaevalist Isabelle Hope Muntz [1907-81] is buried at East Chaldon, beside her sister Elizabeth Muntz [1894-1977], the sculptor. Both were born in Toronto.

Hope Muntz, who never married, researched for years to gather the Dorset-based material which she presented in an epic of saga-style perfection, *The Golden Warrior* [1948], which was translated into German and Scandinavian editions. She also reviewed books, under the pseudonym William Langland, and became Britain's leading scholar on the Battle of Hastings and the Bayeux Tapestry.

The latter influence rubbed off on her sister Elizabeth who produced the primitive nativity picture for the church at East Chaldon which has the barrow-studded escarpment of the Five Marys as its backdrop.

Elizabeth also cut author Llewelyn Powys's grave slab from a block of Portland stone and erected it on the slope overlooking Weymouth Bay.

CHALDON HERRING – see DORCHESTER
for Rothesay House: birthplace of Llewelyn Powys

Chapman – for HESTER WOLFERSTAN PELLATT [1899-1976], known as HESTER CHAPMAN, see LANGTON MATRAVERS

CHETTLE and FARNHAM
Chettle House: Chafin and West.

The Queen Anne style Chettle House, a lofty square of bricks, was built by George Chafin early in the eighteenth century, to designs by Thomas Archer (Ordnance Survey map reference ST 952 133). Chafin died in 1766 and the last member of the family to live in Chettle was William Chafin [died 1818] whose *Anecdotes and History of Cranbourn Chase* has a drawing of a group of deer poachers as its frontispiece.

His successor is better remembered in Canada than in Chettle. Rev John West [1778-1845] was chaplain to the Hudson's Bay Company and first missionary to the North American Indians on behalf of the Church Missionary Society. His Red River Settlement church and school became St John's Cathedral, Winnipeg. He had been rector of Chettle since 1820, leaving a curate to look after the little parish, but on returning in 1828 he found there was religion in its peoples too.

A Brief Memoir of William B ... commemorates the life of a twelve-year-old who died at Chettle in 1831. Such feelings were expanded into a 246 page biography of his wife, Harriet West [1789-1839], *A Memoir of Mrs John West*, in 1840. He regarded her as a saint, and having also become rector of the adjoining parish of Farnham in 1834, he threw the rest of his life into the welfare and teaching of deprived British children. His final good work was a scheme for a Gypsy School at Farnham in the buildings that became the also relatively short-lived Pitt-Rivers Museum.

CHILD OKEFORD
William Kethe: *All people that on earth do dwell.*

> *All people that on earth do dwell,*
> *Sing to the Lord with cheerful voice,*
> *Him serve with fear His praise forth tell,*
> *Come ye before Him and rejoice.*

That is the opening verse of William Kethe's version of the hundredth psalm which is sung to the tune of *The Old Hundredth*. Kethe was rector of Child Okeford, north-west of Blandford, from 1561 until his death in about 1608. He converted twenty-five such psalms into hymns though most remained in obscurity. Before opting for life in the heart of the Dorsetshire countryside

Kethe had been in the mainstream of Protestant theologians and worked in Switzerland with English exiles – he was Scots – on the translation of the Geneva Bible.

There was a talented lighter side to the "no unready rhymer" and he produced some popular ballads, including *A Ballet, declaringe the fal of the Whore of Babylone, intytuled Tye thy Mare, Tom-boye*.

CHILD OKEFORD – see HANFORD
for Where Sullivan composed: *Onward Christian Soldiers*

CHRISTCHURCH (MUDEFORD)
Gundimore: Rose's 'Persian Tent' where Scott and Coleridge stayed.

Gundimore is now known as Scott's House. It overlooks Avon Beach from the sand-dunes of Mudeford and was built in the style of a Persian tent by William Stewart Rose [1775-1843]. With his father he was returned to Parliament from Christchurch in 1796 at the age of twenty-one but opted out via the Stewardship of the Chiltern Hundreds in 1800. Young Rose, an enthusiastic student of mediaeval romance, published a version of the *Amadis* in French in 1803 and struck up a friendship that year with Walter Scott [1771-1832; made baronet 1820].

Gundimore was Rose's villa in the sands, and Scott came there in 1807 and adapted the introduction to *Marmion* to include an allusion to Rose's translation of *Partenopex of Blois*; causing Rose to be unjustly accused of plagiarism from *Marmion*.

In his poem *Gundimore*, a verse-letter to an Italian friend, Rose enthuses over his remarkable house. Its tent drapes are painted deep red with gold edging and frame the doors and fireplace, continuing as a frieze that encircles the room, with tassels and medallions to enhance the effect. The room leads into a circular passage which was built as an open portico and repeats the same design.

Samuel Taylor Coleridge [1772-1834] and Sir Walter Scott frequently stayed at Gundimore and their visits to Christchurch Harbour are commemorated among the *Rhymes* which Rose published in 1837.

CHRISTCHURCH (HIGHCLIFFE)
Chewton Glen: Marryat echoes.

Chewton Glen Hotel overlooks the Walkford Brook which is the point at which Dorset becomes Hampshire (Ordnance Survey map reference SZ 226 941). It was here, when it must have been quite new, that Captain Frederick Marryat [1792-1848] stayed in 1846 and wrote his Civil War period novel *The Children of the New Forest*.

He could return to even greater comfort today. Martin Skan and his brother Trevor bought the house in 1966 and expanded it into an international-class hotel. It won the Egon Ronay "Gold Plate Award" for Britain's hotel of the year in 1976 and has gone on to accumulate a foyer full of presentation pieces.

CHRISTCHURCH
Henry Weekes: sculpture to Shelley in the Priory.

The finest work of art in Christchurch Priory is the outstanding piece carved by Henry Weekes [1807-77] on commission from Sir Percy Florence Shelley of Boscombe Manor in memory of his father, the poet Percy Bysshe Shelley [1792-1822]. It shows the drowned poet's body being lifted by his widow on to an Italian beach.

Engravings appeared in the Art Journal of 1853 and it was intended for St Peter's church in the centre of Bournemouth, but the vicar rejected it, feeling that it would turn his building into a Shelley shrine. So it came to the north wall of the Priory tower. The stanza at the end of the inscription is from Shelley's *Adonais:*

> He hath outsoared the shadow of our night
> Envy and calumny and hate and pain,
> And that unrest which men miscall delight
> Can touch him not and torture not again;
> From the contagion of the world's slow stain
> He is secure, and now can never mourn
> A heart grown cold, a head grown grey in vain,
> Nor, when the spirit's self has ceased to burn
> With sparkless ashes load an unlamented urn.

Ironically, in view of the rejection of the sculpture, Shelley's heart would find its way into a vault beneath St Peter's churchyard, Bournemouth, in 1889.

CHRISTCHURCH
Gleeson White and Baron Corvo: *Hadrian the Seventh.*

Frederick Rolfe [1860-1913] arrived in Christchurch at Toinham [now Tyneham] House in Bridge Street in the summer of 1899 and adopted the name Baron Corvo to the dismay and ridicule of his neighbours. By 7 December 1899 he was in Scots College, Rome, from which he was physically expelled a few months later.

In 1891 he was back in Christchurch and writing in The Artist of experiments with colour photography, writing play critiques, and painting an altar mural of St Michael, modelled for him by Cecil Castle, for the Church of the Immaculate Conception and St Joseph in the village of Purewell which is now a suburb of Christchurch.

Donald Weeks has shown in Dorset County Magazine, issue 82, that Nikolaus Pevsner's suggestion that he also produced the wall painting in Corpus Christi church, Boscombe, is unfounded as it was not completed until 1910 and Rolfe left Christchurch in 1891.

He had by then written the story of an Italian peasant boy, *In His Own Image*, and resurrected the hero, Tito, for a subsequent series of stories. He produced drawings, including "St Sebastian" which became the figure Hypnos for the title page of *Don Renato* in 1909.

By then Rolfe had moved to London and created his masterpiece, *Hadrian the Seventh,* in which he portrayed himself as a mediaeval Pope. The failed priest had made good, and in it and other work there are allusions to Gleeson White [1851-98] and his family who befriended him in Christchurch in 1891. They were stationers in the town, in Caxton House, but their major contribution to cultural life came a little later, after they had moved to Hammersmith, when they were the first to bring the talent of artist Aubrey Beardsley [1872-98] to public attention.

Rolfe abandoned his vow of chastity in 1908 and became openly transvestite, not that he had ever troubled to disguise his homosexual inclinations. He had never had any time for women and had a particular aversion to bird-nest hats. Some regarded him as an "enjoyable freak". His *Venice Letters* show him writing well.

"I want to know more," is the rider to a delicately written admiration of a young docker whom he proposes to find again in the morning. A talent that had touched the point of genius was receding into torment. Unfulfilled, and unrecognised for what he had achieved, Rolfe was to die unloved, in Venice in 1913.

Churchill — for SIR WINSTON CHURCHILL [1874-1965]
see BOURNEMOUTH (WESTBOURNE)

Clark — for CUMBERLAND CLARK [killed 1941]
see BOURNEMOUTH

Clarke — for THOMAS J. CLARKE [executed 1916]
see PORTLAND

Clavell — for JOHN CLAVELL [1603-42]
see KIMMERIDGE (SMEDMORE)

CLIFTON MAYBANK — see SHERBORNE
for Sir Thomas Wyatt: loved Anne Boleyn and gave us the sonnet.

CLOUDS HILL — see TURNERS PUDDLE (CLOUDS HILL)

Coleridge — for SAMUEL TAYLOR COLERIDGE [1772-1834]
see BROADWINDSOR for Racedown: where Wordsworth wrote *The Borderers* and CHRISTCHURCH (MUDEFORD) for Gundimore: Rose's Persian tent, where Scott and Coleridge stayed.

Cooper — for ANTHONY ASHLEY COOPER [1671-1713], third EARL of SHAFTESBURY, see WIMBORNE ST GILES

CORFE CASTLE (ENCOMBE)

Eldon: deprived Shelley of his children.

There is a link between Encombe House, in the deep Golden Bowl of a Purbeck coastal valley (Ordnance Survey map reference SY 944 785) with the poet Percy Bysshe Shelley [1792-1822]. The owner of the house, the first Earl of Eldon [1751-1838], in his capacity as Lord High Chancellor of England, acted to prevent Shelley gaining custody of his two children after the suicide of his first wife, Harriet Shelley, in 1816.

Shelley had written *The Necessity of Atheism*, for which he had been expelled from Oxford, in 1811. His negative religious views were cited by Eldon as the ground for his decision.

Eldon's brother, Sir William Scott, first Baron Stowell [1745-1836] was a close friend of Dr Johnson. Stowell was the draughtsman of the basic international maritime laws.

The Egyptian-style stone needle above Encombe valley (Ordnance Survey map reference SY 946 791), which is forty feet high, was raised in 1835 "in honour of Sir William Scott, created first Baron Stowell".

CORFE CASTLE — see PAMPHILL (KINGSTON LACY) for Henry Bankes: *History of Rome*

CORFE CASTLE — see SWANAGE for Mary Palgrave: Royalist romance

CORSCOMBE and HALSTOCK
Thomas Hollis: endowed Harvard Library.

Fields and farms at Corscombe and Halstock carry names of North American places, persons and ideals of the eighteenth century, together with libertarian echoes from this side of the Atlantic. These were chosen by gentleman scholar and book editor Thomas Hollis [1720-74]. He lived at Urless Farm, Corscombe, and had its church rebuilt in 1746, but would be buried in an unmarked grave, ten feet deep, in the middle of a field either there or at Harvard Farm, above the Dorset corner of Sutton Bingham Reservoir (Ordnance Survey map reference ST 550 095). Legend has it that his horse was shot and buried with him.

The Harvard connection was that his uncle had been its benefactor and Hollis endowed its famous university library. He also gave books to those at Berne and Zurich. His seven hundred acres soon abounded with political tags. Locke Farm, Halstock, was in tribute to the English philosopher. Liberty Farm pre-dates the new American nation of 1776 but has the word in which it would be conceived.

Hollis had tried to reason with William Pitt, the Earl of Chatham, to avoid that colonial war. Field names include the catchwords Reasonableness, Comprehension and Understanding from Locke's works and one addressed to Archbishop Secker, but that was in derision, so Hollis applied it to barren ground. Massachusetts proved too much for the Dorset tongue, as it does for my spelling, and has become "Massy Field".

As a man of letters, Hollis was involved in the editing and publication of several major works, including Toland's *Life of Milton* [1761] and John Locke's *Two Treatises on Government* and his *Letters concerning Toleration*.

Ascetic in all things, Hollis's diet excluded sugar, salt and spices. He drank only water. Urless Farm he regarded as "a most healthy, and, I think, beautiful spot; the very earth itself is sweet beyond a nosegay".

His friend and heir Thomas Brand became Thomas Brand-Hollis "upon succeeding to Mr Hollis's fortune".

Corvo — for BARON CORVO, actually FREDERICK ROLFE [1860-1913], see CHRISTCHURCH

CRANBORNE
Edward Stillingfleet: *Origines Britannicae.*

Born at Cranborne, and educated at its grammar school under Thomas Garden, Edward Stillingfleet [1635-99] would become one of the notable scholarly clerics. Indeed his promotional prospects were ensured by those writings, particularly *Origines Sacrae* [1622], and he plunged into deep controversy during the Church of England's schism of 1664, emerging as chaplain to Charles II [1667] and canon of Canterbury [1669]. He argued theology constantly and made his view that of the establishment as personal advancement continued. From Archdeacon of London [1677] he became Dean of St Paul's [1678] and Bishop of Worcester [1689-99].

His *Origines Britannicae* [1685] is one of the most forceful and important works on the evolution of the early English church to appear in the post-mediaeval period. He had the learning to carry the theology, a combination that would not be matched until the nineteenth century, as is shown by the antiquarian research that went into a *Discourse of the True Antiquity of London*.

Creech — for THOMAS CREECH [1659-1700] see BLANDFORD

Croft-Cooke — for RUPERT CROFT-COOKE [1903-78]
see BOURNEMOUTH

Crowe — for WILLIAM CROWE [1745-1829] see STOKE ABBOTT

Cruickshank — for GEORGE CRUICKSHANK [1792-1878]
see LYME REGIS

Crusoe — for ROBINSON CRUSOE [discovered 1709, re-named 1719]
see POOLE

Curgenven — for THOMAS CURGENVEN [late 17th century]
see FOLKE

Dale — for CHARLES WILLIAM DALE [1791-1872]
see GLANVILLES WOOTTON

Darby — for JOHN NELSON DARBY [1800-82]
see BOURNEMOUTH

Darwin — for CHARLES DARWIN [1809-82]
see BOURNEMOUTH

Day Lewis — for CECIL DAY LEWIS [1904-72]
see STINSFORD

Defoe — for DANIEL DEFOE [?1661-1731] see POOLE for Woodes
Rogers: discovered *Robinson Crusoe*

Dibben — for THOMAS DIBBEN [1695-1741] see MANSTON

Dickens — for CHARLES DICKENS [1812-70]
see SHERBORNE

Dodington — for GEORGE BUBB DODINGTON [1691-1762], first
BARON MELCOMBE, see TARRANT GUNVILLE (EASTBURY)

DORCHESTER

Thomas Locket: spoke for the printer.

Thomas Locket was Dorchester's printer in the period before the Napoleonic wars, in about 1780-98, and in his advertising broadside "Thomas Locket's

Address to his Friends at Dorchester and its Vicinity" he gives us a glimpse of
his workplace and its services to the community:

> Next his Printing Room we view,
> Rolling Press, and Letter new;
> Here he works his Copper-Plates,
> Here he prints his moisten'd Sheets;
> There disposed in Order lie,
> Types by Caslon and by Fry;
> Round the Room behold are hung,
> Songs which fav'rite Bards have sung,
> Party Squibs and Birth Day Odes,
> Epigrams and Episodes,
> Dying Speeches, Friendly Rules,
> Terms at Large of Country Schools,
> Lists of Members — (Votes of Credit),
> How they Voted — why they did it;
> Lists of Boroughs sound and true,
> Names of rotten Boroughs too.

DORCHESTER
Richard Carlile: the imprisoned publisher.

Richard Carlile [1790-1843] languished for six years in Dorchester Prison for
defending the freedom of the press against political interference. He was
brought from London and convicted on six counts of printing and publishing
scandalous, impious, profane and blasphemous libels. His trial in the Shire
Hall courtroom lasted three days in November 1819 and stirred fears in the
aristocracy across Europe.

The Czar of Russia, Aleksandr Pavlovich, banned any report of the proceedings from entering his country. Prison failed to stop Carlile's 1821 *New
Year's address to the Reformers of Great Britain* and a quantity of other pamphlets.

In later life he wondered if it had all been worth the trouble: "I did not then
see what my experience has since taught me, that the greatest despotism
ruling the press is popular ignorance."

DORCHESTER
Peto brought the railway into town: Hardy's 'John Power'.

Samuel Morton Peto [1809-89], a world-class railway builder, brought the
rails from Southampton into Dorchester in 1847. He was a Baptist, benefactor
and Liberal MP; he would be knighted for his engineering achievements.

Already in 1844 he was enjoying his rising wealth and bought Somerlayton
estate in Sussex from Lord Sidney Godolphin Osborne of Durweston — he of
"S.G.O" letters in The Times — who had overstretched himself on the
racecourse.

Sir Samuel Morton Peto was thinly veiled as "John Power" when Thomas
Hardy lifted this industrial baron lock stock and barrel for the father of the
heiress who is his central character in the novel *A Laodicean*. Not that they
shared the same end. Peto over-extended himself towards the finish whereas
Power is allowed to die in full steam. As well as their rails, both left a legacy
of Baptist chapels across the land.

DORCHESTER (FORDINGTON)

Henry Moule: right royal stink in Hardyesque Mill Street.

The desperate conditions of the mid-nineteenth century threw up a courageous champion who fought to save his flock from the squalor and death caused by powerful landowners. This was Rev Henry Moule [1801-80], vicar of Fordington — Dorchester's working class appendage — and the owners he so bitterly attacked were none other than the Royal Family. While moral stalwarts of Dorset society were prepared to flinch, and say nothing, Moule wrote a series of letters vehemently denouncing the long-term maladministration of those controlling the royal lands. He wrote to the man at the top — direct to Queen Victoria's husband, Prince Albert.

The German consort was considered to be more than a figurehead, and Moule would not moderate his words for the royal reader: "During the last twelve days I have passed from house to house of the sick and dying ... the blame of no inconsiderable portion of it lies and the door of those who, for the last sixty or seventy years, have managed this estate of His Royal Highness the Duke of Cornwall."

Henry Moule pre-empted any official cover-up by refusing to accept excuses and without even waiting for the reply.

"I shall publish what I write," he warned in his first letter of 12 September 1854. "At the east end of Dorchester, then, and within a space that can scarcely exceed five acres, about 1,100 persons are congregated in a set of dwellings, many of which are of the most wretched description, and utterly destitute of the ordinary conveniences of life. This space consists of two great divisions, Mill Street, on the one side of a mill pond, and Holloway-row, together with Cuckold-row and Standfast, on the other side.

"In Mill Street, the floors of the houses lie considerably below the highest elevation of the pond, and some of them even below its bed. The other division consists of two, and in part of it, of three rows of cottages, rising one above the other, from the bank of the mill pond, on the side of a chalk hill. In Holloway-row, about twenty of the cottages have a small patch of ground, about eighteen feet square, and a pathway and lane in front of them. They have also a little space hollowed out of the hill behind them. But, with these exceptions, scarcely a cottage in this division (and the same may be said of many in Mill Street) has a single inch of ground beyond that on which it stands.

"Their filth is consequently cast either into the open and wretched drain in the street, or into the mill pond. And into this same mill pond, from which, moreover, the people draw most of their water for washing, and sometimes even for culinary purposes, 'the conveniences' of more than half of these 1,100 people empty themselves together with the filth of the county gaol, and of some portion of the other three parishes of Dorchester. The population, with few exceptions, consists of mechanics, labourers, and paupers from this and many other parishes. Vice, in the worst forms, abounds among them."

The fate of Dorset's poor was to be eclipsed by the military adventure in the Crimea and the slums of Mill Street remained long enough to enter the annals of English literature via *The Mayor of Casterbridge* in which Thomas Hardy called it "Mixen Lane". It features also in *A Changed Man*; Henry Moule is the model for the title character. He reappears, with wife Mary, as the parents of Angel Clare in *Tess of the d'Urbervilles*.

Hardy had more than an academic interest in his "Mixen Lane". Florence Hardy was the chairman of the Mill Street Housing Society which had by 1934 built thirty-four new homes. The practicalities of rehousing schemes came naturally to Florence as her father had been a director of the Enfield Building Society for half a century.

DORCHESTER

John Pouncy: pioneer half-tones in *Dorsetshire Photographically Illustrated.*

Photographic processes of printing illustrations took off in the 1850s. Firmin Gillot [1820-72], working in Paris, devised a method of relief printing from an engraved zinc plate — by etching out with acid the areas required to be left white — in 1850. Wood-engraving was on the way out, particularly after Paul Pretsch [1803-73] arrived in London in 1854 and produced the first relief half-tone block from a photograph.

The first books to utilise the new process were produced in Dorchester in 1857 by photographer John Pouncy. *Dorchester Photographically Illustrated* was advertised as a six part set — though I have only ever been able to acquire volumes one, two and four — and each contained twenty pictures, in a landscape format eleven inches wide and eight inches deep.

To us, they have a stilted tone that looks more like a line engraving than a reproduction of a photographic bromide, and Pouncy was himself at pains to stress they were indeed photographs rather than prints: "The Detail and Touch of Nature faithfully reproduced by a New Process on Stone, by which Views are rendered Truthful, Artistic, and Durable."

DORCHESTER (FORDINGTON)

Horace Moule, Hardy's mentor: buried at Fordington.

Thomas Hardy's greatest male friendship ended in a tragedy that spilled over into his work. When his mentor Horace Moule [1832-73] of Fordington Vicarage, Dorchester, killed himself — as if he were a participant in a Hardy novel — the shock stayed with the novelist.

Yet so many characters would make exits as grim as that of Horace Moule, that one might even wonder whether Hardy planted the nihilistic philosophy that destroyed his closest intellectual friend. Nature prevails in Hardy novels, but there is little future in being human.

Horace's problem with opium and drink is said to have started when he was reviewing books for Macmillan and forced himself to work up to seventy-two hours at a stretch. His exit was grimly Hardyesque. Then 41 years old, employed as a Poor Law inspector, he died at Cambridge on a Sunday in September 1873. Just before eight o'clock, from a next-door room, his brother Charles heard a "trickling not a violent sound". He found Horace "conscious but unable to speak" with an "incised wound across and severing the wind-pipe". There was a razor on the bed. He died about an hour later, and "temporary insanity" was the verdict at the inquest.

"Not one there is among us that understandeth any more," wrote Hardy, quoting the 74th psalm. The burial was at Fordington.

"His last smile" to Thomas Hardy had been in the summer, on 21 June. Horace, at an earlier stage in the author's career, had reluctantly discouraged

Hardy from immersing himself totally in Greek plays, since if he "really had to make an income in some way from architecture in 1862, it would hardly be worthwhile for him to read Aeschylus or Sophocles in 1859-61".

Not that Hardy neglected literature's Greek roots. Fate is the constant and inescapable 'baddie' in Hardy novels as much as she is throughout Greek plays. Two of his major male unfortunates − Angel Clare in *Tess* and *Jude the Obscure* himself, are modelled upon Horace Moule. He is the subject versified in *Standing by the Mantelpiece*.

DORCHESTER

40 South Street: Barnes the schoolmaster.

Dialect poet and schoolmaster William Barnes [1801-86] moved his Academy and family from Mere to Dorchester, to cramped premises in Durngate Street, in 1835. They found more space, if few windows, in Norman's House, adjoining the north side of Napper's Mite almshouses in South Street, from 1838 until 1847. The Academy was then transferred across the road to the new 40 South Street, at the south end of the three-storey brick built terrace on the south side of New Street corner, in 1847. The school itself was an out-house at the back which had hanging slates down the wall and a projecting first storey; this was demolished in 1965.

Barnes's mind kept searching for a wider clientele and the new Victorian age would present him with opportunities for grouping like-minds into a force for the cultural advancement of the masses.

A stone plaque on the building, between the windows of the offices of Hy Duke and Son, has a laurel wreath surrounding an inscription: "William Barnes the Dorset poet lived here. 1847 to 1862."

In 1845, having spearheaded the establishment of what was then known as the Dorchester Museum, he galvanised its efforts into an active environmental campaign. The threat was approaching on two fronts as the railway moguls sliced their way across the county. It was through Barnes's efforts that the Roman amphitheatre of Maumbury Rings (Ordnance Survey map reference SY 690 899) would be saved by a diversion that left the puzzled railway navvies building two widely separated platforms − one of which was a siding to nowhere, and the other a tight curve.

The second fight he thought he might lose. They had missed the deadline for petitioning Parliament against "the threatened intersection" of Pound-bury Camp hill-fort (Ordnance Survey map reference SY 683 911) but a compromise was reached "and we have reason to hope that the earthwork will be tunnelled and therefore remain unmutilated". He thanked other "antiquarian friends" for their "truly good and not-to-be-forgotten endeavours" but it was William Barnes who had been the first Dorset conservationist, and a successful one at that.

As well as schooling the young, Barnes saw Dorchester and the re-education of its adult population as the continuing challenge. He was a co-founder of the Dorchester Institute which was intended as a "literary lecture-hall" for the betterment of working men, via the Dorchester Working Men's Improvement Society. "I am a working man," he reassured them in 1857, "like yourselves."

The days of teaching boys were nearly over for Barnes − though his Academy would struggle on until 1862 − but as with all aspects of his life he could not bring them to a close until he had summed up his experiences in a book. It was *Se Gefylsta: an Anglo-Saxon delectus* [1849] which W.G. Locket would describe in 1893 as "the first practical school primer in the language".

Two of his old boys appear here in the book you are reading – Octavius Pickard of Bloxworth, who later styled himself Octavius Pickard-Cambridge, and Sir Frederick Treves of Dorchester.

[See Winterborne Came for the remainder of William Barnes's story].

DORCHESTER
Leader Scott: Barnes's daughter.

Lucy Emily Barnes [1837-1902], the third daughter of poet William Barnes, was born in Dorchester. She would marry Samuel Baxter in 1867 but it was under her pen-name "Leader Scott" that she wrote her father's biography.

By that time she was an expatriate, absorbed into Florence's literary society and writing on classical architecture and art, with *The Cathedral Builders* [1899] as her major work. The Italians rewarded her with honorary life membership of the Academia delle Belle Arti.

DORCHESTER
St Peter's church: statue of Barnes.

The life-size bronze statue to William Barnes, standing beside the porch to St Peter's church in High West Street, was unveiled in February 1889. It had cost £400 which was raised by public subscription.

DORCHESTER
39 South Street: Hardy the architect.

No 39 South Street is among the shops on the west side of South Street on the opposite corner of New Street from the Post Office, in the centre left of a terrace of three-storey houses that were stone built, with a frontage of Broadmayne brick, in 1847.

It was to this building that Thomas Hardy [1840-1928] came as a boy of sixteen to work as a trainee draughtsman for architect John Hicks. That was in 1856 and he worked here until 1862, and then continued his architectural career in London, with Arthur Blomfield, returning to Hicks in 1867.

DORCHESTER and WEYMOUTH (SUTTON POYNTZ)
The print behind *The Trumpet Major*.

It was in "an old woman's cottage near 'Overcombe'" – as Thomas Hardy called Sutton Poyntz – that in 1880, when he published *The Trumpet Major*, there was still a horror-poster of Napoleon hanging on a wall. Hardy has his character Robert Loveday produce it from a pocket: "The hat represented a maimed French eagle; the face was ingeniously made up of human carcases as to form a physiognomy; a band, or stock, shaped to resemble the English Channel, encircled his throat, and seemed to choke him; his epaulette was a hand tearing a cobweb that represented the treaty of peace with England; and his ear was a woman crouching over a dying child."

Kathleen Strange of Portland discovered a copy of the original cartoon and presented it, in 1957, to the Hardy room in the Dorset County Museum at Dorchester.

DORCHESTER
Shire Hall Place: Hardy's interim home.

In June 1883 43-year-old Thomas Hardy and first wife Emma moved into Shire Hall Place, behind Shire Hall on the north side of High West Street, Dorchester. They were searching for a permanent home, which would become his own designer-villa after the Prince of Wales (later Edward VII) agreed to lease whatever corner of the Duchy of Cornwall lands that the novelist requested. It was a plot opposite the toll house known as Mack's Gate beside the Wareham road on the outskirts of the county town.

DORCHESTER
Thomas Hardy: dug up Roman pots.

Thomas Hardy [1840-1928] exaggerated somewhat when he wrote in the opening of *The Mayor of Casterbridge* [1886] that one could sense old Rome throughout the streets of the town — Roman Durnovaria is not on the visual scale of Chester or York — but in the choice of a building site for his Max Gate house (Ordnance Survey map reference SY 704 899) he had provided himself with some first class antiquities.

They were discovered in 1884 as the workmen dug the trenches for the foundations of his villa. Three burials were in elliptical graves, cut into the chalk, with skeletons contracted in womb-like pose rather than being laid out. One had a bronze brooch — present location unknown — at its head, where it was probably used to fasten the shroud. There were a total of six black-ware pottery vessels in a variety of native Durotrigic or imitation Roman shapes of the first century AD, together with a splendid 22.5 cm high cream-coloured ring-neck flask that had been made at the Corfe Mullen kiln in the time of Claudius, the emperor who had undertaken the AD 43 invasion of Britain.

Other skeletons were found later. From the forehead of one Hardy took a pair of penannular brooches which had been joined by another early Roman fibula of the Maiden Castle class. Nearby, there was a pit with the burnt bones of a horse and an iron spearhead. Covering one of the skeletons was a large sarsen stone which Hardy had "set up at Max Gate as a menhir".

Later finds, from his flower beds and vegetable garden, included decorated sherds of top-class imported Samian pottery from later in the first century. Hardy quite rightly cherished his private collection of conquest-period native and Roman pottery and other finds — they were kept in his private study, the contents of which went to Dorset County Museum in 1936.

DORCHESTER
Max Gate: itself, *Tess*, *Jude* and the poems.

Thomas Hardy is unique as the only major English novelist to design the house in which he was to produce most of his work. Hardy the architect built a large late-Victorian villa, its austere three storey lines being set-back from Alington Avenue, the old Wareham road out of Dorchester (Ordnance Survey map reference SY 704 899), on the west side of its corner with Syward Road and given its initial privacy by a brick wall and its more effective screen by the newly planted trees which grew to match the author's spreading fame.

He called it Max Gate, adopting and improving upon the local name for the spot, derived from the Mack's Gate turnpike toll-house which was demolished in the twentieth century and is now under the present course of the town's A352 approach road. This has moved most of the traffic. Max Gate stands to the east of the Trumpet Major roundabout, behind the wall between Friars Close and Syward Road.

It was Hardy's home from age forty-five on 29 June 1885 until his death there on 11 January 1928. Here he saw *The Mayor of Casterbridge* into print and wrote *The Woodlanders* [1887], *Tess of the d'Urbervilles* [1891], *Jude the Obscure* [1895] and most of his poetry, including the three-part poetic drama *The Dynasts* [1904-08]. Literary visitors included William Barnes, R.L. Stevenson, Lawrence of Arabia, E.M. Forster, Edmund Gosse, John Cowper Powys, A.E. Housman, John Galsworthy, Newman Flower and W.B. Yeats.

The award of the Order of Merit did something to awaken Dorchester folk to Hardy's importance but it was only after the Prince of Wales [Edward VIII] called for tea on 20 July 1923 that they fully realised the unparalleled reputation of the local talent in their midst.

Max Gate was left to the National Trust by Kate Hardy, the author's sister, in 1940, "to retain the same in the present condition as far as possible". It is not open to the public and Hardy's study has been rebuilt as an exhibit in the Dorset County Museum, High West Street, Dorchester.

It is this writer's ultimate ambition that the National Trust will eventually lease Max Gate to the Dorset Natural History and Archaeological Society for them to restore to it Hardy's collection, so that it can resume its rightful and logical rôle as the place of principal literary pilgrimage in the county. The Society can use the space this frees in the County Museum for more traditional antiquities of the sort which its Victorian creators, Hardy included, would have approved.

DORCHESTER

King's Arms: hosted R.L. Stevenson.

En route to Dartmoor, hoping the change of air would help his suffering chest — though Dartmoor would not be everyone's choice for that — Robert Louis Stevenson [1850-94] stayed for a few days in the King's Arms, High East Street, Dorchester. It was in August 1885 and he was living in Bournemouth at the time, completing *Kidnapped* and *Dr Jekyll and Mr Hyde*.

He was one of the first distinguished visitors to Max Gate where the Hardys had just set up their permanent home beside the Wareham road out of town. "He came out to my house unexpectedly," Hardy recalled. "He appeared in a velveteen jacket with one hand in a sling. He particularly wanted to see the room I wrote in, but as I had come into the house quite recently I had not settled into any definite writing place.

"My wife went next day to call on them at the hotel just before they left . . . A letter arrived from Mrs Stevenson three weeks later, dated from an hotel in Exeter, informing me that Louis had been taken ill, and could go no further."

He had prematurely aged, thinning into unspeakable slightness, and smoked heavily. Gastric fever had left him with a frailty against which even Hardy looked fit; yet Stevenson was ten years his junior.

Stevenson, who had published *Treasure Island* in 1883, was working on a string of essays and stories. In May 1886 he would write to Max Gate asking if he might dramatise *The Mayor of Casterbridge* but though Hardy accepted the offer nothing would materialise. His admiration remained, however, despite a loss of confidence over "the morals of *Tess*", as Hardy later put it, and

Edmund Gosse was sent out to scour London for a copy of *The Woodlanders* one Sunday in 1887. Stevenson wanted to take it on his final journey from England to America – from there he would continue to the Pacific, Sydney, and death in Samoa in 1894.

DORCHESTER
Barclays Bank: Henchard's House.

Fact and fiction have been fused, if not confused, at Barclays Bank on the east side of South Street, where the attractive Georgian brickwork carries a blue plaque, set between the arched window, classical doorway and the night-safe:

"This house is reputed to have been lived in by the Mayor of Casterbridge in Thomas Hardy's story of that name written in 1885."

Michael Henchard was the character.

DORCHESTER and STINSFORD
Hardy's statue: by Eric Kennington and rubbished by Augustus John.

There had to be a monument to one of England's greatest writers but Thomas Hardy was not, Augustus John [1878-1961] remarks in *Chiaroscuro*, of "monumental build, though he had a fine head", and his suggestion was for a statue of Tess of the d'Urbervilles instead, to be erected on an elevated point in Egdon Heath. Anyway, as John continues, "my project was turned down, and Tess rejected in favour of the depressing object we now see at the top of the High Street, Dorchester".

Sydney Cockerell [1867-1962], Hardy's literary executor, had also fought for something better. He wrote to The Times on 16 January 1928 suggesting that Hardy should be commemorated by the erection of a tall tower on the heath beside his Stinsford (Higher Bockhampton) birthplace.

He said that Hardy had "a particular objection to what he called 'utilitarian memorials'. In this phrase he condemned the common practice of making the death of a famous person the excuse for raising money for drinking-fountains, lecterns, village halls, and other useful purposes, however commendable they might be on general grounds. He preferred a monument to be commemorative and nothing else.

"As an example he often pointed with approval to the column raised to his famous namesake on a Dorset hilltop within sight of Max Gate" – Vice-Admiral Hardy's Monument above Portesham. "I have heard him admit, when the topic came up in conversation, that if any local memorial were to be raised to him he would like that column to have a fellow."

It was not to be. What we have at Colliton Walks is the bronze of a seated Hardy; offering the interesting if wizened hook-nosed head but diminutive in form, with hat in hand, crossed legged and looking towards the Bridport Road from a plain sarcophagus of a plinth. The casting is by Eric Kennington [1888-1960] and though he had already sculpted the war memorials at Battersea Park and Soissons, France, it is a creation of his early period. The editors of a reprint of *Highways and Byways in Dorset* noted that the author is portrayed in knickerbockers with his feet resting on a heap of horticultural specimens: "Criticism must be respectfully withheld, as it doubtless pleased the committee and subscribers who were responsible for its erection."

Even the unveiling failed to please them. It was carried out in 1931 by Sir James Barrie [1860-1937] who with characteristic puckishness started by saying that at his birth Hardy was such a weakling that the nurse had put him in the washing-basket for dead and directed her attention to the mother instead. Hardy's widow, Florence Hardy, was outraged and later told Barrie that "T.H." had never mentioned the incident:

"I asked Barrie to tell me about it when we returned to Max Gate. I said that I had never heard the story. Then he remarked: 'Well, I put that bit in. It was a good piece of drama. So I put it in!'"

"That," Florence responded, "is how legends begin. Like Wellington's 'Up Guards and at 'em' at Waterloo. I think it monstrous."

DORCHESTER (FORDINGTON)

Handley C.G. Moule: *Dorchester Poems.*

Born at Fordington Vicarage, Handley Carr Glyn Moule [1841-1920] was the youngest son of Rev Henry Moule. He would become his father's curate and issued a collection of *Dorchester Poems* [1878] which are a celebration of the area's proliferation of antiquities.

In the house of the Pilgrimage followed in 1896, from Cambridge where he was Principal of Ridley Hall. This book of sacred verse has some crisp imagery: "On life's Atlantic deep today, we cross another zone; the shore of birth is far away, the further shore unknown."

For Handley Moule the passage was going relatively smoothly and he would be enthroned Bishop of Durham [1901]. He wrote a large number of other religious works and looked back on life in Victorian Fordington in his *Memories of a Vicarage*.

DORCHESTER

Sir Frederick Treves: whose byways returned to St Peter's church.

Sir Frederick Treves [1853-1923] penned the best loved of all guides to Dorset. In 1906, his *Highways and Byways in Dorset* was immediately the most popular book ever written on the county. It is still one of the most sought-after Dorset titles.

Treves was far from a parochial figure. He was the royal surgeon who postponed King Edward VII's coronation in 1902. The king desperately needed an appendicitis operation but strongly opposed going into hospital. "I have a coronation on hand," he protested. But Treves was adamant: "It will be a funeral, if you don't have the operation." Treves won, and the king lived. He did not remove the appendix but carried out an appendicectomy to drain an abcess.

The surgeon's first love was for Dorset and he was a keen photographer. As president and founder of the Society of Dorset Men in London he encouraged other exiles to study their native county. He was born in Dorchester in 1853 and died at Lausanne on 7 December 1923. His funeral took place at St Peter's church, Dorchester, on 2 January 1924 and the king and queen were represented by Lord Dawson. Thomas Hardy attended and chose the hymns. Hardy also wrote a poem for the occasion and had it published in The Times. It starts with the words: "In the evening, when the world knew he was dead."

His ashes were buried in Dorchester (Fordington) cemetery. It would be sixty years later that he returned to fame when his last book, *The Elephant Man*, was turned into a successful film. He also wrote a manuscript on the events surrounding the operation on Edward VII but it was suppressed.

DORCHESTER
Llewelyn Powys: born in Rothesay House.

Only one of the literary four among the Powys brothers was born in Dorset, though all would weave it into their writings and spend much of their lives in the county. The sole Dorsetman was Llewelyn Powys [1884-1939] who was born in Rothesay House, close to Dorchester South railway station, the son of Rev Charles Francis Powys and Mary Cowper Johnson.

They had inherited £40,000 in 1879, which enabled the family to move from Shirley, Derbyshire, to be near an aged parent in Weymouth. In December 1885 the family was on the move again, as Charles Powys took over his own parish as vicar of Montacute, Somerset. Llewelyn went from Sherborne School and Cambridge to stock-farming in Kenya [1914-19] followed by newspaper reporting in New York City [1920-25]. He then felt the need to return to his roots. See his Chaldon Herring entry for the remainder of the story.

DORCHESTER – see DORSET GENERAL (at front of book) for Hardy placenames: a checklist. BERE REGIS for *Chrestoleros*: the crazed vicar. MORETON for Mary Frampton: *The Journal*. STALBRIDGE for wife-selling: as in *The Mayor of Casterbridge*. STINSFORD for Thomas Hardy: his heart in Wessex.

Doyle – for SIR ARTHUR CONAN DOYLE [1859-1930] see BEAMINSTER

Druitt – for MONTAGUE JAMES DRUITT [1888 suicide], Jack the Ripper suspect, see WIMBORNE

DURWESTON
'S.G.O.' told on Dorset's poverty: letters to The Times.

Lord Sidney Godolphin Osborne [1808-89] blew the whistle on Dorset poverty at the start of the Hungry Forties when he arrived at Durweston Rectory. The initials "S.G.O." told the world, via the correspondence columns of The Times, of a landowning class which kept their workers below the poverty line, as he discovered when he started calling on cottagers: "I found the woman with two of the children, eating a few unwholesome potatoes and some bread; a child of nine years of age dead in a coffin close to them; the only ascent to the bedroom by a broken ladder."

S.G.O. thundered: "God will not have the poor oppressed in body or in soul."

As for his peers among the upper classes, they regarded Osborne as a traitor. George Bankes MP tried to get colleagues in the House of Commons to take their side but only succeeded in bringing yet more attention to the

Dorset problems as a result. Osborne withstood the ostracism until 1875, when in Queen Victoria's golden age he retired to Lewes, Sussex. His last letter to The Times was topical – about the activities of Jack the Ripper.

Thomas Carlyle produced this vignette of Dorset's caring parson. Osborne had conducted the marriage of Charles Kingsley to Fanny Godolphin Osborne, his sister, in Bath:

"The strange Rev Lord Sidney, the famous S.G.O. of the newspapers, and one of the strangest brother mortals I ever met; a most lean, tall and perpendicular man, face palpably aristocratic but full of plebeian mobilities, free and easy rapidities, nice laughing little dark grey eyes, careless, honest, full of native ingenuity, sincerity, innocent vanity, incessant talk, anecdote, personal, distractedly speculative, oftenest purposely distracted, never altogether boring. To me his talk had one great property, it saved all task of talking on my part. He was very intrinsically polite too and we did very well together."

Sidney Godolphin Osborne was buried at Lewes, Sussex. The grave at Durweston of Sidney Francis Godolphin Osborne, at the meadow end of a line of four Portland crosses, is that of his eldest son.

DURWESTON and PIMPERNE

Charles Kingsley: lodged at Durweston Rectory.

When Rev Charles Kingsley [1819-75] arrived in Dorset in April 1844, as temporary curate for Pimperne parish, he stayed with his brother-in-law the Hon [later Lord] Sidney Godolphin Osborne [1808-89] at Durweston Rectory. From there (Ordnance Survey map reference ST 858 085) it was a three mile walk, over France Down, to Pimperne. Kingsley found in Osborne a practising prototype for the burst of radical Christian Socialism in which he engaged after returning to Dorset for a second brief period in 1848.

He mused: "How much I should like to preach a sermon on chalk downs and chalk streams; they are so purely beautiful."

Thereafter Kingsley was destined for national fame, with the novels *Yeast* [1848] and *Alton Locke* [1850] and his appointment a decade later as chaplain to Queen Victoria.

Vacillating between nervous restlessness and bouts of intense depression on one hand, and repressed paedophile sexuality on the other, he turned frustration into a classic, *The Water Babies* [1863].

EAST BEXINGTON – see ABBOTSBURY (EAST BEXINGTON)

EAST CHALDON – see CHALDON HERRING (EAST CHALDON)

EAST LULWORTH – see LULWORTH, EAST

EAST STOUR

Church Farm: where Fielding wrote *Tom Jones*.

Henry Fielding [1705-54] was the father of the English novel and his greatest, *Tom Jones, or the History of a Foundling*, was written in the old Rectory at East Stour. It has since been demolished and Church Farm stands now on its site beside the parish church. Fielding was an extravagant cosmopolitan personality. His London life was resented by the local Dorset squires, who probably realised his capacity for poking fun at them. In 1748 he was completing the finest real-life immorality story that England had been treated to since Shakespeare.

The problem for Dorset is that Fielding's Lodge, at Twerton, near Bath, has also been a claimant as the place where *Tom Jones* was written. Certainly Fielding was regularly dining at Twerton with his friend Ralph Allen in 1748. *Tom Jones*, however, is more than a year's work in the life of an exceedingly busy man. Fielding may have polished off the manuscript at Twerton but it was created and the main writing done in Dorset, as he himself indirectly confirms in the dedication to the first edition, published on 28 February 1749. There he describes it as the "labour of some years of my life" which puts it firmly into his Dorset period. *Tom Jones* was as instant a success as one could hope for in the eighteenth century, editions having been said to have been delivered to the shops at breakfast and been sold out by tea-time. That was not only in London. It was the hottest literary product in Europe, with translators working at their copies in cities from Madrid to Moscow. *Tom Jones* was also dramatised as a stage comedy at Covent Garden, and in Paris and Germany.

Fielding never lived to enjoy his fame from a Dorset country retirement. In 1754 he left London for Lisbon in a hopeless attempt to regain his health which was tortured by concurrent asthma, dropsy, gout and jaundice. Two months later he was buried among other English exiles in the Estrela cemetery. One of the relics of his days at East Stour is a table from the old Rectory which is in Somerset County Museum at Taunton Castle.

EDMONDSHAM – see SHAFTESBURY
for Sanderson Robins: *Necessity of State Education*

Embleton – for RONALD S. EMBLETON [1930-87]
see BOURNEMOUTH (SOUTHBOURNE)

ENCOMBE – see CORFE CASTLE (ENCOMBE)

Falkner – for JOHN MEADE FALKNER [1858-1932]
see FLEET

FARNHAM and TOLLARD ROYAL
Pitt-Rivers: Father of Archaeology.

Lieutenant-General Henry Lane Fox [1827-1900] served in the Crimean war. Life took a very different course when, against all the odds and after the unexpected deaths of other contenders, he inherited his great-uncle George's estate. His 29,000 acres spread out from Cranborne Chase as far as the eye could see across great tracts of Dorset and Wiltshire. George Pitt had been the second Baron Rivers, so his great-nephew assumed the name Pitt-Rivers. When he first visited Cranborne Chase there were twelve lives between him and his succession – there followed accidents; "incidents" (whatever that means); the fifth Lord Rivers having only eight daughters; the sixth Lord Rivers dying childless. If it all sounds rather familiar remember that there were only eight heirs to be worked through in *Kind Hearts and Coronets*.

In 1880, bingo! Hereon he acted out his destiny and began the *Excavations in Cranborne Chase* which were a magnum opus that set the whole foundation of scientific archaeology. As an anthropologist he was scathing about how fellow antiquarian landowners had wasted their opportunities: "In only one instance Sir Richard Colt Hoare describes a skeleton, saying that it 'grinned horribly a ghastly smile . . . a singularity that I have never before noticed.' No doubt the skeleton must have been laughing at him for his unscientific method of dealing with it, and when one thinks of the large amount of racial evidence that he destroyed in this way, and the comparatively small number of skeletons that have remained in the barrows to be examined since, it is almost enough to give any lover of antiquity a ghastly smile!"

Pitt-Rivers has to be seen in another class. To quote Warwick Bray and David Trump: "In 1880 he inherited a large estate in Cranborne Chase and in the next ten years applied to excavations there the experience gained in his military career and museum collections. The result was to advance excavation to a scientific technique, characterised by precise work, meticulous recording of all details, emphasis on the apparently trivial, complete study [in contrast to the usual sampling of his time], and full and rapid publication. In these, his example was hardly equalled until the 1920s, and is rarely improved upon today."

What Pitt-Rivers brought to the subject was simple logic, with his observation that "common things are of more importance than particular things, because they are more prevalent". Thinking of archaeology, he wrote at the end of his life that "if ever a time should come when our illustrated newspapers take to recording interesting and sensible things, a new era will have arrived. Let us hope for an evolution in this as in all other things".

Leslie Grinsell has used the most fitting analogy: "Of Pitt-Rivers alone can it be said, as Matthew Arnold said of Shakespeare, that 'others abide our question: thou art free'."

Perhaps the greatest surprise is in how archaeology reacted to the advancements he brought. Sir Mortimer Wheeler summed it up: "Then what? Nothing. Nobody paid the slightest attention to the old man. One of his assistants [Harry St George Gray] even proceeded to dig up a lake village [at Glastonbury] . . . like potatoes. Not only had the clock not gone on, but it had been set back."

This remarkable man excelled in other fields, with a menagerie for experiments in hybridisation, and he established on the county boundary between Farnham and Tollard Royal the Larmer Tree Grounds where thousands came from Bournemouth and Salisbury in the course of the summer to picnic among an exotic assortment of buildings including a temple, open-air theatre, rustic bandstand, Indian teahouses, skittle-alleys and summer-houses. There is no general public access these days but the grounds still come to life for conferences (Ordnance Survey map reference ST 941 170).

To the south of the village of Farnham (Ordnance Survey map reference ST 957 147) the Pitt-Rivers Museum — built as a gypsy school but the children played truant — became the most famous one-man collection in the kingdom. It closed in the 1960s and the contents were dispersed, with Mrs Stella Pitt-Rivers selling most of the huge collection of ethnology at Sotheby's, though the General's own finds from Cranborne Chase were deposited with Salisbury Museum.

He has left, however, a spirit that can still be felt around the Iron Age settlement at Woodcutts, a mile north of the hamlet and the B3081 (Ordnance Survey map reference ST 963 181) and others of the places he unearthed.

Jaquetta Hawkes has written: "Had he lived in the Middle Ages he would perhaps have become a legendary figure, the hero of many stories and with his name attached to antiquities or natural features of his countryside."

His mortal remains are in Tollard Royal church, next to King John's House, where Michael Pitt-Rivers told me of the little altercation between the General and his wife. He was a passionate advocate of cremation, then not yet in vogue, and she was determinedly not of like mind. "Damn it woman, you shall burn!" he thundered. In the end she didn't. He went first on that last journey to Woking, the nearest crematorium, and returned as ashes to a classical urn.

FARNHAM — see CHETTLE for Chettle House: Chafin and West

Felix — for NICHOLAS WANOSTROCHT [1804-76], known as NICHOLAS FELIX,
see WIMBORNE

Fielding — for HENRY FIELDING [1707-54]
see EAST STOUR

FLEET

Fleet Chapel: *Moonfleet*
of John Meade Falkner and real-life sea stories.

Fleet Chapel is the remnant of a church destroyed by a hurricane in 1824 when the sea swept over the Chesil Beach. Some houses below the church-yard were also washed away. A terrace is all that survives of the hamlet of East Fleet, along the lane signposted to the Moonfleet Hotel from a mini-roundabout on the B3157 at Chickerell, two miles north-west of Weymouth.

The cottage and Fleet Chapel are just off from the first corner (Ordnance Survey map reference SY 636 801) in half a mile. There is a footpath beside the cottages to the chapel and the shore of the Fleet lagoon.

There was a young eye-witness to the events of about 8 am on 23 November 1824: "Most so soon as twas light a lot of us boys was out where we be a-standing, for to look at the seas what was coming over the ridge. Then after we'd been a-looking a goodish bit a thing happened differ'nt altogether. Twern't a sea — not a bit of it — twer the great sea hisself rose up level like, and come on right over ridge and all, like nothing in this world . . . we runned like mad . . . till we was nigh up in Chickerell. When we comed back, where was the church? — all but thic firm little chancel — all sucked away by that terrible rise of the sea; went up to that there linchet, he did."

The ruins of the nave were demolished in 1827 and the mediaeval chancel, with an original gable-cross, was rebuilt as a chapel. It contains attractive brasses to members of the Mohun family, Margaret [died 1603] and Maximilian [1612], whose vault is beneath the floor. A legend of a secret passage between the church and a house was developed by John Meade Falkner [1858-1932] into the classic Victorian smuggling adventure story, *Moonfleet*. It was given a degree of substance in 1925 when a channel was found two feet below the ground: "The tunnel had solid walls, cemented on the inside, about five feet high and two feet wide, and was traceable across the church-yard."

Fishing was often only a pretext for being near this coast and the coastal economy owed much to smuggling and the plunder of shipwrecks. On 22 December 1756 the vicar of Fleet, Rev Thomas Francklyn, preached a sermon that reminded his parishioners of the Acts of Parliament relating to ships that are stranded on the coast and in particular the penalties for the plunder of merchant goods: "This has long been looked upon as a thing right and lawful to be done by them who received it from their forefathers, and practised it betimes. And, indeed, nothing can reconcile an act so shocking to any one's reason and conscience, but the frequency of committing."

The greatest of all such events anywhere along the Dorset coast happened here after 16 January 1748 when the *Hope*, returning to Amsterdam from the Spanish South American colonies, was driven on to the Chesil Beach.

"A vast concourse" of some 4,000 people from the villages and Portland, Wyke and Weymouth held the beach for several days and appointed Portland labourer Augustin Elliott as custodian of the loot: "The pillaging parties threw all they could snatch in to one heap, for the security of which the prisoner at the bar was posted, as commander of an armed select party. As soon as the reflux of the sea had made the ship accessible, the scattered bands again united, in a hostile manner, armed with cutlasses, clubs, hooks and such like. They marched down to the ship swearing it was a wreck and if not so they could make it a wreck. Shocking to relate! From curses and menaces they proceeded to offer violence and outrage to those persons, whom even the merciless and furious seas had left unhurt! ... the injury of strangers in distress is adding barbarity to iniquity and committing an act exceedingly sinful in the sight of both God and man."

Not that Elliott was a prisoner for long: "As at a moderate computation 10,000 from all parts of the county, of farmers, tradesmen, labourers with one L..d of a M...r, have been concerned either in carrying away part of the property of this ship themselves, or in purchasing the same off them that did so; it is therefore far from being any matter of wonder to find the j..y under a strong disposition to favour such, as were tried for offences of this kind."

The Dutchmen reckoned their loss at £25,000; a fortune in the then value of money, and into the twentieth century the boys and fishermen of this area went on to the Chesil Beach after severe gales to search for gold coins washed up from the dozens of rich wrecks in "Dead Man's Bay" and glistening between the pebbles.

FLEET

Moonfleet Hotel: fiction into fact.

Moonfleet Hotel is at the end of the Fleet lane, where it reaches to the lagoon (Ordnance Survey map reference SY 617 806). Its name has been changed to put fiction into fact. This was Fleet House, built by Maximilian Mohun in 1603, of the family that gave its name to Hammoon in the Blackmore Vale. Their home beside the Fleet had passed to other hands in 1774 and was remodelled in characteristic eighteenth century style by either John Gould or George Gould from Upwey.

That it is now Moonfleet is a mark of the impact that John Meade Falkner's classic smuggling story made on Victorian and Edwardian minds, and its inseparable links with this coast. *Moonfleet* is based upon Mohun family traditions and the fact that smuggling was the main trade hereabouts. It is set in 1757 and tells the story of John Trenchard who discovers a locket with a puzzling message in the vaults of Moonfleet church. The actual church at Fleet was largely swept away by a flood in 1824 [see its entry] and this event is also woven into Falkner's story. John is befriended by local innkeeper Elzevir Block, joins the dangerous world of the smugglers, takes part in a skirmish with the militia, and is blamed for the killing of the hated magistrate, Maskew.

It is all a rattling good yarn, revived for our generation by BBC television under the title of *Smugglers' Bay*.

Moonfleet Hotel has not lost its grip on these literary associations. In 1970, Bruce Hemingway converted the extensive cellars beneath the hotel into a dive-bar called Blackbeard's Vaults and the atmosphere was helped by a large stone trough, iron water pump, boat, kegs, smuggling notices, lantern, church-pew type seating and a coffin.

Flower — for SIR NEWMAN FLOWER [1879-1964]
see FONTMELL MAGNA for Brewery to Cassells and STUDLAND for Old Harry: ashes of H.G. Wells.

FOLKE and SHERBORNE

Thomas Curgenven: classical scholar.

Rev Thomas Curgenven was rector of Folke in the late seventeenth century but was remembered as a brilliant classical scholar. Not that much of his own work survives but as master of Sherborne School he skilfully passed on his enthusiasms to a talented new generation.

In particular he was instrumental in helping Thomas Creech [1659-1700] of Blandford upon what became a career of translating. His assistance is acknowledged in the latter's works on Theocritus and Horace.

FOLKE — see LONG BURTON for Charles Herbert Mayo:
Bibliotheca Dorsetiensis

FONTMELL MAGNA and TARRANT KEYNESTON

Sir Newman Flower: Brewery to Cassells.

Sir Newman Flower [1879-1964] was one of the top publishers of the twentieth century. He nurtured giants for the Cassells list, including Winston Churchill's story of *The Second World War*, Arnold Bennett's plays, and the later output of H.G. Wells. Newman Flower, Wells wrote, "incubates others when he ought to be incubated".

He was born at Fontmell Magna where his father owned the Brewery. It was in 1896 that London called: "Out of my village of Fontmell Magna there is a long white road that leads over the hill. There was a legend that no native of the village who went up that long white road ever came back to live in the village again unless he was a failure."

His returns were from the pinnacle of his profession, befriending Thomas Hardy and Sir Frederick Treves, until half a century later he was back "in that corner of Dorset which seemed to belong to me because my youth had never left it". He had retired to Tarrant Keyn[e]ston House in the valley on the other side of Blandford.

Flower's own books included *George Friderick Handel, Franz Schubert, Sir Arthur Sullivan, Through my Garden Gate, Crucifixion, Red Harvest, Is God Dead?* and the autobiographical *Just as it Happened* [1950].

FONTMELL MAGNA — see MANSTON for Thomas Dibben:
translated *Carmen Seculare*

FONTMELL MAGNA − see STUDLAND
for Old Harry: ashes of H.G. Wells.

FORDE − see THORNCOMBE (FORDE)

FORDINGTON − see DORCHESTER (FORDINGTON)

Forster − for WILLIAM FORSTER [1818-86]
see BRADPOLE

Fowles − for JOHN FOWLES [born 1926]
see LYME REGIS

Frampton − for MARY FRAMPTON [1773-1846]
see MORETON

Freke − for WILLIAM FREKE [1662-1744]
see HINTON ST MARY

Fuller − for THOMAS FULLER [1608-61]
see BROADWINDSOR

Garnett − for DAVID GARNETT [1892-1981]
see CHALDON HERRING (EAST CHALDON)

Gerard − for THOMAS GERARD [1592-1634]
see TRENT

GLANVILLES WOOTTON

C.W. Dale: butterfly man.

Charles William Dale [1791-1872] of Glanvilles Wootton had the distinction of
having added a new butterfly to the British list. He was the first to record
Thymelicus acteon, henceforth the Lulworth Skipper, after taking his first
specimen at Durdle Door on 15 August 1832. Dale became one of the most
eminent Victorian entomologists though it was only posthumously that most
of his work appeared in print, including the popular *History of our British
Butterflies* [1890].

He was also a parochial naturalist of the finest quality and painstakingly
collected records of all forms of wildlife in his Blackmore Vale parish. *The
History of Glanville's Wootton* [1878] is not at all what it sounds − it is for the
most part a list of thousands of insect species that Dale had collected. It
would have no popular appeal, but Dale had achieved the most comprehensive
record list to be compiled during the nineteenth century for any spot on
earth.

Glisson − for FRANCIS GLISSON [1597-1677]
see RAMPISHAM

Godwin − for FRANCIS GODWIN [1562-1633]
see SANDFORD ORCAS

Godwin − for MARY WOLLSTONECRAFT GODWIN [1759-97]
see BOURNEMOUTH

Godwin — for WILLIAM GODWIN [1756-1836]
see BOURNEMOUTH

Guest — for CHARLOTTE ELIZABETH BERTIE [1812-95], known as
LADY CHARLOTTE GUEST [from 1833] and LADY CHARLOTTE
SCHREIBER [from 1855]
see POOLE (CANFORD MAGNA)

Hall — for MARGUERITE RADCLYFFE HALL [1886-1943]
see BOURNEMOUTH

HALSTOCK — see CORSCOMBE for Thomas Hollis: endowed
Harvard Library

Haly — for WILLIAM TAYLOR HALY [1818-74]
see POOLE

HANFORD and CHILD OKEFORD

Where Sullivan composed: *Onward Christian Soldiers.*

Sir Arthur Sullivan [1842-1900] composed the hymn tune *Onward Christian
Soldiers* whilst staying at Hanford House, beside the River Stour between
Child Okeford and Stourpaine (Ordnance Survey map reference ST 845 111).
Or rather he composed *St Gertrude* as it was originally named, in praise of his
hostess, Mrs Gertrude Clay-Ker-Seymer. At the time he was collaborating
with W.S. Gilbert in the production of *Thespis* and the partnership would lead
to the Savoy operas.

Onward Christian Soldiers was sung for the first time by the choir at St
Nicholas church in Child Okeford [1871].

Hannay — for JAMES OWEN HANNAY [1865-1950], writing as
GEORGE A BIRMINGHAM,
see LULWORTH (WEST)

Harcourt — for SIR WILLIAM HARCOURT [1827-1904]
see BLANDFORD

Hardy — for THOMAS HARDY [1840-1928] see DORSET GENERAL,
at front of book, for Hardy placenames: a checklist. See
DORCHESTER for Peto brought the railway into town: gave Hardy
'John Power'; 39 South Street: Hardy the architect; The print behind
The Trumpet Major; Shire Hall Place: Hardy's interim home; Thomas
Hardy: dug up Roman pots; Max Gate: itself, *Tess, Jude* and the
poems; King's Arms: hosted R.L. Stevenson; Barclays Bank:
Henchard's House; Hardy's statue: by Kennington and rubbished by
Augustus John. See DORCHESTER (FORDINGTON) for Henry
Moule: right royal stink in Hardyesque Mill Street; Horace Moule,
Hardy's mentor: buried at Fordington. See HOOKE for Westcombe:
Hardy's Norcombe. See MINTERNE MAGNA for High Stoy: Hardy's
favourite view. See STINSFORD for Hardy's Cottage: *Under the
Greenwood Tree*; Hardy and Julia Martin: rustles in *Desperate Remedies*;
His heart in Wessex. See STALBRIDGE for wife-selling as in *The
Mayor of Casterbridge*. See STURMINSTER MARSHALL for Thomas

Hardy Memorial Cottages; see STURMINSTER NEWTON for Hardy's Riverside plaque: on the wrong house. See SWANAGE for West End Cottages. See Weymouth for Hardy's lodgings: 3 Wolperton Street. See WIMBORNE for Llanherne: Hardy's home in Avenue Road.

Hearne — for SAMUEL HEARNE [1745-92]
see BEAMINSTER

Henty — for GEORGE ALFRED HENTY [1832-1902]
see WEYMOUTH

Higgenbotten — for J.C. HIGGENBOTTEN [early 20th century], known as ORME ANGUS,
see WAREHAM

HIGHER BOCKHAMPTON — see STINSFORD (HIGHER BOCKHAMPTON)

Highmore — for NATHANIEL HIGHMORE [1613-85]
see PURSE CAUNDLE

Hill — for ROBERT YOUNG [1811-1908], known as RABIN HILL,
see STURMINSTER NEWTON

HINTON MARTELL

Henry Bickersteth: *Peace, Perfect Peace.*

Though it was as a vicar in Hampstead that Henry Bickersteth [1825-1906] wrote the hymn *Peace, Perfect Peace*, this was the product of reflection upon his less demanding years as rector of the east Dorset country parish of Hinton Martell [1852-55]. Likewise the preface to his epic poem *Yesterday, Today and For Ever* [1866] acknowledged that it was the result of ideas "laid up in my heart".

It was compared with Milton's *Paradise Lost* and was an instant and lasting success, going through twenty-four editions during the author's lifetime and securing his appointment as Bishop of Exeter [1885-1900].

HINTON ST MARY

William Freke: mystic dream-writer.

In 1696, William Freke [1662-1744] came to the Manor House at Hinton St Mary and stayed for the rest of his life. He was notorious as a pamphleteer of material that London society could hardly ignore but did not know quite what to do with. To ensure that it received a reaction, Freke circulated a tract to members of both Houses of Parliament; it was ordered to be publicly burned by the hangman in Old Palace Yard, Westminster.

The author was eventually fined £500, forced to recant, and to give sureties of good behaviour. He later called himself a "master in the holy language" and compiled a dictionary of the imagery of dreams, *Lingua Tersancta*. By 1709 his mysticism was out of all control and he saw himself as "the great Elijah". Later topics for his pamphlets included *The Prophetick Foreknowledge of the Weather* [1719].

As for local affairs, Dorset made him a Justice of the Peace, from about

104

1720. His wife, Elizabeth, put up with an unhappy marriage and gave him twelve children. William Freke died at Christmas 1744 and was buried next door, in Hinton St Mary church, on 2 January 1745.

Hollis — for THOMAS HOLLIS [1720-74]
see CORSCOMBE

HOLNEST — see LONGBURTON for William Sharpe: *Treatise upon Coal Mines*

HOOKE and PUDDLETOWN
Westcombe: Hardy's Norcombe.

Not only are Burnt Bottom and Westcombe Coppice at Hooke (Ordnance Survey map reference ST 527 016) the probable model for Thomas Hardy's thinly disguised Norcombe in *Far from the Madding Crowd* but the hamlet also seems to have provided the novel's principal male character, Gabriel Oak. He was Robert Walden, the farm bailiff half a mile west at Toller Whelme in 1850, who later moved to the house around which Hardy set the book. That is Waterston House, two miles upstream from Puddletown in the Piddle valley, which in the novel becomes Weatherbury Farm (map reference SY 734 952).

In 1851, at the age of thirty, Robert Walden plucked twenty-one-year-old domestic servant Martha Bailey to be his wife. They married at Puddletown; as did the fictional Gabriel Oak and Bathsheba Everdene. Hardy himself, writing in the preface when the manuscript was published in 1874, says that despite the passing of time there is sufficient reality left for certain identifications to be made with persons and places.

What perhaps clinches the matter, which came to light when Geoffrey Thompson of Yeovil was compiling his own family tree more than a century later, is that there used to be Hardys at Toller Whelme. Thomas Hardy satiated himself with Victorian works on the county's history and spotted Thomas Hardy, Edmund Hardy and Edwin Hardy appearing at Toller Whelme in *The Visitation of Dorset* [1514-1623]. Thomas Hardy, the novelist, liked to imagine that they were his ancestors.

A further link between the hamlet in this remote valley and the novel is that it is a coppice away from the mill to which Bathsheba rode to fetch oatmeal. That, and a flaxmill, were on the Hooke river.

Hutchins — for JOHN HUTCHINS [1698-1773]
see WAREHAM

Irving — for SIR HENRY IRVING [1838-1905]
see BOURNEMOUTH (BOSCOMBE)

IWERNE MINSTER
John Willis: first usable shorthand.

Rev John Willis [?1570-1628], the stenographer who invented the first practical system of shorthand, is said to be buried at Iwerne Minster. His *Art of Stenographie* [1602] went to numerous editions and was complemented by a teaching guide, *The Schoolemaster to the Art of Stenographie* [1623].

His other profession was the cloth. He became rector of a London parish in 1601 and moved to Bentley Parva, Essex, in 1606.

IWERNE MINSTER

Mark Beaufoy: first with the Union Jack on Mont Blanc.

Mark Beaufoy [1764-1827] lost the race to conquer Mont Blanc to Switzerland's Saussure but six days later, on 9 August 1787, he had the consolation prize of being the first Englishman to reach the summit.

The son of a Quaker brewer, from Lambeth, he had been sent to school in Dorset, at Iwerne Minster. He became an astronomer and figured out the orbits of Jupiter's moons, utilising a superb mathematical mind, though his major work, *Nautical and Hydraulic Experiments*, was not published until seven years after his death.

He was shown in 1857 to have been only two years out in his calculation of the maximum westward diurnal variation in the earth's magnetic field as calculated from England. He went for magnetic north at 24° 41' 42'' W in March 1819; the maximum had, however, been achieved in 1817.

IWERNE STEPLETON

Peter Beckford: hunting classics.

Peter Beckford [1740-1811] of Stepleton House (Ordnance Survey map reference ST 862 113) wrote the classic book on foxhunting. His *Thoughts upon Hare and Fox Hunting* [1781] was the first properly detailed account of the pursuit of hunting with hounds. He also wrote *Essays on Hunting* which had an introduction explaining how hares were hunted by the Greeks.

His grave, in the church beside the house, has an epitaph that ignores the power of the printed word: "We die and are forgotten; tis Heaven's decree; Thus the fate of others will be the fate of me."

His accomplishments and linguistic talent have not passed unrecorded. It was said that he would bag a fox in Greek, find a hare in Latin, inspect his kennels in Italian and direct the management of his stables in exquisite French.

Jardine — for DAVID JARDINE [1794-1860]
see SWANAGE

Jellicoe — for ANN JELLICOE [born 1927]
see LYME REGIS

John — for AUGUSTUS JOHN [1878-1961] see POOLE (ALDERNEY)
for Margaret Kennedy: *The Constant Nymph*. See DORCHESTER for
Hardy's statue: rubbished by Augustus John.

John — for JOHN OF FORDE [?1140-1214]
see THORNCOMBE (FORDE)

Jourdain — for SILVESTER JOURDAIN [early 17th century]
see LYME REGIS

Keats — for JOHN KEATS [1795-1821]
see LULWORTH, WEST

Keble — for JOHN KEBLE [1792-1886]
see BOURNEMOUTH

Kennedy — for MARGARET KENNEDY [1896-1967], known also as
LADY DAVIES,
see POOLE (ALDERNEY)

Kethe — for WILLIAM KETHE [died 1608]
see CHILD OKEFORD

Kilvert — for FRANCIS KILVERT [1840-79] see WINTERBORNE
CAME for Francis Kilvert's visit. See MARSHWOOD for comment on
Lambert's Castle.

KIMMERIDGE (SMEDMORE)

John Clavell: poetic robber.

John Clavell [1603-42], the nephew of Sir William Clavell, of Smedmore
House, Kimmeridge, was a gentleman, a poet, and a robber. He boasted of
his abilities in all three pursuits, publishing in 1628, as "John Clavell, Gent",
a volume entitled *A recantation of an ill-led Life; or a Discoverie of the Highway
Law, in verse*.

His contribution to the highway code was dated "from my lonely chamber
in the King's Road, October 1627". He had been captured earlier that year
and sentenced to death, but was saved through his connections with other
gentlemen, by a royal pardon from Charles I.

The poem may have helped, or that at least was what he claimed in the
accompanying blurb — "approved by the King's most excellent majesty and
published by his express command". It would be a success, being reprinted
in 1628 and 1634.

Kingsley — for CHARLES KINGSLEY [1819-75]
see DURWESTON

KINGSTON LACY — see PAMPHILL (KINGSTON LACY)

KINGSTON MAURWARD — see STINSFORD (KINGSTON
MAURWARD)

KINGSTON RUSSELL

John Lothrop Motley: *The Rise of the Dutch Republic.*

John Lothrop Motley [1814-77] was elected to the American Hall of Fame in
1910, but he already had an English memorial in the house where he died,
with an inscription by its owner, the Duke of Bedford: "John Lothrop Motley,
Minister of the United States, Historian of the Dutch Republic, died at
Kingston Russell House, 29 May, 1877."

He was a diplomat, having been secretary of the United States legation in
St Petersburg [1841] and the ambassador to Austria [1861-67] and then Lon-
don [1869-70]. Since 1847 he had been studying the history of the Nether-
lands and publication of *The Rise of the Dutch Republic* [1856] was followed by
The History of the United Netherlands in two volumes [1860-61] and *The Life and
Death of John of Barneveld* [1874].

The classical lines of Kingston Russell House stand in the Bride valley to
the south of the A35 road seven miles west of Dorchester (Ordnance Survey
map reference SY 573 895).

LANGTON MATRAVERS

Hester Chapman: born at Durnford School.

Hester Wolferstan Pellatt [1899-1976] was born at Durnford Preparatory School, Langton Matravers. Her father was a master there. His daughter would spring to fame as Hester Chapman, in the 1930s with the novels *She Saw Them Go By* [1932] and *To Be a King*, [1934] and have a varied war helping the Free French and the American Red Cross, and then as a canteen waitress for Combined Operations. Meantime she produced *Long Division* [1943], *Will be Good* [1945] and *Worlds Apart* [1947] before embarking on the string of historical biographies for which she is remembered.

They began with *Great Villiers* [1949] and went on to deal with *Mary II* [1953], *Queen Anne's Son* [1954], *The Last Tudor King* [1958], *Two Tudor Portraits* [1960], *Lady Jane Grey* [1962], *The Tragedy of Charles II* [1964], *Lucy* [1965], *Privileged Persons* [1966], *The Sisters of Henry VIII* [1969], *Caroline Matilda* [1974] and *Four Fine Gentlemen* which was being printed at her death.

Hester Chapman, who had been twice married but was childless, was complimented by J.H. Plumb on her "rare insight into the vagaries of the human heart". It was, he noted, a quality frequently lacking in historians.

Between the histories there had been a few more novels: *Ever Thine* [1951], *Falling Stream* [1954], *The Stone Lily* [1957], *Eugéine* [1961], *Fear No More* [1968] and *Limmerston Hall* [1972].

As for her birthplace, Durnford School ceased to exist with the Second World War and its buildings became a ramshackle out-station of the Air Ministry's Telecommunications Research Establishment, devising Britain's wartime airborne radar systems [1940-42]. The buildings were in a poor state and partial demolition took place in the 1950s. Durnford House is on the north side of the High Street, the B3069, towards the top end of the village, opposite the eastern part of St George's playing fields.

Locket — for THOMAS LOCKET [flourished 1780-98]
see DORCHESTER

LONG BURTON, HOLNEST, CASTLETON and LEWESTON

William Sharpe: *Treatise upon Coal Mines.*

Rev William Sharpe [1724-83] was born in Houghton le Spring in the Durham coalfield. As vicar of Long Burton and Holnest, in the countryside south of Sherborne, he retained a vision of pit-heads and slag heaps which he was sure would come to this green and pleasant land. He arrived in 1763 and published his *Treatise upon Coal Mines* in 1769. The following year he documented previous prospecting failures with *An Appendix to a Treatise on Coal Mines, containing an historical account of the several attempts formerly made to find coal in the environs of Sherborne, interspersed with remarks upon the imperfection and inefficacy of those attempts.*

The favourite location for a dig was among the old marble quarries of Highmore's Hill, in the parish of Castleton, on the ridge east of Oborne. The main road passes into Somerset here at Crackmore Rocks. Above the road, on the south side, the hilltop (Ordnance Survey map reference ST 666 181) is capped with a fossiliferous deposit of Forest Marble mixed with a blue clay almost indistinguishable from that found in true mining districts. That, and a fair amount of greed, was enough to trigger five attempts at sinking a mineshaft; around the years 1690, 1705, 1717, 1720 and 1740.

Another outcrop of the Forest Marble is on West Hill to the south of Sherborne, in Castleton parish, where the old turnpike road can be traced as a sunken trackway to the west of the present A352 main road, which dates from 1848 (Ordnance Survey map reference ST 640 146). Here the diggers at least found something which might burn, but the smell was offensive; as Sharpe says "a foul kind of coal was found and arrived at Sherborne and burnt upon the hearths".

This area towards Leweston was also explored at Dykehead (Ordnance Survey map reference ST 641 120) in about 1705 by Henry Thynne, son of the first Viscount Weymouth. Dr Hugh Torrens has shown that with all these attempts there was probably enough fossil wood found to keep the search alive by at least producing something that might just about burn.

There was a dig into different strata at Holnest Common (Ordnance Survey map reference ST 650 090) in 1765 but the Oxford clay looks much like the Forest Marble. That too was a waste of time; coal in Dorset remained at eighteen pence a bushel compared with fourpence in the Somerset coalfield.

LONG BURTON and FOLKE

Charles Herbert Mayo: *Bibliotheca Dorsetiensis.*

Rev Charles Herbert Mayo [1845-1929] of The Retreat at Long Burton was the son of Folke's rector, William Mayo, and almost followed his footsteps, becoming vicar of Long Burton [1872-1912]. He devoted his life to studying local history and encouraging others to do the same. This was achieved by the compilation of the first bibliography of the county's books, *Bibliotheca Dorsetiensis* [1885] which remains the standard reference work on Dorset's antiquarian books and has helped me, for one, to search out and acquire about 130 of them.

He was also the first Dorset editor of *Notes and Queries for Somerset and Dorset* [1888-1921]. He assembled and published the *Municipal Records of the Borough of Shaftesbury*, the Civil War *Minutes of the Dorset Standing Committee, 1646-50* and *A Genealogical Account of the Mayo and Elton Families* plus their own biographies for a couple of distinguished kinsmen. Not being married is the probable answer to how he found time to amass the largest quantity of Dorset research since John Hutchins.

LONG CRICHEL

Raymond Mortimer: book reviewer.

Raymond Mortimer [1895-1980], the literary editor of The Nation, and a reviewer for a wide range of quality newspapers and journals, retired to Long Crichel House. He had worked with the French Red Cross through the Great War and was an Officier de la Légion d'Honneur.

His writings included *The Oxford Circus* [1922], *The French Pictures: a Letter to Harriet* [1932], *Channel Packet* [1942], *Try Anything Once* [1976], and a compilation of *Poems by Tennyson* [1958].

Loveless — for GEORGE LOVELESS [1797-1874]
see TOLPUDDLE

LULWORTH, EAST

John Fitzgerald Pennie: *Modern Genius.*

John Fitzgerald Pennie [1782-1848] was East Lulworth's noted writer. He was born at the Vicarage, where his parents seem to have been in domestic service, and though self-taught he had by the age of fifteen produced a tragedy, *The Unhappy Shepherdess*, and a neighbour, Captain Hay Forbes, had sufficient confidence in Pennie to arrange for him an interview with the manager of the Covent Garden Theatre. He told him to return to Dorset and write another play, and Pennie was to find his way into a travelling band of players. His first attempt at producing his own comedy, at Shaftesbury in 1810, was a dismal failure and left him in poverty. A benefit performance of his own *Gonzanga* was given at Chepstow in 1814 and little more attention was given him until *Ethelwolf, or the Danish Pirates* was put on in Weymouth in 1827.

Pennie published his first epic, *The Royal Minstrel* in 1817 and started a school at Lulworth, but it had closed by 1828 when he moved to Keysworth Cottage, north of Wareham. His life's achievement dated from his time at Lulworth; the publication in 1827, under the name of Sylvaticus, of *The Tale of a Modern Genius*, the autobiographical account of an aesthete's bitter struggle against abuse and neglect, with descriptions of Purbeck. From Keysworth he moved to Stoborough Heath where friends had helped him build a cottage which he called 'Rogvald' after his second epic which had been published in 1823. The rest of his life was marred by debt, on behalf of his family, and he died within a couple of days of his wife in 1848. They were buried at East Lulworth.

LULWORTH, WEST

John O'Keeffe: *Rambles in Dorsetshire.*

The Irish playwright John O'Keeffe [1747-1833] visited West Lulworth in 1791 and stayed at the Red Lion, the house which is now known as 'Churchfields'. It also served for a time as the toll-gate. The innkeeper was William Randall [1728-94] with his wife Ann, who had five daughters and one son. Randall was to provide O'Keeffe with his central character John Barleycorn for the farce *The London Hermit, or Rambles in Dorsetshire, A Comedy in Three Acts, as performed with Universal Applause at the Theatre Royal, Haymarket,* to quote its first edition title page of 1793. It is dedicated to Rev John Ball of Winfrith.

O'Keeffe remembered William Randall in his *Recollections,* published in 1826:

"The greatest original in person, manner and dress ever seen. He was tall, thin and bony with a long shallow face and staring eyes. His dress usually a white flannel coat, scarlet waistcoat with brass buttons, brown corduroy breeches, brown thread stockings and thick solid shoes with iron buckles. Besides performing the duties of innkeeper to perfection he was a man of all trades. He farmed the land, mended the doors and windows and repaired roofs. He painted names on the stern of the local fishing boats charging a penny a letter. He was adept at cobbling shoes and had painted the 'Red Lion' on his own sign board. To amuse himself he strummed a bass viol, and Sundays sang in the Church choir. If need arose, he was always ready to act as courier carrying messages to Poole, Blandford or Dorchester. When speaking he gesticulated wildly, swinging his arms and head about, and continually stammering over the many long and fine sounding words with which he attempted to embellish his speech."

Paul Randall writes about the characterisation of his ancestor and his family in issue seventy-five of Dorset County Magazine:

"The comedy is set in and around the Red Lion which is specifically mentioned, as is Lulworth in the script. William Randall figures under the name of John Barleycorn and his daughter, Kitty, is a principal character.

"She is described as a girl educated beyond her station which may well have been near the truth.

"The play is somewhat dated but the minor characters are delightful. The Boots, 'John Grum', is shown as a real country bumpkin whose only lines consist of 'Ah' or 'Um'. Apparently on the first night his appearance was so droll and the applause was so great that he needed to say nothing.

"One wonders if 'John Barleycorn' was sufficiently interested in his representation to persuade his family to see the play in town on the boards of the Haymarket Theatre but William's first visit to London was such that he probably preferred to stay at home."

In his *Recollections* O'Keeffe recalled his morning dips in Lulworth Cove, and how he had asked a fisherman why he did not bathe. He was told: "Not I, master, I keep out of the water as much as I can, and I am sure I cannot see why, for my part, you London folks come down here at a vast expense, to souse and sop yourselves in salt water."

LULWORTH, WEST
John Keats: last moments in England.

The last hours on English soil of the poet John Keats [1795-1821] seem to have been spent at Lulworth Cove on 30 September 1820. It is said to have been there that he regained sufficient composure to write his final poem, the sonnet, "Bright Star, would that I were steadfast as thou art".

He was on board the *Maria Crowther*, bound for Italy, and Captain Walsh was waiting for a favourable wind and thought it wise to let his passengers go on shore at intervals to improve their morale.

The landing place has been subject to conjecture, with Studland Bay and Holworth at Ringstead having their supporters, but tradition, boosted by a poem from Thomas Hardy, favours Lulworth.

Hardy's poem of September 1920 asks, "You see that man?" and answers: "That man goes to Rome — to death, despair; And no one notes him now but you and I: A hundred years and the world will follow him there, And bend with reverence where his ashes lie."

LULWORTH, WEST
Newlands Farm: where Bertrand Russell brought his loves.

Newlands Farm, on the downs a mile west of West Lulworth (Ordnance Survey map reference SY 811 811), was the principal holiday haunt of the promiscuous philosopher and mathematician Bertrand Russell [1872-1970]. The rather bland eighteenth century building has rendered walls and its beauty is in the setting into which it looks, particularly the view of the whole length of Bindon Hill which was the external attraction of Russell's favourite bedroom, on the east side of the farmhouse.

There he had all the major lovers of his life, from 1916 until the mid-thirties, including Lady Ottoline Morrell, Colette O'Neil (Lady Constance Malleson), Dora Black, Katherine Mansfield, Vivien Eliot (first wife of T.S. Eliot), Dorothy Wrinch and Patricia ("Peter") Spence. Several of them, and members of their various cliques, went for nude bathes in Lulworth Cove, and otherwise scandalised the village with activities that are hinted at in the novel which Colette O'Neil wrote around their relationship.

Russell became Earl Russell on his brother's death in 1931. He was a prolific writer on mathematical and philosophical subjects, branching out with books on *Marriage and Morals* and *In Praise of Idleness*, but it was for his pacifism that he would be famous in old age. As the leading figure in the anti-nuclear Committee of One Hundred he was frequently imprisoned during the civil disobedience campaigns of the 1960s.

LULWORTH, WEST
James Owen Hannay: *Bindon Parva.*

It was whilst on holiday at Lulworth Cove in September 1923 that Rev James Owen Hannay [1865-1950] started to write the novel *Bindon Parva*. It is about a parson of a Purbeck parish who celebrates communion with his dead parishioners, an unseen congregation of all classes who span the centuries and whose lives and doings he feels are absorbed into the very fabric of the building. Hannay was at that time the chaplain to the British community in

Budapest. From 1924-35 he was rector of Mells, near Frome, Somerset. His fiction appeared under the pseudonym George A. Birmingham. *Bindon Parva* was published in 1925.

LYME REGIS and WHITCHURCH CANONICORUM

Silvester Jourdain: inspired Shakespeare to *The Tempest.*

The adventures of Sir George Somers [1554-1610] and the *Sea Venture*, which was wrecked in 1609 on an uninhabited chain of islands in the mid-Atlantic, were recorded in 1610 by another Lyme man, Sylvester Jourdain. A copy of his account, *A Discovery of the Bermudas, otherwise called the Isle of Devils*, found its way to William Shakespeare [1564-1616], who was inspired to write *The Tempest.*

Somers, who had bought Berne Farm, between Charmouth and Whitchurch Canonicorum (Ordnance Survey map reference SY 388 944) in 1587, had been brought out of retirement to relieve the beleaguered Jamestown colony in Virginia. He would not get beyond Bermuda, dying there on 9 November 1610 "of a surfeit of eating of a pig", and his embalmed body would be brought home by his nephew, Matthew Somers, for a military funeral in the church at Whitchurch Canonicorum.

Later in 1611, Shakespeare performed *The Tempest.*

LYME REGIS and BETTISCOMBE

James Strong: *Feminine Valour.*

Royalist forces led by Prince Maurice of the Rhine besieged the Cromwellian town of Lyme Regis for eight weeks in 1645. They failed however to take the Cobb harbour which was then a detached quay separated by an area of foreshore from the mainland. The town's fleet of boats broke the land blockade and thatch was stripped from roofs to reduce the danger of flaming arrows that rained down on the town from the attackers on the hill.

Exchanges of musket-fire at the earthwork defences to the town amounted to litte more than mutual harassment though an evening raid killed Lyme's bravest defender: Captain Pyne commanded its cavalry detachment and had for a year taken the Civil War into the Royalist camp with repeated sallies against their positions.

The other heroes were the town's determined womenfolk who sustained the resistance and produced a minor epic of the English Civil War, in a set of verses that established them as a legend for Puritan London. Rev James Strong, the rector of Bettiscombe, penned *Joanereidos*. Its sub-title summarises the content, though for the sake of communication I shall convert the spellings into modern style:

"Feminine valour: eminently discovered in Western Women: as well as by defying the merciless enemy at the face abroad, as by fighting against them in the Garrison towns, sometimes carrying stones, anon tumbling of stones over the Works on the enemy, when they have been scaling them, some carrying powder, others charging of pieces to ease the soldiers, constantly resolved for generality, not to think any one's life dear, to maintain that Christian quarrel for the Parliament. Whereby, as they deserve commendations in themselves, so are they proposed as example unto others."

The siege was abandoned on 16 June 1645.

LYME REGIS
Within this place Lives Doctor Case.

John Case of Lyme Regis [flourished 1680-1700] did not, unfortunately, make his name in the town. It was in London that he wrote his 1695 *Compendium Anatomicum nova methodo intitutum* and followed it with *Ars Anatomica breviter elucidata* and *Flos Aevi, or Coelestial Observations* [1696]. The following year his *Angelical Guide* appeared and in 1698 the *Medical Expositer*.

Joseph Addison wrote in The Tatler that Case had made more money from a distich above his door that Dryden had managed from all his works:

> *Within this place*
> *Lives Doctor Case.*

He had a quick wit. Once three doctors were at supper together and John Radcliffe toasted Case's health: "Here's to all the fools, your patients, brother Case."

"I thank you, good brother," Case replied. "Let me have all the fools, and you are heartily welcome to the rest of the practice."

LYME REGIS
Jane Austen: *Persuasion.*

Jane Austen [1775-1817] stayed at Lyme Regis, apparently in November 1803, when she witnessed a huge fire, and returned in September 1804. Her tart view of Lyme's society was developed for the novel *Persuasion*, which was published posthumously in 1818.

Where she stayed arouses controversy. John Oldfield and John Fowles have shown that she could not possibly have stayed in the house called Wings, demolished in 1945, on Lyme's Marine Parade, as it was not built until after 1827.

Their "logical preference" is for Hiscott's lodging house in Broad Street which was demolished and replaced by the new Three Cups in 1807. The evidence is from the novelist herself, writing from Lyme Regis in 1804, as she described a walk that could have been that from the Assembly Rooms, up the Bell Cliff steps and along the unlit Middle Row alley, above the Shambles, to Hiscott's: "The ball last night was pleasant but not full for Thursday. My father stayed contentedly till half past nine (we left a little after eight) and then walked home with James and the lanthorn, though I believe the lanthorn was not lit, as the moon was up, but this lanthorn may sometimes be of great convenience to him."

The other contender, the old Three Cups, can be eliminated as it stood on the other side of the road from the Assembly Rooms.

LYME REGIS
The Jane Austen Garden.

Beside the promenade which leads from the Cobb to the Marine Parade and the town of Lyme stood the weather-boarded villa known as Wings.

Having previously lambasted the local councillors for perpetuating the myth that it was here Miss Austen had stayed, an error that had gone into stone on a plaque beside the site of the seaside house, I must record the present (acceptable) wording. The spot is now a small public open space, as the replacement plaque explains:

"The Jane Austen Garden. Lyme Regis, was part of the setting for the novel *Persuasion* by Jane Austen who lodged in the town in 1804. The garden was opened by Sir Hugh Smiley, Bt., Chairman of the Jane Austen Society, on the 23rd April 1975."

The ceremony was one part of a series of events to mark the two hundredth anniversary of the author's birth.

LYME REGIS

George Cruikshank: satire on nude bathing and 'Sub-Lyme' Burke.

An engraving by George Cruikshank [1792-1878] that was published in London on 8 September 1819, and is on display in Lyme Regis Museum, shows the bathing machines on the beach beside the Cobb harbour at Lyme Regis, with the ladies, as was the custom, taking to the water without a costume among them.

The title *Hydromania! or a Touch of the Sub-Lyme and Beautiful* was satirical, being a comment both upon the unfathomable fashion for cold water and Edmund Burke's essay *On the Sublime and Beautiful* [1756].

LYME REGIS

John Gould: discovered the world's birds.

John Gould of Lyme Regis [1804-81] went into the world and returned as the supreme ornithologist of all time. He discovered and described more species of birds than anyone else — hundreds of them — and left too few for his total to be matched until someone finds birds on another planet.

Gould's hunting ground spanned Asia and Australasia from the Himalayas to New Guinea and the islands of paradise. His meticulous drawings, taken from the skins he procured or was sent — at some cost, as three of his collectors lost their lives in the process — were to fill volumes.

There are 2,999 of his bird illustrations. The volumes of hand-coloured lithographs have been the target of house decorators, broken up and put into frames, to the extent that they now rate among the world's rarest and most sought-after books. The price of a set reached £400,000 in 1987.

His other claim to fame is that he introduced the budgerigar to England.

LYME REGIS

Palgrave: *Golden Treasury.*

Francis Turner Palgrave [1824-97] was the most eminent of Dorset's Victorian literati, from the moment he settled in Little Park, Haye Lane, Lyme Regis, in 1872. A close friend and travel companion of Tennyson he was also a poet, whose *Visions of England* [1880-81] were followed by *Amenophis* [1892] and volumes of literary criticism, such as *Landscape in Poetry* [1897]. From 1885-95 he was Professor of Poetry at Oxford.

What he would be remembered for is not his own work, however, but a colossal series of anthologies entitled the *Golden Treasury of the Best Song and Lyrical Poems in the English Language* [1861, extended in 1897]. Some of the religious omissions made it into the sequel, the *Treasury of Sacred Song* [1889]. His brother Reginald lived at Swanage.

LYME REGIS

John Fowles: Belmont House, *The French Lieutenant's Woman* and 'Allsop Island'.

Belmont House is an imposing eighteenth century mansion set back from Pound Street, which takes the Exeter road up the hill out of Lyme, at the junction with Cobb Road. It has panoramic views over the little stone harbour and the expanse of Lyme Bay, across its own lawn and grounds, and was the home of an enterprising lady, Eleanore Coade [died 1796] who invented the terracotta-making process used to cast the decorations inset around Belmont's facade and a far larger symbol to the nation, the imposing red lion that stood at the entrance to Waterloo Station until 1966, when it was moved to the south end of Westminster Bridge.

Belmont's twentieth century lion of literature has been John Fowles [born 31 March 1926] who moved here (Ordnance Survey map reference SY 338 920) in the 1960s from Underhill Farm, on the edge of the miles of Undercliff National Nature Reserve (Ordnance Survey map reference SY 327 915) after a couple of its fields landslipped towards the sea.

Built rather like Orson Welles, plus a Solzenytzin beard, he was already a cult figure — studied in universities in Europe and America — with deep novels such as *The Collector* [1963], *The Aristos* [1965] and *The Magus* [1966].

Two had been made into films but his wider fame would follow in 1969 with publication of *The French Lieutenant's Woman* which is not only set in Lyme Regis, in Napoleon's time, which would be Hardyesque in itself, but has the distinction of being the first Dorset novel to upstage the work of Thomas Hardy and extend the bounds of literary devices. It was for its innovative skills, seen as advancing the craft, that it won the Silver Pen of 1969 and the W.H. Smith Award of 1970, and would be a major success in the cinema, with Meryl Streep and Jeremy Irons.

Its author went on to write *The Ebony Tower* [1974] and *Daniel Martin* [1977], and in the 1980s *The Maggot*, but he also exercised his scholar's brain on the monument that has perplexed antiquarian thought, *The Enigma of Stonehenge* [1980] which invited, as he put it to me, "the ritual slaughter of John Fowles by the new Druids (or archaeological pro's)". We were then working together on the first publication of John Aubrey's vast compendium of notes [see Blandford entry] entitled *Monumenta Britannica* [1980-82] which had lain untranscribed in the Bodleian Library for nearly three centuries.

I wondered why he needed the time consuming torment of trying to unravel obscure abbreviations, a jumble of Latin and post-mediaeval English, and often disappeared bits of ancient Britain. "I do it as an alternative to the crossword," he replied.

The mind games could only be punctuated by botany or spider-hunting. "Belmont Botanical Gardens" I jokingly called his grounds when plant collecting was at its height, including specimens plucked from great gardens the world over, but in later years it was reclaimed by nature and visited only by the badgers.

John Fowles provided the means and influence to acquire the toy of my middle years, the island of Steep Holm five miles out in Bristol Channel, which we turned into "Allsop Island" as a memorial to Dorset author and naturalist Kenneth Allsop [see Powerstock entry]. But that, as they say, is another story.

LYME REGIS

Ann Jellicoe: *The Knack.*

Playwright Ann Jellicoe [born 1927] came to fame with *The Knack* which with both content and timing [1961] spearheaded the Swinging Sixties. Its transition from the stage to the cinema [1965] captured pop culture at its climax.

Locally, from Colway Manor, Colway Lane, Lyme Regis, Ann Jellicoe has brought community theatre to west Dorset — choosing subjects that have shaped its history such as the 1685 rebellion in support of the Duke of Monmouth and having the descendants as the players — and expanded one-off performances into the Colway Theatre Trust. She has also been at the forefront of the regional efforts by South West Arts. Her second marriage [1962] is to photographer Roger Mayne.

LYTCHETT MINSTER

Sir Francis Younghusband: 'Forbidden City' gravestone.

The Potala, the monastic palace of the former Dalai Lamas in Lhasa, Tibet, is featured in bas-relief on a gravestone in Lytchett Minster churchyard. It is to Lieutenant-Colonel Sir Francis Edward Younghusband [1863-1942] who was born at Murree in the Punjab. He explored the fringes of the "Roof of the World" in 1886-87 and penetrated its secret places with the Tibet Mission in 1903-04.

This force of 1,150 men was intended to bring about the installation of a British diplomatic presence in Lhasa but the Tibetans regarded its incursion across the border from Sikkim in December 1903 as an act of hostility and they mounted attacks. These were little more than harassment as far as the highly-disciplined and well-armed column of Sikh, Gurkha and British troops were concerned.

Lieutenant-Colonel Younghusband reached the "Forbidden City" of Lhasa on 3 August 1904, but the Dalai Lama was absent. He was able, however, to bring about an Anglo-Tibetan treaty which was signed on 7 September 1904 in a tripartite form endorsed by the Chinese. Fears that Tibet had already fallen under Russian influence proved to be groundless; it was still an independent buffer state between three great powers.

Younghusband returned to India and a knighthood. In 1917 he was rewarded with the Star of India for his war service in the India Office. In retirement he became chairman of the Mount Everest Committee, but did not live to see the conquest of the mountain.

His books include *Heart of a Continent* [1898], *India and Tibet: Within* [1912], *Everest: the Challenge* [1936], *A Venture of Faith* [1937], and *The Sum of Things* [1939].

Macgregor — for JOHN MACGREGOR [1825-92], known as ROB ROY, see BOURNEMOUTH (BOSCOMBE)

Macready — for WILLIAM MACREADY [1793-1873] see SHERBORNE

Mansel-Pleydell — for JOHN CLAVELL MANSEL-PLEYDELL [1817-1902] see WINTERBORNE WHITECHURCH

MANSTON and FONTMELL MAGNA

Thomas Dibben: translated *Carmen Seculare*.

Thomas Dibben [died 1741] was born at Manston. He became a fellow of Trinity College, Cambridge, in 1698 and in 1700 translated Matthew Prior's *Carmen Seculare* into Latin verse. Dibben was appointed rector of Great Fontmell — now known as Fontmell Magna — in 1701.

He was chaplain to the Bishop of Bristol, Dr John Robinson, and became precentor of St Paul's Cathedral in 1714.

MAPPOWDER

T.F.Powys: one decent wish.

Ousted from his Chaldon Herring home on Dorset's potential invasion coast by the fear that accompanied the long, hot summer of 1940, author Theodore Francis Powys [1875-1953] came to the Blackmore Vale to embark on his final reflections. He had already, he told John O'London's Weekly in 1936, entered a stage where he would probably never write again. He had enough behind him in *Interpretation of Genesis, Soliloquies of a Hermit, Mr Tasker's Gods, The Left Leg, Black Bryony, Mark Only, Unclay, Fables, John Told and the Worm, Kindness in a Corner,* and, above all in terms of popularity, *Mr Weston's Good Wine.*

It was mood-writing, agile and precise in construction but abstract in meaning, that tried to reconcile earthly humanity with the divinity that co-exists with life. The words brought neither a cure for depression nor a blissful uplift from their value. He still "went searching for God", as his brother Llewelyn Powys put it.

At Mappowder Theodore's last home was the little stone lodge-like building beside the churchyard. It was to the church that he went for contemplation but was always the absent parishioner on a Sunday. The other days of the week, when religion could be personal rather than communal, he rang the bell for Compline and often settled into one of the pews.

Those who entered his world found a certain sadness, if not utter pessimism, and it was in Mappowder churchyard that he would achieve what, to quote one of his characters, "all men and women have in their hearts, through all their foolishness, one decent wish — to be buried".

Marryat — for CAPTAIN FREDERICK MARRYAT [1792-1848]
see CHRISTCHURCH (HIGHCLIFFE)

MARSHWOOD

Kilvert's visit: to Lambert's Castle.

A fine fresh air blew from the sea
over the high furzy moor.

— Rev Francis Kilvert [1840-79] visiting Lambert's Castle Hill (Ordnance Survey map reference SY 370 988), 2 August 1871. It hardly suffices to bring Dorset into the Kilvert Country though there might have been more as the accidental destruction of the typescript of his diaries was one of the literary tragedies of the twentieth century.

Mayo – for CHARLES HERBERT MAYO [1845-1929]
see LONG BURTON

MELCOMBE HORSEY and WEST STAFFORD

Reginald Bosworth Smith: birds and Allah.

Reginald Bosworth Smith had been assistant master of Harrow School. From the old thatched rectory at West Stafford (Ordnance Survey map reference SY 724 895) he had moved to the aristocratic mansion of Bingham's Melcombe Manor in the upland parish of Melcombe Horsey (ST 772 022). He described it in *Bird Life and Bird Lore* [1905]: "Its old grey walls and its surroundings seem to enhance the charms, and even to some extent, to modify the habits of the birds which haunt them; while they, in their turn, lend something of life, of activity, of enjoyment, of music to the atmosphere of peace and undisturbed repose which always seems to hover over its ancient precincts."

Aware that birds of prey were being edged towards extinction, he called for private country estates to be managed as wild life (then two words) sanctuaries, with the New Forest as a public one.

He was also ahead of his time in lecturing the Royal Institution on the implications of "Allahu Akbar" and the "inexhaustible vitality" of the "wild crusade" of Islam. *Mohammed and Mohammedanism* was published in 1874. He also wrote *Carthage and the Carthaginians* and *The Life of Lord Lawrence*, Governor-General of India. "Too eulogistic," the *Dictionary of National Biography* calls the latter.

Millar – for GEORGE MILLAR [born 1910]
see SYDLING ST NICHOLAS

MINTERNE MAGNA

High Stoy: Hardy's favourite view.

When Thomas Hardy [1840-1928] was asked to name the best views in Dorset he put the one from High Stoy first in the list. Given the same question, Sir Frederick Treves [1853-1923] said that the countryside seen from High Stoy made it the finest inland view in Dorset. "High Sty" the locals call it. "The High Stoy view is in all probability one of the most magnificent landscape views in the south of England, and I believe that if put to the vote of the county it would take chief place," stated the writer of a patriotic article about the county in 1914.

A lane off the A352 Dorchester-Sherborne road turns towards Hermitage and skirts the foot of High Stoy (Ordnance Survey map reference ST 649 057). The trees on its steep flank rise to a rounded chalk summit at 846 feet. It is the highest and finest of a series of hilltops amid the sudden change of scenery, from the head of the Cerne valley at Minterne Magna to the Blackmore Vale at Middlemarsh. Because of the classical acclaim given to the hill, no better description is possible than that of Sir Frederick Treves:

"... the most engaging of all Dorset hills – a hill of 800 feet made up of green slopes, a cliff, and a mantle of trees ... From the crest of High Stoy is a view to the north, the east, and the west which is not likely to be forgotten. It embraces the north of Dorset, the south of Wiltshire, and ranges over Somerset to Glastonbury and the Mendip Hills. Whether it is possible, as some declare, to see the two Holmes in the Bristol Channel I am unable to say."

You can — the larger one being Steep Holm and the lesser Flat Holm, though only in the rare moments of superb clarity that follow a storm.

Mitchell-Hedges — for FREDERICK MITCHELL-HEDGES [1882-1959] see POOLE (SANDBANKS)

MORETON and DORCHESTER

Mary Frampton: *The Journal.*

Mary Frampton [1773-1846] of Moreton House (Ordnance Survey map reference SY 806 892) had posthumous fame. Her diary would be published as *The Journal of Mary Frampton* and fascinate the Victorians with its lush picture of high fashion and country house living, interspersed with visits to London and court anecdotes, both from there and the royal travelling circus to Weymouth, plus touches of fear when prestige and power were threatened by the mob — she was in Town during the Gordon Riots, and trembling behind the shutters at Moreton during the Captain Swing fires of 1830.

She displays high Toryism, a strong will, and a capacity for observation, but there is the standard feminine interest in weddings and the general social round. Paradoxically, though she was at the centre of the county's social set, Mary would never marry.

Her father, James Frampton, died in 1784 and two years later Mary moved with her mother, Phillis, to Wollaston House, Dorchester, where the parties went on as before. Phillis Frampton lived to be ninety-two and died in 1829. Mary's niece, Harriot Georgina Mundy, would prepare the journal for publication in 1885.

MORETON — see TURNERS PUDDLE (CLOUDS HILL) for T.E. Lawrence: *Seven Pillars of Wisdom*

Mortimer — for RAYMOND MORTIMER [1895-1980] see LONG CRICHEL

Motley — for JOHN LOTHROP MOTLEY [1814-77] see KINGSTON RUSSELL

Moule — for HANDLEY CARR GLYN MOULE [1841-1920], Bishop of Durham, see DORCHESTER (FORDINGTON)

Moule — for HENRY MOULE [1801-80] see DORCHESTER (FORDINGTON)

Moule — for HORACE MOULE [1832-73] see DORCHESTER (FORDINGTON)

Muntz — for ISABELLE HOPE MUNTZ [1907-81] see CHALDON HERRING (EAST CHALDON)

OBORNE — see CASTLETON (OBORNE) for Robert Goadby's memorial: just an empty space

O'Keeffe — for JOHN O'KEEFFE [1747-1833] see LULWORTH, WEST

Osborne — for LORD SIDNEY GODOLPHIN OSBORNE [1808-89]
see DURWESTON

Palgrave — for FRANCIS TURNER PALGRAVE [1824-97]
see LYME REGIS

Palgrave — for SIR REGINALD PALGRAVE [1829-1904]
see SWANAGE

Palgrave — for MARY PALGRAVE [daughter of Sir Reginald]
see SWANAGE

PAMPHILL (KINGSTON LACY), CORFE CASTLE and WIMBORNE

Henry Bankes: *History of Rome.*

Henry Bankes MP [1757-1834] of Kingston Lacy House represented the family ruin of Corfe Castle in Parliament for nearly half a century [1780-1826] and then held one of the Dorset seats [1826-30].

Bankes was also the Parliamentary mouthpiece for the British Museum trustees. In 1818 he published *A Civil and Constitutional History of Rome, from the Foundation to the Age of Augustus.* He was buried in Wimborne Minster.

PARKSTONE — see POOLE (PARKSTONE)

Parry — for SIR HUBERT PARRY [1848-1919]
see BOURNEMOUTH

Peacock — for THOMAS LOVE PEACOCK [1785-1866]
see WEYMOUTH

Pennie — for JOHN FITZGERALD PENNIE [1782-1848]
see LULWORTH, EAST

PENTRIDGE (WOODYATES)

Ancestors of Robert Browning.

A memorial tablet on the north wall of Pentridge church records the connection between the Browning graves in the churchyard and the poet Robert Browning [1812-89]:

"To the memory of Robert Browning of Woodyates, in this parish, who died November 25th 1746 and is the first known forefather of Robert Browning, the poet. He married Elizabeth Pethebridge who died in 1759, and their son Thomas [born 1721] of Woodyates Inn was the poet's great-grandfather. This tablet was erected by some of the poet's friends and admirers, 1902."

Woodyates Inn (Ordnance Survey map reference SU 029 193), an extensive eighteenth century coaching house, had a thatched former tavern — which had provided the last night of freedom for the fugitive Duke of Monmouth in 1685 — facing it on the opposite side of the main road. Both buildings were demolished in the 1950s.

It is only in Pentridge that Browning links remain (map reference SU 033 178). In the churchyard there is a memorial to Jane and Thomas Browning [died 1773 and 1794 respectively] and "William Browning their Son, an officer in His Majesty's ship Sybil and who was unfortunately drowned in St John's Harbour, Antigua, 21st December 1781. Aged 22." In fact Browning, who was the master's mate, drowned in English Harbour, which was the naval anchorage of the Carribean island.

Their stone is still perfectly clear-cut, unlike the description of a gravestone their descendant would put in his poem *Fame*:

> *How the minute grey lichens, plate o'er plate,*
> *Have softened down the crisp-cut name and date!*

Pickard-Cambridge — for SIR ARTHUR PICKARD-CAMBRIDGE [1873-1952]
see BLOXWORTH

Pickard-Cambridge — for WILLIAM ADAIR PICKARD-CAMBRIDGE [1879-1957]
see BLOXWORTH

Pickard-Cambridge — for WILLIAM ADAIR PICKARD-CAMBRIDGE [1879-1957]
see BLOXWORTH

PIDDLETRENTHIDE — see PUDDLETOWN for Ralph Wightman: *Abiding Things*

PIMPERNE — see BLANDFORD for Christopher Pitt: translated Virgil; and DURWESTON for Charles Kingsley

Pitt — for CHRISTOPHER PITT [1699-1748]
see BLANDFORD

Pitt-Rivers — for LIEUTENANT-GENERAL HENRY LANE FOX PITT-RIVERS [1827-1900]
see FARNHAM

Pococke — for RICHARD POCOCKE [1704-65]
see CERNE ABBAS

POOLE

Woodes Rogers: discovered *Robinson Crusoe*.

Captain Woodes Rogers [?1697-1732] was apparently born in Poole. His father, certainly, was born in the town and lived there with his wife, Frances, prior to moving to Bristol. Their son became a leading sea-captain, who rose in status through his marriage in London to Sarah Whetstone, the daughter of Sir William Whetstone.

What he is remembered for, however, was his accidental discovery on 31 January 1709 of a white man, dressed in goatskins, on the uninhabited far-south Pacific island(s) of Juan Fernández. This individual, who spoke only broken English, turned out to be a Scotsman, Alexander Selkirk [1676-1721], who had been marooned there some four years earlier after a row with his captain, Thomas Stradling.

The story captured the British imagination. Richard Steele [1672-1729] told it in the Englishman Journal of 1713 and then Woodes Rogers wrote up his own *Cruising Voyage Round the World* [1718].

The version, however, that the world now knows is that published in 1719 by Daniel Defoe [?1661-1731]. Alexander Selkirk had become *Robinson Crusoe*, and his stay on that re-located island (it is now in the North Atlantic) had stretched to twenty-eight years.

The Chileans, who own the actual island, have solved the identification problem delightfully. There are in fact two islands in the sea at about 79° west / 33° south. The larger, eastern, one is called Isla Robinson Crusoe. The higher, western, one is known as Isla Alejandro Selkirk. You can take your choice!

POOLE (CANFORD MAGNA)

Lady Charlotte Guest: translated the *Mabinogion*.

One of Britain's leading industrialists, Sir Josiah John Guest MP [1783-1852] — owner of Dowlais Ironworks, Merthyr Tydfil, which produced the rails for the railways — ploughed his excess £350,000 into buying Canford Manor and its thousands of acres in 1845. The estate ran from Wimborne to the sea — hence Canford Cliffs. Guest had the house enlarged by Sir Charles Barry who was at the time also rebuilding the Houses of Parliament.

In 1833, Guest married the daughter of the ninth Earl of Lindsey, Charlotte Elizabeth Bertie [1812-95], who would give him ten children in the next thirteen years. She also found time to be one of the great Welsh scholars of all time, translating the manuscripts that formed the *Mabinogion*, published between 1838 and 1849. These provided her friend Alfred Tennyson [1809-92] with the Arthurian legends that formed the basis for his *Idylls of the King* [1859].

Charlotte's second marriage, to Charles Schreiber in 1855, ended with his death in 1884.

She also made a major impact upon British culture by one of her "good works", a shelter for London cabmen which was kept supplied with newspapers; this helped to create one of the most articulate and opinionated groups of people in the land.

Her porcelain collection was presented to the Victoria and Albert Museum, in memory of second husband Charles, and she then published two lavish volumes on her collection of painted fans, in 1888-90. The fans were then given to the British Museum in 1891.

POOLE

Thomas Bell: footsteps of Gilbert White.

Thomas Bell [1792-1880], the son of a Poole surgeon, became a dentist and produced a study on tooth decay in 1829. His main interest, however, was zoology and in the early Victorian period he published three standard works as something between textbooks and popular guides to the country's animal life. These were the *History of British Quadrupeds* [1837, expanded 1874], the *History of British Reptiles* [1839] and the *History of British Stalk-eyed Crustacea* [1853].

In 1860 he retired to The Wakes at Selborne in Hampshire, which had been the home of naturalist Gilbert White [1720-93] and immersed himself in his predecessor's memorabilia. Bell prepared a biography of White and re-issued his *Natural History of Selborne* in what, in 1877, was soon acclaimed as its classic edition.

POOLE (BRANKSOME PARK)

Hugh Mulleneux Walmsley: *Branksome Dene.*

Sir Joshua Walmsley [1794-1871], a leader of the Anti-Corn Law League and close friend of railway pioneer George Stephenson, retired to Branksome Park after falling out with Leicester's electorate in 1857. His *Life* would be compiled by his son, Colonel Hugh Mulleneux Walmsley of the Ottoman Imperial Army.

Hugh had already written a smuggling and shipwreck adventure story spun around Isaac Gulliver and Branksome Chine in the Napoleonic wars. The three volume work, written at the suggestion of Richard Bentley, is entitled *Branksome Dene: a Sea Tale* [1872]. His other books included *The Lifeguardsman* and *The Chasseurs de' Afrique.*

Branksome Dene, built by the Guest family of Canford Manor, is now the Royal Masonic Benevolent Institution's Zetland Court retirement home.

POOLE

William Taylor Haly: the would-be MP.

William Taylor Haly [1818-74] was born in Poole and is buried in its cemetery. In his boyhood he travelled with his father, Lieutenant Richard Standish Haly RN, in the Carribean, and then stayed in the United States. His father protested against the press-gangs with a 44-page publication on *Impressment: An Attempt to Prove Why it Should and How it Could be Abolished.*

William Haly also established a reputation as "an extreme radical" and went on to write "a perfect encyclopaedia of political knowledge" which was how The Times praised his book on *The Opinions of Sir Robert Peel* in 1843. He also produced a study on *Education: Showing What is done; What is not done; What we can do; to Educate the People* in which he urged an extension in primary education — though well short of suggesting it should be compulsory.

By 1852 he was attempting to get into Parliament, on a ticket for free trade, anti-window tax, set three-year terms for government, against state moneys for the Church, and in favour of wider voting rights. That was in an entertaining campaign in Paisley where he lost by 374 votes to 496.

In 1857 he brought his "advanced Liberal" ideas to Poole and took on the establishment sitting Liberal, Henry Danby Seymour. It was a three-cornered fight for the town's two seats and Seymour went back to Westminster with 211 votes, as did the Tory, George Franklyn, with 189 votes. Haly had only 98 votes.

He returned north on the death of his previous opponent at Paisley and saw his former support just about wiped out — probably because he had turned his back on Scotland and returned to Poole. So once again he came back south, in 1859, but to no avail — the votes were Franklyn 208; Seymour 193; Haly 143. His political career was over before it had started.

POOLE (CANFORD MAGNA)

Sir Henry Austen Layard: 'Discoverer of Ninevah'.

A red-granite tombstone in Canford Magna churchyard makes two false claims — one in words, the other by being there at all: "The Right Honourable Sir Henry Austen Layard GCB, the Discoverer of Ninevah. Sometime a Member of Parliament, and H.M. Ambassador at Constantinople. Born at

Paris 5 March 1817. Died in London 5 July 1894."

Dorset does not, however, have his bones. He was cremated at Woking and his ashes are buried there.

The other exaggeration is the claim that he discovered Ninevah. He thought he had, and indeed wrote books on *Ninevah and its Remains* [1848-49] and *Ninevah and Babylon* [1853], and brought home massive Assyrian bas-reliefs and cuneiform inscriptions which he presented to the British Museum. The inscriptions were later to prove that the four palaces he had dug up in 1845 were in fact in the Assyrian city of Calah. The mounds of the lost Ninevah lay undisturbed twenty miles away.

Sir Henry's connection with Canford is that he married one of its young ladies, Mary Evelyn Guest, in 1869. The east end of Canford Manor was transformed into Ninevah Court to house Layard's matchless collection of Assyrian antiquities. Note that I do not say "priceless" collection. For in art everything has a price. Most went to the Metropolitan Museum, New York.

POOLE

Augusta Webster: *Housewife's Opinions.*

Mrs Augusta Webster [1837-94] was born in Poole. Her father, Vice-Admiral George Davies [1800-76], was a hero for saving lives in shipwreck.

His daughter published *Blanche Lisle, and other Poems* in 1860, under the name Cecil Home, but her abiding concern was for social causes. Her essays in The Examiner were reprinted as *A Housewife's Opinions* in 1878 and produced as leaflets by the Women's Suffrage Society. She was hardly an average housewife, putting herself forward in 1879 for the Chelsea seat on the London School Board and winning it with 3,912 votes to spare.

POOLE (BROADSTONE)

Alfred Russel Wallace: Broadstone fossil tree.

Alfred Russel Wallace [1823-1913] of the Old Orchard at Broadstone has a fossil tree standing on his grave in the Dunyeats Road cemetery. He had died in the full glory of being one of the world's leading naturalists, rewarded with the Order of Merit in 1910, and remembered as the man who could have been Darwin.

For Wallace had been thinking along the same lines and it was as a joint paper that Charles Darwin and Alfred Russel Wallace published their pamphlet *On the Tendency of Species to form Varieties* in 1858. Only two copies survive. It would be Darwin's work *On the Origin of Species* that would appear the following year and popularise the theory of evolution for general consumption and lasting memory.

Wallace had not been that slow in going into print: he had already published *Travels on the Amazon* and *Palm Trees of the Amazon* [1853], but his later works show a determination to grasp new ground and pre-empt the competition. Diverse subjects included *The Malay Archipelago* [1869], *Natural Selection* [1870], *Miracles and Modern Spiritualism* [1874], *The Geographical Distribution of Animals* [1876], *Tropical Nature* [1878], *Australasia* [1879], *Island Life* [1880], *Land Nationalisation* [1882], *Bad Times* [1885], *Darwinism* [1889], *Vaccination a Delusion* [1898] and *The Wonderful Century, its Successes and Failures* [1898].

He had the vision to see some of our preoccupations in the next. *Studies, Scientific and Social* [1900] led to *Man's Place in the Universe*, and an ambitious question-mark for a new century that was trying to push the bounds of powered flight over distances in excess of twenty-five miles — *Is Mars Inhabitable?* appeared in 1906. *The World of Life* followed in 1910.

Wallace had one of the great minds of the age. His views on medical vaccination are now outdated, and as President of the Land Nationalisation Society he is unlikely to have a successor until the twenty-first century, but between games of chess and tending his Broadstone garden he encouraged others to expand the frontiers of science.

POOLE (BRANKSOME PARK)

Edgar Wallace: *Mr Justice Maxell.*

The last link with the demolished Branksome Towers (Ordnance Survey map reference SZ 067 899), the setting in 1922 for Edgar Wallace's *Mr Justice Maxell,* were lost in 1975 when Poole Council pulled down its lodge at County Gates, Westbourne, to mark the start of European Architectural Heritage Year.

The philistines on the council achieved a remarkable double as 1975 was also the centenary year of the thriller-writer's birth. He died in 1932.

Dorset devotees should be aware of the tendency for the odd cherished corner to disappear whilst the visitors are home for the winter.

POOLE (ALDERNEY)

Margaret Kennedy: *The Constant Nymph.*

Welsh impressionist painter Augustus John [1878-1961] moved to Alderney Manor, between Poole and Wallisdown, in 1911, after the death of his wife, Ida Nettleship in 1907. Lady Wimborne, of Canford Manor, rented him this crenellated piece of Victorian Gothic, in sixty acres of heathland on what is now the St Barnabas church side of the corner of Alderney Avenue and Ringwood Road, opposite the drive to Alderney Isolation Hospital (Ordnance Survey map reference SZ 044 943).

Local society would soon resent his pacifism and be outraged by the multiplicity of lovers. The debauchery of Alderney, in which second wife Dorelia and Augustus John set the pace for the artists of the Swinging Twenties, was inevitably affecting the quality of his work. "He is unquestionably the greatest painter in England today," Christopher Wood wrote in 1922, "and if he hadn't drunk so much would have been greater than Leonardo da Vinci or Michelangelo."

The smart-set at Alderney were immortalised by Margaret Kennedy [1896-1967] in *The Constant Nymph,* the best-seller of 1924. The novel satirised one of the key members of the John entourage, Dorelia's fancy man Henry Lamb, as the character Lewis Dodd, who would later be played by Noel Coward [1926].

Lady Wimborne died in 1927. The lease was terminated and Alderney Manor demolished. The John family and sycophants moved to Fryern Court, Fordingbridge.

POOLE (SANDBANKS)

Frederick Mitchell-Hedges: *Battling with Sea Monsters.*

On 21 February 1927 the Daily Express published allegations that Frederick

126

Mitchell-Hedges [1882-1959], the explorer, author and lecturer, of the Bridge House, Sandbanks, had staged a bogus highway robbery to draw attention to a device known as a 'Monomark' and gain himself fraudulent notoriety. The first article was headed : "Robbery on the Ripley Road. True story of the great midnight hold-up. A pure fake."

The alleged incident happened on the night of 14 January when Mitchell-Hedges was accompanied by Colin Edgell on a car journey from the National Liberal Club in London to his home at Sandbanks. They were stopped on the outskirts of Ripley by a person who said a man was ill and needed assistance.

This they said was a trap, reporting that a skirmish then took place, in which the attackers tied up the chauffeur with a rope. They then ran off with Mitchell-Hedges's attache case which, he said, contained "four reduced heads of human beings" which had been obtained on his travels, and various documents.

Mitchell-Hedges claimed to hold several world records for the capture of giant fish and to have discovered a new race of people in Panama in 1921. He credited himself with discovering the ruins of the vast Maya lost city of Lubaantum in 1924. As he arrived back at Paddington station from Venezuela a snake escaped from his carriage; it was 18 feet 6 inches long. A Daily Mail reporter and Lady (Richmond) Brown helped him put it back in its box. When it finally reached London Zoo seven men were needed to deal with it. Mitchell-Hedges's financial affairs also attracted attention as he was declared bankrupt in 1912.

His books were pure gung-ho stuff: *Battles with Giant Fish, The White Tiger, Land of Wonder and Fear, Battling with Sea Monsters* and *Danger My Ally.* Undaunted by the troubles of either 1912 or 1927 he was off again to Central America in 1930 and Tanganyika and the atolls of the Indian Ocean in 1950.

POOLE (LILLIPUT)
Mary Butts: born at Salterns.

The "maggot-knot of dwellings" beside Poole Harbour at Salterns, in the heart of Lilliput's yacht-land (Ordnance Survey map reference SZ 037 897) was the birthplace of Mary Butts [1890-1937]. She anguished at a new barbarism that was changing the face of rural England from the cherished Edwardian water-colour vision of her childhood into the harsh mechanised sprawl of the suburbanised Twenties and Thirties.

Returned washed-out from a mad fling in Paris, where she had published *Imaginary Letters* in 1928, she wanted the security of old England and found it to an extent with next husband Gabriel Aitken in Cornwall. Fictional work included *Ashe of Rings* [1925] and *Death of Felicity Taverner* [1932] and led to an investigation of Alexander the Great, *The Macedonian* [1933]. *The Crystal Cabinet*, her autobiography, would appear posthumously.

POOLE (PARKSTONE)
Ivan Ruff: *Blood Money.*

Thriller writer Ivan Ruff [born 1945] wrote *The Dark Red Star, Dead Reckoning* and *Blood Money* in Parkstone, at Furze Hill Drive. He sent me a copy of *Blood Money* [1988] with the explanation that although it appeared to be "set in a mythical all-purpose England" it is actually Dorset and "from first page to last the place is there".

He paid me the compliment of having borrowed a "nuclear neighbour" phrase from an old issue of Dorset County Magazine, a reference to Winfrith, and was the only person to elevate that journal's haphazard publication schedule during my twenty year regime into a virtue by saying "the absence of date and the irregular publication were in character with the timeless subject matter".

His own "barely disguised Dorset bits" are sharply defined with the clarity and pace that only an accomplished crime writer can manage. The plot puts the edge on the topography; it's nice to know that my ramblings have been of use. Ivan Ruff came to Dorset in 1973 and has had encouraging national reviews.

POOLE (BROADSTONE) — see BLOXWORTH for W.A. Pickard-Cambridge: *Dorset Carols*

Poor — for BISHOP ROGER POOR [died 1237] see TARRANT CRAWFORD

Pope — for ALEXANDER POPE [1688-1744] see CASTLETON (SHERBORNE CASTLE)

Potter — for BEATRICE POTTER [1858-1943] see PORTLAND (once, she said)

PORTLAND
Pennsylvania Castle: John Penn's drama.

Pennsylvania Castle, among Penn's trees which are the sycamores of the only wood on the island, at the south end of Wakeham's wide street, was built for John Penn [1760-1834] to the designs of eminent architect James Wyatt [1746-1813] in 1800. It is Gothic mock-fortification with matching embattled parapets to the gateway (Ordnance Survey map reference SY 695 711).

The double pun in the name was that Penn's grandfather William Penn [1644-1718] had founded Pennsylvania.

As for John Penn of Portland, he was a reasonably prolific writer, poet and dramatist. In 1817 he formed a "matrimonial society" to improve the domestic life of married persons. It became the Outlinian Society, 1818-25. Penn himself was unmarried.

He was something of a playwright, with *The Battle of Eddington or British Liberty* being performed at Windsor, the Haymarket, Covent Garden and Sadler's Wells. He also translated Virgil and wrote his own poems, published on the private press at his other seat, Stoke Poges Park in Buckinghamshire. There is a memorial to him in St George's church, at Reforne on Portland.

PORTLAND
'Abergavenny' wreck: claims a Wordsworth, inspires the *Happy Warrior.*

The East Indiaman *Abergavenny*, outward bound, sailed on to the Shambles sandbanks off Portland Bill through a pilot's error, on 5 February 1805. John Wordsworth, the commander, faced the tragic consequences with great courage and was among more than two hundred who perished. Captain Wordsworth, who was born in 1772, was the poet's brother.

William Wordsworth [1770-1850] attempted a commemorative poem but was too distressed to conclude it, though he did produce elegaic verses referring to his last parting with John, near Grisedale. There are many references to John in William's poems and the *Happy Warrior*, inspired by Nelson's death, incorporates aspects of his brother's character.

PORTLAND
Beatrice Potter: 'see Portland once'.

Beatrice Potter [1858-1943] took her father to see Portland on 11 April 1895 but saw no point in going again: "Portland Island is a curiosity to see once. Very like Gibraltar only flat-topped. The top is one vast quarry and stony wilderness. The convicts did not particularly appeal to me."

PORTLAND
A.E. Housman's convict.

The realities of a Portland convict's life interrupt the rural progress of *A Shropshire Lad* by A.E. Housman [1859-1936] which was published in 1896:

> *The star-filled seas are smooth to-night*
> *From France to England strown;*
> *Black towers above the Portland light*
> *The felon-quarrier stone.*

> *On yonder island, not to rise,*
> *Never to stir forth free,*
> *Far from his folk a dead lad lies,*
> *That once was friends with me.*

Portland Prison then comprised the buildings at The Grove (Ordnance Survey map reference SY 700 726) which are now the Borstal. Its convicts were there for hard labour — raising the stone that would enclose four square miles of sea inside the breakwaters of Portland Harbour.

PORTLAND
Thomas J. Clarke: declared Irish independence.

Thomas J. Clarke, convicted under the name of Wilson, arrived at Portland Prison — the buildings at The Grove which are now the Borstal — in 1884 with a life sentence for conspiring with the Fenian or Irish Revolutionary Brotherhood to dynamite public buildings in England. He was released under an amnesty in 1898.

On 23 April 1916 Clarke issued his own death warrant, in the form of the first and only issue of *Irish War News*, which had as its sub-title the words "The Irish Republic" and was released in Dublin to announce the Sinn Fein Easter uprising.

"The following have been named as the Provisional Government:- Thomas J. Clarke . . ." His was the first of seven names. Two thousand rebels held the centre of the city for a week. Martyrdom came for Clarke on 3 August 1916.

PORTLAND

Portland Museum: gift of birth-control advocate Marie Stopes —
Love Songs for Young Lovers.

Dr Marie Stopes [1880-1958] became the country's youngest doctor of science in 1905, but it is not as a paleobotanist that she is remembered. In 1921 she founded Britain's first family planning clinic, the Mothers' Clinic for Constructive Birth Control, and chose Portland for a holiday home. This was the derelict Avice's Cottage at Wakeham — a Portland rarity as it is thatched — which was the home of Avice Caro, the heroine, in Thomas Hardy's novel *The Well-Beloved* [1897]. Marie Stopes would give the cottage (Ordnance Survey map reference SY 697 713) to the island for use as a museum [1929].

Meanwhile, throughout the 1920s, she brought out a stream of books on her chosen subject and became its leading pundit. *Married Love* of 1918 was followed by *Wise Parenthood and Radiant Motherhood* [1920], *Contraception, its Theory, History and Practice* [1923], *Sex and the Young* and *Enduring Passion* [both 1928], and *Sex and Religion* [1929].

Her own life failed to run the rails of textbook romance. Marie's first kiss did not come until the age of twenty-four. She married the Canadian botanist R.R. Gates in 1911 but obtained an annulment in 1916 on the claim of non-consummation. She then married the aviator Humphrey Verdon Roe [1878-1948] from the famous family of A.V. Roe and the Avro planemaking company. His money launched the family planning clinics and in 1923 he gave Marie her only son, Harry Verdon Stopes-Roe, on whom she would inflict a bizarre choice of clothing, non-education and the cruel interference in his choice of mate on the grounds that the girl was short-sighted and therefore genetically unfit for breeding.

By the time Harry was conceived the pair had moved to Portland's former Upper Lighthouse (Ordnance Survey map reference SY 677 693). She refused to wear a bra or corset and threw her physical energy into swimming the treacherous tide-race off Portland Bill which one day almost claimed her life.

Portlanders would remember her wild red hair and recall with distaste the open philandering with young men. She exalted them in *Love Songs for Young Lovers*, by which time the morality of the public Stokes, that of the string of books, was only a memory or less. H.V. Roe added a sad postscript to them with a letter written in "The Old Lighthouse" at Portland Bill:

"Five years ago when I told you I wanted no more sex union and that I should not object if you decided to have a lover to replace my deficiency — you were very hurt and answered that it was unthinkable. Now that you have suffered sex deprivation for all these years you may feel differently, and I wish to put it on record that if you did it would not in any way alter our existing relations ... as I have long considered a wife whose husband is incapable of coitus has every right to supplement his deficiency without breaking up the home."

Marie apparently dictated it. She was ahead of her time in managing two failed marriages and for setting the twentieth century ethos that sex is a gift for enjoyment that seldom has to be complicated by procreative considerations. It was all a bit risqué for Portlanders, but this harsh landscape captured her heart and on her death at seventy-eight her ashes would be cast by Harry from Portland Bill into the waters from which she had once been so lucky to escape.

POWERSTOCK and BEAMINSTER

Thomas Russell: young poet.

There is a tablet to the poet Rev Thomas Russell [1762-88] in the tower of Powerstock parish church. The son of a rich Beaminster lawyer, he had gone from New College into the church and was at the beginning of what would have probably been a life of sonnets, when he fell ill at the age of twenty-six and died whilst undergoing treatment at the Hotwells in Bristol.

Wordsworth incorporated four lines from Russell's work in his sonnet *Iona (upon landing):*

> *Hopes, perhaps, more heavenly bright than thine,*
> *A grave by thee unsought and unpossest,*
> *A faith more fixed, a rapture more divine*
> *Shall gild their passage to eternal rest.*

POWERSTOCK (WEST MILTON)

Kenneth Allsop: 'Tonight' to *In the Country* and saviour of Powerstock Common.

"I am happiest here in the intricate and moody countryside of South Wessex," Kenneth Allsop [1920-73] wrote in his last book, *In the Country*, which describes a year around his Milton Mill home in the deep valley at West Milton, a mile west of Powerstock (Ordnance Survey map reference SY 496 963). He brought to it one of television's most unforgettable faces. It became national property with 'Tonight', which in 1960 was the BBC's first evening news magazine.

Boyish looks and a soft voice camouflaged a searching interviewer whose mind flowed hyperactively with a passionate intensity that frequently spilled over, off the camera, into agonies of depression. He cared above all for the countryside, particularly its bird life, and from his latter-life retreat in west Dorset he spearheaded the country's emergent environmental movement. He fought bitterly to prevent the Forestry Commission from clear-felling what is now the nature reserve on Powerstock Common (Ordnance Survey map reference SY 540 963).

In the process he concealed the physical pain lingering from an RAF assault course injury in 1943 which had led to one of his legs being amputated, at his request, in 1945. His last article in the Sunday Times concerned the distressful effects of agricultural insecticides on the breeding of the majestic peregrine falcon which had been brought to the edge of extinction. He despaired at any bird suffering but generally endured his own. Ken Allsop's life ended with a drugs overdose one May morning when his valley was shrouded in a rain-cloud. He is buried in Powerstock churchyard, beneath the medlar tree which he had ordered only a couple of weeks earlier for his mill-house grounds.

Fate, ironically, would be kinder to those peregrines. They were set to make a recovery along the western coasts in the mid-1970s and had by the end of the decade returned to breed on the island of Steep Holm, off Weston-super-Mare, which had been bought in 1976 for a nature reserve in Allsop's memory. That would have delighted him.

Powys — for JOHN COWPER POWYS [1872-1964]
see ABBOTSBURY

Powys — for LITTLETON C. POWYS [1874-1955]
see SHERBORNE

Powys — for LLEWELYN POWYS [1884-1939]
see DORCHESTER for entry on birth: in Rothesay House;
CHALDON HERRING for the main entry.

Powys — for THEODORE FRANCIS POWYS [1875-1955]
see CHALDON HERRING (EAST CHALDON) for Beth Car: *Mr
Weston's Good Wine*; MAPPOWDER for T.F. Powys: one decent wish.

Prior — for MATTHEW PRIOR [1664-1721]
see WIMBORNE

PUDDLETOWN and PIDDLETRENTHIDE
Ralph Wightman: *Abiding Things.*

"The Dorset farmer" was how Ralph Wightman [1901-71] was known though
he used to point out that he had never actually farmed. He was an agricultural adviser who in 1942 was heard over the wireless on the BBC's "Country
Matters" programme which had already established A.G. Street and S.P.B.
Mais as the voices of rural England. Ralph Wightman was to excel, his natural
dulcet tones captivating the professional broadcasters, the nation, and even
that most influential section of the listening world — he delivered 270 conse-
cutive weekly broadcasts to Americans from the English countryside at war.

He was a genuine son of the Dorset soil, born at Piddletrenthide where his
father was a farmer and his elder brother would be the butcher, who had
settled into the sixteenth century stone mullioned and thatched roofed Tudor
House in Puddletown. For nearly three decades his soft voice was synonymous with Dorset in the national mind, specialising in what many would
regard as sound commonsense to punctuate the politics on "Any Ques-
tions".

Ralph Wightman did not trouble to make the transfer to television and
instead worked at home, to convey the impressions and values of his Dorset
through a string of books that often captured in print the same relaxed style
he had on the air — *Moss Green Days* [1948], *My Homeward Road* [1950], *Arable
Farming* [1951], *Watching the Certain Things* [1951], *Livestock Farming* [1952],
Days on the Farm [1952], *The Seasons* [1953], *The Wessex Heathland* [1953], *Rural
Rides* [1957], *Abiding Things* [1962], *Portrait of Dorset* [1965],*Take Life Easy* [1968]
and *The Countryside Today* [1970].

PUDDLETOWN — see HOOKE for Westcombe: Hardy's Norcombe

Pulteney — for RICHARD PULTENEY [1730-1801]
see BLANDFORD

PURSE CAUNDLE and SHERBORNE
Nathaniel Highmore: *Corporis Humani.*

Nathaniel Highmore MD [1613-85], the rector's son from Purse Caundle, pushed forward the frontiers of medicine in 1651 with his treatise on the structure of the human body, *Corporis Humani disquisitio anatomica in que sanguinis circulationem prosequuutus est*.

In it, he writes of an "alexipharmaca dispositio vitalium" which he says enabled a student, when he was at Oxford, to eat spiders with impunity. He relates how the cavity in the superior maxillary, an air pocket in the cheek-bone — since known as the "antrum of Highmore" — was brought to his attention by a lady patient, whose abcess he had drained by removing her left canine. He also writes of dissecting an ostrich.

Dr Highmore's surgery was in Sherborne. He is buried inside the church at Purse Caundle, on the south side of the chancel (Ordnance Survey map reference ST 696 176).

RACEDOWN — see BROADWINDSOR (RACEDOWN)

Radclyffe Hall — for MARGUERITE RADCLYFFE HALL [1886-1943] see BOURNEMOUTH

RADIPOLE — see WEYMOUTH (RADIPOLE)

Raleigh — for SIR WALTER RALEIGH [?1552-1618] see CASTLETON (SHERBORNE CASTLE)

RAMPISHAM

Francis Glisson: *De Rachitide* on rickets — the disease he discovered in Dorset, and Britain's first medical textbook.

Noticing the bent bones and swollen joints of the chidren of his native county, Francis Glisson [1597-1677] of Rampisham became the first man in England to recognise and fully describe the symptoms of rickets and scurvy. Several years of study and consideration led in 1650 to his publication of *De Rachitide sive morbo puerili qui vulgo The Rickets dicitur. Tractatus*. The following year its first English translation appeared in *A Treatise of the Rickets: being a Disease common to Children*.

Its 416 pages of detailed observations were the first monograph about any disease to be published in the British Isles. That he put its cause as "some errors in point of diet" was as close as he could come in an age before vitamins had been identified. Rickets is caused by a deficiency of Vitamin D and a related complaint, infantile scurvy, is also described for the first time in the book (it being due to a lack of Vitamin C).

A Treatise of the Rickets, to quote the *Dictionary of National Biography*, "will always remain one of the glories of English medicine".

In his next book, *Anatomia hepatis* in 1654, Glisson gave such an exact description of the fibrous sheath of the liver that it would become known as "Glisson's capsule". By 1667 he had become President of the College of Physicians.

His 1672 *Tractatus de Natura Substantiae Energetica* is a metaphysical plunge into Aristotelian philosophy. It is dedicated to Anthony Ashley Cooper [1621-83], first Baron Ashley and first Earl of Shaftesbury, of Wimborne St Giles. Glisson was his physician, so continuing a link with Dorset, but little is known about the doctor's life which ended in London in 1677. He is buried in St Bride's church, Fleet Street.

Reeve — for HENRY REEVE [1813-95]
see BOURNEMOUTH (SOUTHBOURNE)

Richards — for JOHN RICHARDS [died 1720]
see WARMWELL

Ripper — for MONTAGUE JAMES DRUITT [1888 suicide], JACK the
RIPPER suspect,
see WIMBORNE

Robins — for SANDERSON ROBINS [1801-62]
see SHAFTESBURY

Robinson — for both SIR CHARLES ROBINSON [1824-1913] and son
CHARLES EDMUND ROBINSON [1853-1913], later known as
CHARLES EDMUND NEWTON-ROBINSON,
see combined entry under SWANAGE

Rolfe — for FREDERICK ROLFE [1860-1913], alias BARON CORVO,
see CHRISTCHURCH

Rogers — for WOODES ROGERS [?1697-1732]
see POOLE

Rose — for WILLIAM STEWART ROSE [1775-1843]
see CHRISTCHURCH (MUDEFORD)

Ruff — for IVAN RUFF [born 1945]
see POOLE (PARKSTONE)

Russell — for BERTRAND RUSSELL [1872-1970], third EARL
RUSSELL, see STUDLAND for Cliff End: Russell's seduction; WEST
LULWORTH for Newlands Farm: where Bertrand Russell brought his
loves.

Russell — for THOMAS RUSSELL [1762-88]
see POWERSTOCK

SANDBANKS — see POOLE (SANDBANKS)

SANDFORD ORCAS

Francis Godwin: *The Man in the Moone.*

The young rector of Sandford Orcas in 1585-89 was Francis Godwin [1562-
1633] who used the comparative respite of his time in the hills north of
Sherborne to compile a *Catalogue of the Bishops of England* [1601]. He also had
what the locals would have regarded as a fertile imagination, had they known
that he would leave a manuscript which is the first work of science fiction in
the English language. It was published posthumously.

  *The Man in the Moone, or a Discourse of a Voyage thither by Domingo Gonsales,
the Speedy Messenger* [1638] showed he understood Copernican astronomical
orbits. It was to have an influence on three subsequent writings in the genre
— John Wilkins's *The Discovery of a World in the Moone, or a Discourse tending to
prove that 'tis probable there may be another Habitable World in that Planet* [also
1638], Savinien de Cyrano de Bergerac's *Voyage to the Moon* [1656] and Jona-

than Swift's *Gulliver's Travels* [1726].

As for Godwin, he did reasonably well on the present planet, becoming Bishop of Llandaff and then of Hereford, and is remembered in Sandford Orcas by the naming for him, in Victorian times, of its inn − the Mitre.

Scott − for LUCY EMILY BARNES [1837-1902], Mrs SAMUEL BAXTER, known as LEADER SCOTT,
see DORCHESTER

Scott − for SIR WALTER SCOTT [1771-1832]
see CHRISTCHURCH (MUDEFORD)

Selkirk − for ALEXANDER SELKIRK [1676-1721] see POOLE for Woodes Rogers: discovered *Robinson Crusoe.*

SHAFTESBURY and EDMONDSHAM

Sanderson Robins: *Necessity of State Education.*

Rev Sanderson Robins [1801-62] was rector of Edmondsham [1826-40] but it was from his next parish, Shaftesbury [1840-54], that he wrote an influential pamphlet, issued in 1851 and reprinted that year, which basically set out the system of state education that would be enshrined in the Education Act of 1870. It was entitled: *A Letter to Lord John Russell on the Necessity and Mode of State Assistance in the Education of the People.*

Robins also produced a number of tracts on matters of church politics but he was careful in his educational argument to suggest that religious teaching "should stop short of the doctrinal differences which divide Christians".

Sharpe − for TOM SHARPE [born 1928]
see BRIDPORT

Sharpe − for WILLIAM SHARPE [1742-83]
see LONG BURTON

Shelley − for MARY WOLLSTONECRAFT SHELLEY [1797-1851]
see BOURNEMOUTH

Shelley − for PERCY BYSSHE SHELLEY [1792-1822]
see CORFE CASTLE (ENCOMBE) for Eldon: deprived Shelley of his children. See BOURNEMOUTH for entry on Frankenstein's author, plus women's rights mother and her anarchist husband buried with Shelley's heart in St Peter's churchyard; CHRISTCHURCH for Henry Weekes: sculpture to Shelley in the Priory.

Shelley − for SIR PERCY FLORENCE SHELLEY [1819-89]
see BOURNEMOUTH (BOSCOMBE)

SHERBORNE

Saint Aldhelm: verses enthralled Alfred.

Saint Aldhelm [?640-709] was, as Bishop of Sherborne, England's leading intellectual in the period when learning went out of fashion across Europe.

He kept the light flickering for Alfred [849-901], king of the West Saxons and the first effective monarch of all England, to rekindle the flames and translate and popularise imported works.

William of Malmesbury, the Norman chronicler, records that Alfred praised Aldhelm's English verses in the lost *Manual of Alfred*. Aldhelm is also known to have written heavier pieces in a mixture of Greek and Latin. His *De Laude Virginitatis* was addressed to the Abbess of Barking and her nuns. Nothing lighter has survived, though there are some Latin verses that celebrate the completion of Sherborne Abbey; which used to be thought to refer to Rome rather than his Dorset church dedicated to Saints Peter and Paul. He also created the Romanesque church of St Mary at Wareham which was one of Britain's most substantially intact Saxon churches until it was pulled apart in the name of restoration in 1841.

Aldhelm was an arbiter in defusing the fall-out from one of the great schisms of the early Church — the method of calculating the date of Easter — and it was through his intervention that the Welsh finally conformed to the prevailing method.

He made regular journeys, by foot, across his diocese and it was on one of these, at Doulting near Wells, that he died. Aldhelm was buried at Malmesbury, Wiltshire, where he had built two churches. He would be held as a Saint and his day is 25 May.

SHERBORNE
Adam of Barking: lost writings.

Adam of Barking, a Benedictine monk at Sherborne Abbey in about 1217, was to be praised by John Leland, Henry VIII's historian, for his promise as a writer of both prose and verse. Leland mentions his scholarly side and others his moral zeal.

The titles of many of his works are known, including the prose *Super Quatuor Evangelia* and verses *De Natura divinâ et humanâ* and *De Serie Sex Aetatum*, which were in Leland's time still at Sherborne, but just about all his manuscripts were subsequently lost.

SHERBORNE
Sifrewas and Whas: *Sherborne Missal.*

The Sherborne Missal was the fifteenth-century mass-book of Sherborne Abbey and it is preserved at Alnwick Castle, Northumberland. It is among the finest mediaeval manuscripts to have survived. Comprising 690 pages of vellum it is 15 inches wide by 24 inches deep and weighs a fraction less than 50 pounds.

It was largely the work of Dominican friar John Sifrewas, regarded as "the greatest of English limners" [illuminators] who embellished his sections with forty-six pictures of birds, captioned with their dialect names. The script has been attributed to John Whas, a Benedictine monk at Sherborne.

Their sponsors were Richard Mitford, Bishop of Sherborne, and Robert Bruning, Abbot of Sherborne.

From about 1400 to the dissolution of the monasteries in 1539 the book was used by the priest in the celebration of mass at Sherborne Abbey. It turned up in France in 1703 and was bought by Hugh Percy, second Duke of Northumberland, in 1800, for £215.

SHERBORNE and CLIFTON MAYBANK

Sir Thomas Wyatt: loved Anne Boleyn and gave us the sonnet.

Buried in Sherborne Abbey is Sir Thomas Wyatt [?1503-42] who pioneered the sonnet in England. His life, however, had its own touches of physical passion. He was, as a boy, the lover of Anne Boleyn, who "sweetly did me kiss, and softly said, 'Dear heart, how do you like this?'"

In 1533, when that was a memory and he had a flowing black beard, a bald head, and vast wealth, Wyatt was appointed a Privy Councillor. Wyatt was the perfect gentleman, admitting the pre-marital alliance and successfully walking the tightrope as the head of Henry VIII's diplomatic corps until, in 1541, he was imprisoned for a time whilst the king satisfied himself as to Wyatt's connections with Thomas Cromwell, the beheaded Earl of Essex.

Wyatt was thirty-nine when he suffered a sudden fever whilst passing through Sherborne on the king's business, en route from Falmouth to London. He was taken to Clifton Maybank (Ordnance Survey map reference ST 576 140) and died there. None of his literary work had been published in his lifetime.

The manuscripts included translations of Petrarch's sonnets, a penitential selection of *Certayne Psalmes* [1549] and, influentially, *Songes and Sonettes* which was published as Richard Tottel's so-called *Miscellany* — in which ninety-six out of a total of 310 are credited to Sir Thomas Wyatt.

Wyatt's memorial at Sherborne reads: "In memory of Sir Thomas Wyat (sic), poet and statesman, who died at Clifton Maybank, the house of his friend Sir John Horsey, 11th Oct. 1542 and was buried in the vault in this chapel.

Wyat resteth here,
that quick could never rest.

SHERBORNE

Dickens and Macready: back from America.

Leading character actor William Macready [1793-1873], Charles Dickens's closest friend, toured the United States and became embroiled in a tiff with his critics, during which he was called a "superannuated driveller", and appeared as Macbeth on New York's Broadway on 10 May 1849 to the worst recorded riot in theatrical history. Some seventeen people were shot dead when troops opened fire.

Macready returned to England and in 1851 "withdrew" to his home in Sherborne. This was the impressive classical three-storey Sherborne House, built about 1720, on the north side of Newland (Ordnance Survey map reference ST 639 169). Lord Digby's School for Girls would move into it in 1931.

"Mac", as he was known to Dickens [1812-70], had already prevailed upon the famous author to come down to read his novel *A Christmas Carol* at a literary institute "in the busy town of Sherborne, in Dorsetshire". The novelist, his wife and sister-in-law stayed a couple of days, until 23 December 1846, and then went home for Christmas.

Dickens had written *The Lamplighter*, a play, for Macready in 1838, for a performance at the Covent Garden Theatre. It was never acted, and in 1841 Dickens rewrote it as "The Lamplighter's Story" in *The Pic Nic Papers* and donated the proceeds to a trust fund for the widow and children of publisher

John Macrone, who had died in poverty.

The novelist named his second daughter Kate Macready Dickens, for the actor, in October 1839. That month Macready attended the dinner in celebration of the completion of *Nicholas Nickleby*, at the Albion, Aldersgate Street, near the Barbican. "You must come and see my house when we have it to rights," Dickens wrote to Macready in November 1839. That was No 1 Devonshire Terrace, Regents Park, which the author would occupy until 1851.

Macready and the Irish revolutionary Daniel O'Connell were among those distressed in 1840 by the killing-off of Little Nell in *The Old Curiosity Shop*. Not that the tragic ending was the author's idea; it had been suggested to him by biographer John Forster.

Dickens cited Mac's company as a reason for staying home in July 1841. "The moral of all this is that there is no place like home," he wrote to Forster, on being told he had been invited to a dinner in his honour in Glasgow. "I sigh for Devonshire Terrace and Broadstairs, for battledore and shuttlecock; I want to dine in a blouse with you and Mac."

The Macreadys looked after the four children when Mr and Mrs Dickens visited America in 1842. Disappointed with what they found, Dickens told Macready that the republic was not that of his imagination, being defective even in comparison with England, "bad and faulty as the old land is". As for "freedom of opinion", it did not exist, and he had been advised not to put his views of America on paper because the Americans could not bear to hear of their faults. They were, however, acceptable as individuals, and the scenery was immense to an extent beyond description, as with the endless solitude of the prairies.

In June 1843, Dickens was at the head of the table for a dinner at the Star and Garter, Richmond, in honour of Macready, when the actor retired from the Drury Lane Theatre and was about to set off on his first tour of America. Dickens was the life and soul of a birthday party for one of Macready's children, dancing — in the novelist's words — like "a country gentleman of independent property, residing on a tip-top farm, with the wind blowing straight in my face every day". He and John Forster performed conjuring tricks, producing a plum-pudding "from an empty saucepan, held over a blazing fire kindled in Stanfield's hat without damage to the lining" and changing a box of bran "into a live guinea-pig" to the "unspeakable admiration of the whole assembly".

When they were not together they kept up a constant correspondence. "Between *Copperfield* and *Household Words*, I am as busy as a bee," Dickens wrote to Mac on returning from Brighton in June 1850. "May the former be as good a book as I hope it will be for your children's children to read."

Dickens organised the staging of Macready's last public performance at Drury Lane, and a public dinner, on 1 March 1851, that was presided over by Sir Edward Bulwer Lytton.

The novelist told Macready that he was tempted on laying down his "book-pen" to "run out on the breezy downs here, tear up the hills, slide down the same, and conduct myself in a frenzied manner, for the relief that only exercise gives me".

He was also using his pen politically, pointing out to Lord Lyttelton on 16 August 1855 that although Macready, as an actor manager, had faced opposition for "rigorously weeding out that great indecency" of prostitution in the theatre, he persisted throughout the time of his management. Subsequently, Webster had managed to cleanse the Haymarket and rescue 'the saloon and passages from the defilement, and made the house quite reproachless in that particular".

Similarly with the Adelphi, but Dickens went on to note that the problem had transferred itself to "a certain Dancing Establishment ... (I mean a Ball Room) which great numbers of women regularly frequent". The police were showing "a sound discretion in not interfering with it" and "it drains off the stragglers" who might otherwise frequent theatres with lax managers, with Dickens taking a pragmatic view: "It is always to be borne in mind that, in a great city, prostitution will be somewhere."

In 1856, on describing the civil service as the 'Circumlocution Office" Dickens wrote to Mac that it had been necessary to let off "a little indignant steam which would otherwise blow me up".

Later in the year that "book-pen" was in full flow: "Calm amidst the wreck, your aged friend glides away on the *Dorrit* stream, forgetting the uproar for a stretch of hours, refreshing himself with a ten or twelve miles' walk, pitches headforemost into foaming rehearsals, placidly emerging for editorial purposes, smokes over buckets of distemper with Mr Stansfield aforesaid, again calmly floats upon the *Dorrit* waters."

Macready remarried in 1860 and moved to Cheltenham. Dickens continued to write. On 18 October 1869 he described to Mac his "preliminary agonies of a new book" which turned out to be *The Mystery of Edwin Drood*. Dickens died before it was finished.

The actor followed in 1873 and is buried at Kensal Green. He was said to have led his life in a manner that was often indistinguishable from his acting persona, being at best introspective, and frequently "unamiable and almost morose as well as violent". Both on stage and off his behaviour was marked by instant changes from one extreme to the other, from curses to courtesies, and he could physically work himself into a frenzy for a performance.

SHERBORNE
Horace Annesley Vachell: *The Other Side.*

Prolific, which is something of an understatement, Horace Annesley Vachell [1861-1955] of The Priory House at Sherborne spent all of his long adult life writing, from the *Romance of Judge Ketchum* [1894] to *Quests* sixty years later. By then he had just about reached his ambition of a hundred titles and came reasonably close to celebrating his own centenary.

Many of the works are plays. *Her Son* was also turned into a novel. The story *Quinney's*, on the other hand, was then dramatised [1915]. Other plays included *Count X* [1921] and *Plus Fours* [1923]. He was also an essayist, with *My Vagabondage* [1936], *Little Tyrannies* [1940] and *A Writer's Autobiography*.

The best known of his novels are *Whitewash* [1920], *Quinney's Adventures* [1924], *Vicar's Walk* [1933] and *Quinneys for Quality* [1938]. There are many allusions to Sherborne in his work and the spiritualist story *The Other Side* [1910] is set in the town.

SHERBORNE
Littleton C. Powys: *The Joy of It.*

The Powys brother who usually rates only a literary footnote is Littleton C.

Powys [1874-1955] of Quarry House, in The Avenue, at Sherborne. He edited *The Letters of Elizabeth Myers* and his own life, mostly spent as a master at Sherborne School, went into two volumes — *The Joy of It* [1937] and *Still the Joy of It*, which despite the optimism of the title was published posthumously in 1956. Rugby and cricket provided most of the happiness but autobiography aside the lasting interest in the books is for their sidelight on the remarkable brothers.

SHERBORNE

Hugh Thomas: *Unfinished History of the World.*

Sherborne School deserves mention for the academicians it has set in the making. One of the best of the twentieth century, historian Hugh Swynnerton Thomas [born 1932], went on to Cambridge and the Sorbonne, emerging in the Cold War as a preacher of disarmament and a student of revolution and conflict.

His numerous studies include *The Spanish Civil War* [1961] and, brilliantly conceived, *An Unfinished History of the World* [1979]. He was given a life peerage, becoming Baron Thomas, in 1981.

SHERBORNE — see ABBOTSBURY for ashes of John Cowper Powys

SHERBORNE — see BLANDFORD for Thomas Creech: a classic exit

SHERBORNE — see CASTLETON (SHERBORNE CASTLE) for Alexander Pope: seat and words

SHERBORNE — see FOLKE for Thomas Curgenvan: classical scholar

SHERBORNE — see PURSE CAUNDLE for Nathaniel Highmore: *Corporis Humani*

SHERBORNE CASTLE — see CASTLETON (SHERBORNE CASTLE)

Sherer — for JOSEPH GODFREY SHERER [flourished around 1800] see BLANDFORD

SHILLINGSTONE

Hintock: Dorset's first 'fictional' telephone exchange.

One of Thomas Hardy's placenames has gone from fiction into reality. The invented Hintock, from *The Woodlanders*, was chosen in 1977 for Shillingstone's new telephone exchange. A second exchange was needed for the area after Child Okeford's ran out of three-figure numbers.

For the first time in Dorset, the Post Office chose its name from a novel instead of the map. Hintock, to a stranger, will not look less natural than either Hazelbury Bryan or Holnest, which are either side of it in the dial-code list.

Purists, however, may recall that Hardy's actual name was plural, the Hintocks, and his individual ones were Great Hintock (Minterne Magna), King's Hintock (Melbury Osmond) and Little Hintock (Stockwood or Hermitage). So dial-a-Hintock (025883) has strayed ten miles. That is what geographical etymologists call a "transferred name".

Sifrewas — for JOHN SIFREWAS [flourished around 1400]
see SHERBORNE

SIXPENNY HANDLEY

Maxwell Staniforth: translated *Meditations*.

Whilst living at Sixpenny Handley, in 1962, the classical scholar Maxwell
Staniforth translated the *Meditations* of the Roman Stoic Marcus Aurelius for
Penguin Classics. It had slipped from its late-Victorian status of required
reading, and that the emperor's "humane wisdom and gentle charm" have
had something of a twentieth century revival is due to Staniforth's skill in
providing "a plain and honest version for the Greekless reader".

The work has been known as the *Meditations* since the Middle Ages, but
that ironically is itself a mistranslation. Its true title means *To Himself* but,
Staniforth observed, there is a point at which usage takes precedence over
pedantry. Marcus Aurelius has some marvellous musings, such as this on the
meaning of life: "The performance is always the same; it is only the actors
who change."

Slade — for MATTHEW SLADE [1569-?1628]
see SOUTH PERROTT

SMEDMORE — see KIMMERIDGE (SMEDMORE)

Smith — for REGINALD BOSWORTH SMITH [late 19th century]
see MELCOMBE HORSEY (BINGHAM'S MELCOMBE)

Southey — for ROBERT SOUTHEY [1774-1843]
see BURTON

SOUTH PERROTT

Matthew Slade: 'walking library'.

The son of its rector, Matthew Slade [1569-?1628] of South Perrott would
become one of the leading scholars of the seventeenth century, "a walking
library" according to Anthony Wood.

He plunged into heated religious rows, siding with the orthodox Calvinists
against the break-away Arminians who had taken issue with them over pre-
destination. The result was Slade's *Cum Conrado Vorstio de Blasphemiis Haeresi-
bus & Atheismis a rege Jacobo I,* which was published in Amsterdam in 1612.

Sprat — for THOMAS SPRAT [1635-1713], DEAN OF
WESTMINSTER, see BEAMINSTER

STALBRIDGE

Robert Boyle: he of Boyle's Law.

Stone lions flanking the gates beside the A357 just north of the little Blackmore Vale town of Stalbridge are a reminder that the park behind this high
stone wall was special. It lost its great country house, which had a dozen
small chimneys (Ordnance Survey map reference ST 731 182), in a fire in

1822. Not only was it a splendid building but it was Dorset's link with one of the all-time greats in the world of science.

Robert Boyle is somewhere in all our schooldays remembered for Boyle's Law, the enunciation that the volume of a gas varies inversely to its pressure.

John Aubrey wrote of him: "He is very tall (about six foot) and straight, very temperate and virtuous, and frugal: a bachelor; keeps a coach; sojournes with his sister, the Lady Ranelagh. His greatest delight is chemistry. He has at his sister's a noble laboratory, and several servants (apprentices to him) to look to it. He is charitable to ingenious men that are in want, and foreign chemists have had large proof of his bounty, for he will not spare for cost to get any rare secret: see Oliver Hill's book, where he is accused of gross plagiarism."

Boyle was born at Lismore Castle in the Irish province of Munster on 25 January 1627. He was studious from an early age, mastering Latin, French algebra and mental arithmetic long before he was ten. Three years at Eton, started at the age of eight, were followed in 1638 by the move to Stalbridge Park, an estate recently bought by his father. In Dorset his education continued, under a minister named Douch and a French tutor, Marcombes.

In October that year, at the age of twelve, Robert left Dorset with the tutor and his elder brother, Francis Boyle, and travelled through Paris and Lyons to Geneva, where they settled for twenty-one months. There he was converted to religion. They spent the first part of 1642 in Florence and Rome, and arrived in Marseilles in May where they heard that their expected finance from Ireland had been embezzled. The party lived on credit in Geneva for two years. England and Ireland were meanwhile slipping into the rebellion and turmoil of Civil War. The two brothers returned to England in the summer of 1644, to the news that their father was dead.

Robert had inherited the manor of Stalbridge, but it was four months — because of the chaos and restrictions — before he could reach Dorset. From this point there emerged Robert Boyle, physicist and chemist. He was becoming, from the age of eighteen, the leader of modern scientific thought. In 1645 he attended the lectures in London of the Philosophical College, which was the forerunner of the Royal Society.

"Vulcan has so transformed and bewitched me," he wrote from Stalbridge to Lady Ranelagh in 1649, "to make me fancy my laboratory as a kind of Elysium". It was with considerable reluctance that he left Dorset in 1652-53 to sort out the problems of his Irish estate, which he described as "a barbarous country, where chemical spirits were so misunderstood, and chemical instruments were so unprocurable, that it was hard to have any Hermetic thoughts in it". Instead, he used the time, accompanied by Sir William Petty, in dissections — establishing to his satisfaction the circulation of the blood.

By the end of the decade the results of Boyle's experiments were beginning to appear in print, on a scale that was unmatched in the scientific world. John Aubrey rightly observed: "His works alone may make a library." There were more than forty of them, and many broke new ground. In *New Experiments Physico-Mechanical* [1660] he invented an air pump. Boyle's law of gases [volume being reciprocal to pressure] first appeared in a revised edition of this work [in 1664]. His *Experiments and Considerations Touching Colours* [1664] provided many leads that were later developed by Newton in his *Optics*. Boyle was the first to notice the chemical indicators, changing colour in the presence of acidic or alkaline substances. In *New Experiments Touching Cold* [1665] he gave the first description of a graduated thermometer.

He pointed out in *Hydrostatical Paradoxes* [1666] that "water may be made as well to depress a body lighter than itself, as to buoy it up". With *Tracts containing New Experiments* [1672] he gives what amounts to the modern theory of oxidation —just — as Boyle's notes say that eleven adjoining pages were lost by the printer. *Essays of the Strange Subtility of Effluviums* [1673] investigated the results of heating metals in air, noting that they increased measurably in weight. *Tracts Consisting of Observations about the Saltness of the Sea* [1674] showed Boyle's mind at its best. *Experiments, Notes about divers Qualities* [1676] is the first work on electricity in the English language.

But for Dorset people there is one work that belongs in county collections, though it is a £2,000 book in 1989. *Occasional Reflections upon Several Subjects* [1665] is a lighter weight collection of thoughts, mainly inspired by rural subjects such as horseshoes, rivers and boys swimming with air bladders. To quote a Sotheby catalogue: "Part of this book was written on a holiday at Stalbridge and shows Boyle in one of his happiest moods. It inspired Jonathan Swift [1667-1745] to his satirical *Occasional Meditations on a Broomstick.* Some sections deal with angling and the book was once wrongly attributed to Izaak Walton."

At one point you have the sharp taste of raw Dorset blue-veined cheese: "We detest and despise some other nations, for feeding upon caterpillars, grasshoppers, and other insects; and others, for feeding upon carrion, and stinking food. And do not many of us do as bad, when we not only eat, but extoll, rotten cheese, whose livid colour sufficiently betrays its putrefactions, and whose odious smell offends most men's noses, and turns some men's stomachs? Nay, when this cheese is grown to that high degree of rottenness that our critical palates like it best in, we then devour whole hundreds of mites, which are really crawling insects, bred out of putrefactions and these too are so numerous and little, that our greediness makes us swallow many of them alive."

He develops his argument: "But lastly, as the highest degree of brutishness, our travellers mention the practice of the Soldanians at the Cape of Good Hope, who not only eat raw meat, but if they be hungry, eat the guts and all of their cattle, with the dung in them. I will not answer, that I know several among us (and perhaps some fair ladies too) that to prevent the scurvy and the gout, drink their own or boy's urine: nor that women themselves take Parmacitty inwardly, though the Latin name (Sperma Ceti) sufficiently declares what excretion of a whale it is (though perhaps mistakenly) believed to be: nor yet that under the name of Album Craecum, dogs' dung is commonly given to patients of all sorts and qualities against sore throats: nor will I mention, that in Holland 'tis usual as I have seen myself, to mingle sheeps' dung with their cheeses, only to give them a colour and as a relish . . ."

Robert Boyle, one of the greatest men of science, died at his sister's house in London on 30 December 1691. His sister, Catherine Lady Ranelagh, had died only a week before, on Christmas Eve. Boyle was nearly 65. He is buried at St Martin-in-the-Fields, beside Trafalgar Square.

STALBRIDGE, DORCHESTER and STINSFORD

Wife-selling: as in *The Mayor of Casterbridge.*

Thomas Hardy [1840-1928] fictionalised wife-selling in his novel *The Mayor of Casterbridge.* It may have seemed far-fetched to readers in Victorian high society in London but there had been documented examples of the practice from the Dorset countryside in the early nineteenth century.

One took place at Stalbridge market on a Tuesday in April 1814. The vendor was Thomas Tuffen of Henstridge, Somerset, who with his wife had been in the habit of attending local fairs and markets to sell gingerbread. On this occasion he contracted with Joseph Cains, a sawyer, for the sale of his wife, together with a basket and goods. Tuffen delivered her in a halter to Cains, who led her to his home.

Nor was this the only Stalbridge custom that Hardy was to incorporate into *The Mayor of Casterbridge*. He started writing it in 1884, and may well have preserved newspaper clippings about "skimmington riding" which was still prevalent in the Dorset countryside. The carnival of anger took place to show communal disgust at behaviour that had offended against the moral code. One of these parades took place through Melbury Osmond in November 1865 but the police intervened to prevent effigies being burned.

Lucy Taylor [1879-1947], living in Stalbridge, recalled a similar procession of local people disguised with sacking over their heads and beating saucepans with tongs and spoons. They escorted a conveyance with caricatures of the guilty pair. These effigies were burned at The Ring, the village green (Ordnance Survey map reference ST 737 175). No one in the village next day was prepared to admit knowing who had taken part in the event.

STALBRIDGE and STURMINSTER NEWTON
R.L. Stevenson: *The Wrecker.*

The narrator's search for the crooked mate of *The Flying Scud*, alias Elias Goddedal, in *The Wrecker* by Robert Louis Stevenson [1850-94] ends with him being found at "Stallbridge-le-Carthew" and unmasked as "Norris Carthew, Stallbridge, Dorset". The real Stalbridge (one 'l') is barely disguised at all.

Sturminster Newton is also brought in, as "Stallbridge Minster" where the searchers "were set down by a dilatory butt-end of a local train on the untenanted platform" and he describes the town as "ancient and compact; a domino of tiled houses and walled gardens, dwarfed by the disproportionate bigness of the church".

There are also descriptions of Stallbridge-le-Carthew where the road "deserts the valley of the river", which is called "the Stall", and where the Carthew seat stood "in the hollow of a bosky park" − a nice expression for a thicket. The Carthew Arms is but "a mere appendage of the family whose name it bore. Engraved portraits of bygone Carthews adorned the walls ... and I was not surprised to learn that the landlord was an ex-butler, the landlady an ex-lady's maid, from the great house."

It could have been inspired by so many places in feudal Dorset where to this day there are the Drax Arms (two of them), Bankes Armes (also two of them), Weld Arms, Rivers Arms, Hambro Arms and Digby Tap as the watering holes in the ancestral acres. There is no record of Stevenson's visit to Stalbridge but he probably passed through as he was living in Bournemouth at the time and his wife thought the country air might bring some relief to his chronic smoker's chest. *The Wrecker* was finished off by his stepson, Lloyd Osbourne, in 1892.

STALBRIDGE

Inter-galactic specimens: *Hitchhiker's Guide.*

The real-life prototypes for the somewhat OTT (over the top) characters in Douglas Adams's radio serial *The Hitchhiker's Guide to the Galaxy* are said to have been found in Stalbridge. He wrote the book in the late 1960s whilst staying at his parents' cottage in Gold Street.

Staniforth — for MAXWELL STANIFORTH [20th century] see SIXPENNY HANDLEY

Steele — for SIR RICHARD STEELE [1672-1729] see POOLE for Woodes Rogers: discovered *Robinson Crusoe*

Stevenson — for ROBERT LOUIS STEVENSON [1850-94] see BOURNEMOUTH (WESTBOURNE) for Skerryvore: the site of R.L. Stevenson's 61 Alum Chine Road; DORCHESTER for King's Arms: hosted R.L. Stevenson; STALBRIDGE for R.L. Stevenson: *The Wrecker*.

Stillingfleet — for EDWARD STILLINGFLEET [1635-99] see CRANBORNE

STINSFORD (HIGHER BOCKHAMPTON)

Hardy's Cottage: *Under the Greenwood Tree.*

The birth of Thomas Hardy [1840-1928] took place at Stinsford in the last thatched cottage of Cherry Lane, Higher Bockhampton, which is now preserved as "The Birthplace" by the National Trust (Ordnance Survey map reference SY 728 925). That event, upstairs, above the living room, was on 2 June 1840. He who would become the greatest English novelist and poet of the age, out-ranking and then outliving his contemporaries, came into the world as a frailty which the nurse feared was dying.

The birth room is the central upstairs window, the middle one as you look at the cottage from its garden. To its right is what would become Thomas's room. That window seat has a view across the Dorchester countryside to Vice-Admiral Hardy's monument [1846] on the hills above Portesham. In his room, which was above the kitchen in Victorian times (that has now been shifted south into the former wash-room), Hardy produced his first literary work.

This began from the perspective of an entirely different career, with an *Essay on Coloured Bricks and Terra-cotta Architecture* which won him a prize and medal from the Institute of British Architects [1863]. He read an article in the Examiner magazine in 1867 that was headed "The Wessex Labourer" and this gave the "territorial definition" for the "realistic dream-country" that his next creations would inhabit. He was a compulsive reader and scavenger of newspapers for detailed facts around which his thinly disguised characters would face life's opportunities and tragedies in a landscape that is conveyed with the precision of a Constable rather than the impressionism of a Turner.

The first works of the young part-time Wessex novelist that appeared in the London bookshops, facing an initially reluctant public, were *Desperate Remedies* [1871] and *Under the Greenwood Tree* [1872].

See under Hardy for a short-list of the multiplicity of other places that make up the Hardy Country, and the beginning of the book for a gazetteer of his semi-fictional placenames. Hardy's Cottage was bought by the National Trust in 1948, under the provisions of the will of Hardy's sister, Kate Hardy. It then had an acre of garden, but a second acre was bought by the Trust in 1967.

STINSFORD (KINGSTON MAURWARD)

Hardy and Julia Martin: rustles in *Desperate Remedies.*

At one or two points in his lifetime, the novelist and poet Thomas Hardy [1840-1928] came near to confessing that his infant affair with Mrs Julia Martin, at Kingston Maurward, involved sexual love on both sides, but near the end of his life, when he concocted with his wife, Florence, the "official biography" that was designed to frustrate investigation by biographers after his death, he and she decided to put a more innocent face on it. But the circumstantial evidence is strong. Strong enough, for instance, to have caused Robert Gittings, in his authoritative biography, *The Older Hardy*, to refer to his "juvenile love-affair with the lady of the manor, Julia Augusta Martin".

The Kingston Maurward estate, around the eighteenth century house of that name at Stinsford (Ordnance Survey map reference SY 716 911) was purchased in 1844, when Hardy was four years old, by Francis Pitney Brouncker Martin, a well-off and well-educated man with an inclination to experimental farming and amateur science. He took up residence with his wife, Julia Augusta, then in her thirties and earnestly devoted to the practice of the Anglican Christian religion.

Since they were the kind of couple who would have wanted to have children, and perhaps even felt an obligation to, it is reasonable to speculate on the reason for their childlessness, which could have a bearing on what happened after their arrival at Kingston Maurward.

As occupants of the cottage on the estate in which Hardy was born, his family were life tenants of the Martins: and Hardy's father was a self-employed builder who was sometimes engaged to do maintenance work at the "big house". They were therefore in a world below the Martins in social class, on the wrong side of a barrier across which there could be little more than polite exchange of courtesies. In spite of this Julia began to develop an intense personal interest in little Hardy, of a kind which was quite inappropriate to her social relationship to his family, and therefore suspect as to motive. This interest started soon after her arrival at Kingston Maurward, and before anything more than a formal acquaintanceship, as between lady of the manor and a tenant's wife, could have developed between her and Jemima Hardy, Thomas's mother.

Freud did not invent infant sexuality. It existed before he wrote about it, and was exploited then as now by adults of both sexes.

It is on record, and never denied by Hardy, that Julia was "accustomed to take [him] into her lap and kiss [him] until he was quite a big child"; and that he responded to these caresses as a lover. In his thirties he recalled "the thrilling 'frou-frou' of her four grey silk flounces when she used to bend over him". She would have known of this effect on him, and attired herself accordingly.

This was not just a passing phase. Julia's behaviour persisted for four years until, when Hardy was nine years old, Jemima put a sudden and decisive end to this alliance between an ostensibly innocent child and an ostentatiously religious woman in her late thirties.

When at the age of eight he was sent from the day of its opening to the new Stinsford parish Anglican school, the cost of building which had been paid by Mrs Martin, the children chanted at him a cruel rhyme with a reference to "kissing". This is significant, as children invariably choose as their victim for this kind of treatment one of their number against whom a black mark has been placed for some supposed social non-conformity.

They would have heard gossip and criticism among their parents, many of whom were related to the Hardys, and some of whom were ill-disposed towards them, about his visits to the "big house". One can imagine the effect this mockery must have had on Hardy, who at that time was a painfully shy and withdrawn little boy. He would have arrived home from school in a state of distress.

It may well have been this which caused his mother to decide to take him away from the school. It was in September, 1849, at the beginning of his second year at the school, that Jemima took him away, and he never attended the school again. And later she took him away from the village, on a pro-tracted visit to her sister at Hatfield in Hertfordshire, thus cutting him off completely from the influence of Mrs Martin.

This was only part of the drastic action she took. The family transferred itself from the Stinsford parish church, where the rustle of Julia's clothing as she brushed past the font had excited Hardy, to the one at Fordington, to avoid encountering her at Sunday services. Hardy's father apparently stopped doing maintenance work at Kingston Maurward. After their return in January 1850 to Bockhampton, Jemima kept Thomas away from school altogether, until he entered the Dorchester school at the beginning of the autumn term.

On Hardy's statement that his mother "stood up to" Julia Martin, biogra-phers have based the legend of a row between the two women, caused by Jemima's decision to take the boy away from the village school and send him to a non-conformist school in Dorchester. It is highly unlikely that there was a row. It is more likely that Jemima took action without any reference to Mrs Martin, and forbade her son to see her again. Julia's reaction on encountering the boy by chance a year later would confirm this. Even so it was a brave action indeed for a woman of her class to defy the lady of the manor in this way; and it would have needed more than a desire to transfer her son to an academically superior school to cause her to do so.

In fact teaching at the village school was exceptionally good, and Hardy had benefited from it. So keen was Jemima on the boy's continued education that she sent him to the local school at Hatfield for the short period they were there. She had obviously powerful reasons for keeping him away from the village school, with no alternative school to send him to, for best part of a year. At that time Thomas was still considered to be not very strong. She would have taken a long time to come round to the notion of sending him to Dorchester in spite of the almost impossible distance he would have to walk each day.

In 1850, when Hardy was ten years old and already attending the Dorches-ter school, an astonishing event occurred.

For a year he had not seen Julia, and his mother no doubt made sure that he had no opportunity to see her; but one Saturday afternoon in autumn, when his mother was away from the house, the teenage daughter of a neighbouring smallholder called and offered to take him to the annual har-vest supper in a large barn on Kingston Maurward estate, to which she had been invited. He accepted the offer and went as an uninvited guest to the party, doubtless not thinking that Julia Martin would be there.

However, at the height of the festivities Mr and Mrs Martin made their appearance, in the role of the lord and lady of the manor making sure the estate workers and their guests were enjoying the feast. She must have been amazed to find there the boy who had been kept away from her for a year, but she kept her composure and decided to punish him publicly, as an unfaithful lover.

"Oh Tommy, how is this?" she exclaimed. "I thought you had deserted me!" Utterly devastated, he tried to defend himself, and burst into tears.

Preoccupied with the soldiers who had been invited from Dorchester barracks, the young woman who had brought him failed to take him home, and he had to wait until after midnight for her to do so, apparently too shocked and upset to venture near the food-tables.

With unbelievable ingenuousness, Florence Hardy comments in her biography of Hardy: "What the estate owner's tender wife would have given had she but known of his hunger and thirst, and how carefully have sent him home had she been aware of his dilemma!" And she had the nerve to suggest, in conversation with Richard Little Purdy, that Hardy's poem, *In her precincts*, in which he dwells on "the gloom of severance", refers not to Julia Martin, but to a young girl subsequently living at Kingston Maurward, with whom he was infatuated.

The influence on Hardy of the affair with Julia Martin, and the manner of its ending, was profound and lifelong. He must have known that it was an illicit relationship, and it seems to have left him with an incurable yearning for such relationships with women, which could have no satisfactory outcome, and over which he suffered feelings of guilt.

More important was the effect on his work, for he was quite unable to keep out of his writings his most intimate and secret private feelings. Illicit sexual relationships, love across the barrier of class and their ruthless ending by conformist social forces is a theme of his novels from the first one, *The Poor Man and the Lady*. In the poem *In Tenebris III* he writes of himself, "the smallest and feeblest of folk" as "weak from my baptism of pain", and more than hints at a suicidal impulse.

The clothes-fetishism to which he admitted, and which finds expression in, for instance, his novel *Desperate Remedies*, would have had its origin in the rustle of and contact with Julia's silken dresses. And he seems to have had analogous feelings of erotic association with the house itself, since so many of the objects of his amorous daydreams came from Kingston Maurward.

STINSFORD

His heart in Wessex.

Thomas Hardy [1840-1928] wished for a Stinsford burial and had discussed it with the vicar, Rev H.G.B. Cowley. Not that it was a reversion to religion from one who had called God "that vast imbecility". The village churchyard (Ordnance Survey map reference SY 712 910) was necessary for Hardy's sense of history and family. "I shall sleep quite calmly at Stinsford, whatever happens," he had written.

Others thought differently. Sydney Cockerell and Sir James Barrie intervened with the Dean of Westminster to arrange an Abbey funeral.

The Hardy family were enraged, with cousin Theresa telling reporters: "I am grieved that they are going to take poor Tom away to London. He wanted, I know, to lie with his own folk in the churchyard yonder."

It was Cowley, the Stinsford vicar, who suggested what Robert Gittings calls "a gruesome though historic compromise".

The heart was to be cut out, to go to Stinsford, and the body would be cremated at Woking, on 14 January 1928, with the ashes being taken to Westminster Abbey, for burial the following day in Poets' Corner.

This solution ignored the weight of popular superstition, firmly rooted in the peasant stock of Hardy's family, that a body should be buried intact. Kate Hardy found it "another staggering blow", and Edward Codd called it "repellent". The pubs of Dorchester relished the whole bizarre concept, with jokes ranging from one about a cat jumping on to the mortuary slab and eating the freshly removed heart, to problems at the resurrection: "Almighty, he'll say, 'Ere be the 'eart, but where be the rest of 'ee?'"

The Abbey service, Robert Gittings writes in *The Older Hardy*, was organised by Macmillans and became a shambles, with a "chaos of wrong invitations and uninvited gate-crashers, 'a sick horror' for years to Florence".

Neither did the weather help. "Before the service was due to start the colour overhead had deepened to a brown such as London often suffers on dull days," The Times reported.

It was not quite what Hardy had expected: "And mourn the yellowing tree: for I shall mind not, slumbering peacefully".

STINSFORD

Cecil Day Lewis: Poet Laureate.

Poet Laureate Cecil Day Lewis [1904-72] is buried at Stinsford beneath his own words: "Shall I be gone long? For ever and a day. To whom there belong? Ask the stone to say. Ask my song."

His work included the *Transitional Poems* [1929], *From Feathers to Iron* [1931], *The Magnetic Mountain* [1933], *A Hope for Poetry* [1934], *Time to Dance* [1935], *Overtures to Death* [1938], *Child of Misfortune* [1939] and *Poems in Wartime*.

With *Noah in the Waters* he produced a modern morality play. The 1930s Oxford poet also wrote detective stories under the pseudonym Nicholas Blake.

That someone with no earthly Dorset connection would presume to end up beside the Hardy grave in what the great author called Mellstock churchyard was predicted by Sir John Betjeman in his poem *Dorset*. Parodying Hardy, his refrain to one of the stanzas runs: "Tranter Reuben, T.S. Eliot, H.G. Wells and Edith Sitwell lie in Mellstock Churchyard now."

Terry Coleman raised the point in an interview with Betjeman for The Guardian: "At the time he wrote that, the last three were alive, and nor are they buried there now. He says the names were put in out of euphony, not malice. But Mellstock is really Stinsford, where Hardy's heart is buried; and beside his grave in that churchyard C. Day Lewis, Betjeman's predecessor as Poet Laureate, really does lie."

STINSFORD – see DORSET GENERAL (at front of book) for Hardy placenames: a checklist

STINSFORD – see DORCHESTER for Max Gate: itself, *Tess* and *Jude*, and for Hardy's statue: by Kennington and rubbished by Augustus John.

STINSFORD – see STALBRIDGE for wife-selling: as in *The Mayor of Casterbridge*

STOKE ABBOTT

William Crowe: peak acclaim for *Lewesdon Hill*.

In the spring of 1788 the Clarendon Press at Oxford published anonymously the romantic poem *Lewesdon Hill* which describes a climb on a May morning to the top of the woody summit near Broadwindsor (Ordnance Survey map reference ST 437 013) and its delightful prospect and associations.

There was such acclaim for this harmonious blank verse that a second edition followed, which identified its author as William Crowe [1745-1829], the rector of Stoke Abbott. It was praised by Tom Moore for imagery "of the highest order" and by Samuel Rogers for "noble passages"; Wordsworth, Coleridge and Bowles also acknowledged it as an important contribution to the Romantic Movement.

Stopes – for MARIE STOPES [1880-1958]
see PORTLAND

STOUR PROVOST (STOUR ROW)

Mildred Cable: *The Gobi Desert*.

Mildred Cable [1878-1952] retired to Willow Cottage at Stour Row (Ordnance Survey map reference ST 820 210) in about 1935. There she wrote the book that recorded one of the most amazing explorations undertaken in the twentieth century. She had been the first woman from the western world to cross the Gobi Desert and her principal book, *The Gobi Desert*, was published in 1942.

She reflected in Dorset upon a life spent trying to wean the Chinese from opium to Christianity. Hers was a practical application of the Christian teaching, to the extent that she brought home to Dorset a Mongolian orphan who was deaf and dumb. Topsy was the subject of a book for children written by Mildred Cable and her other inseparable companion, Francesca French, in 1937: *The Story of Topsy, Little Lonely of Central Asia*.

Strong – for JAMES STRONG [17th century]
see LYME REGIS

STUDLAND (BROWNSEA ISLAND)

William Benson: argued the divine right of kings.

William Benson [1682-1754] moved into Branksea Castle on Brownsea Island, in Poole Harbour, in about 1710. He then created a national stir with his *Letter to Sir Jacob Bankes* [1711] which argued that kings were accountable only to God. It sold 100,000 copies.

He sponsored the arts by printing Samuel Johnson's *Psalms* and erected the monument in Westminster Abbey in memory of the poet John Milton who had died in 1674. For these two acts he was lampooned by Alexander Pope: "On two unequal crutches propp'd he came, Milton's on this, on that one

Johnson's name." Pope rammed the point home: "On poets' tombs see Benson's titles writ."

Frederick, Prince of Wales, was among his visitors to Brownsea Island. He was a popular heir apparent but he would never take the throne as he failed to outlive his unpopular father. Benson's life was also sliding into obscurity and after serious mental illness in 1741 his former love of books had turned into hatred and he was known as "Mad Benson".

STUDLAND

Cliff End: Russell's seduction.

One of the sleazier of Dorset's literary associations concerns Cliff End, an Edwardian villa in the trees between the Bankes Arms and Studland beach. Here an eminent 38-year-old mathematician and philosopher, Bertrand Russell [1872-1970], seduced Lady Ottoline Morrell, the wife of a Liberal MP, during the Easter holiday of 1911.

Philip Morrell [1870-1943] had rented the house. Russell's affair with his wife simmered for a few years and finally extinguished itself when Russell was dismissed from his post at Trinity College, Cambridge, in 1916 as a result of his pacifist opposition to the Great War. Bertrand would become the third Earl Russell on the death of his older brother in 1931.

'Men Like Gods' — title-page inscription from author H.G. Wells (ashes at Old Harry Rocks) to publisher Newman Flower (born at Fontmell Magna). See below and also page 101

STUDLAND and FONTMELL MAGNA

Old Harry: ashes of H.G. Wells.

The ashes of the novelist and futurist Herbert George Wells [1866-1946], who is best remembered for *The War of the Worlds* [1898], were cast into the sea off Old Harry Rocks. He produced science fiction for half a century, from *The Time Machine* in 1895, to *The Shape of Things to Come* [1933], *The New World Order* [1940], and *The Phoenix* [1942]. His radical works included *Ann Veronica* [1909] which promoted feminism. Pot-boilers were issued under the pseudonym Reginald Bliss.

At his memorial service, a passage had been read from his work that concluded: "We are all things that make and pass, striving upon a hidden mission, out to the open sea."

This persuaded the family to have his ashes scattered at sea. Son Anthony and half-brother Gip chartered the *Deirdre* from Poole Quay. They found themselves "pitching nastily" off the Bar, beyond the harbour entrance. Anthony recalled the moment when the ashes were released, for Anthony West's biography of the author:

"The wind took them off as a long veil that struck the pale green water with a hiss. The *Deirdre* wallowed as Captain Miller put her about and I had a moment of agony. He was really gone now."

Sir Newman Flower [1879-1964], of Fontmell Magna, had been Wells's publisher at Cassells and remembered him as a "most untidy writer" who filled the margin with afterthoughts that would collide. Each was in a "balloon" and lines trailed across the page to show where they were to be inserted. Wells, however, was more than a match for Flower's strictures:

> *I sell my books to Flower,*
> *I give my books to Flower,*
> *He kicks and beats me, drives me, starves me;*
> *He has me in his power.*
> *Christian, dost thou hear him?*
> *He prowls, and prowls, and prowls!*
> *Still, I give my books to Flower.*

STURMINSTER MARSHALL
Thomas Hardy Memorial Cottages.

The range of eight thatched cottages opposite the church are under one long roof of thatch. They were built early in the 1700s with cob walls and were at one time owned by a former neighbour of mine in Bournemouth who used to call to collect the shilling-a-week rents. Church Cottages, they were called in his day.

By the 1960s they were semi-derelict and threatened with demolition, but the Society for the Protection of Ancient Buildings stepped in and renovated them as a memorial to the author Thomas Hardy [1840-1928].

A decade later they were gutted by fire and this time had to be totally rebuilt. So this attractive backdrop to the churchyard, with look-alike rebuilds of its brick and half-timbering, has survived against all the odds.

STURMINSTER NEWTON (BAGBER)
William Barnes: born at Bagber Common.

The birthplace of the Dorset poet, William Barnes [1801-86] was the scattered hamlet of Bagber, a mile west of Sturminster Newton. The site of the suitably humble cottage, which was pulled down before 1850, lies in Barnes's Orchard, beside the droveway — a wide grassy track used for herding stock to market — that twists between the pastures to the east of the road across Bagber Common.

Turn north off the A357 at Bagber and proceed along this straight lane for a mile. A bridleway then branches off to the right, just before Rushy Cottages, and you walk along this. Pass the Dairy House and Pleak House Farm. The site of the Barnes holding is 150 yards after the farm, on the left (Ordnance Survey map reference ST 769 147).

STURMINSTER NEWTON
Penny Street: Barnes as schoolboy and clerk.

Penny Street and Tanyard Lane, which are on the eastern side of Sturminster Newton town centre, have numerous associations with the boyhood and youth of Dorset poet William Barnes [1801-86]. He walked into town each day to the Boys' School, from Bagber which lies a mile and a half to the west, and entered beneath its motto: "The foundation of God standeth sure."

Opposite the old school, at the bottom of Penny Street, stands Vine House, the home for generations of the Dashwood family, where the young Barnes would work for three years as a solicitor's clerk. He then moved to the Wiltshire town of Mere to establish a school [1824-35] and returns to our story as a poet, with entries under Dorchester and Winterborne Came.

His memorial at Sturminster Newton is a carved oak lectern in the parish church which was bought by public subscription.

STURMINSTER NEWTON
Hardy's Riverside Plaque: on the wrong house!

In 1985 I published Professor Michael Millgate's protest, regarding Hardy's Sturminster Newton house, that "as I have demonstrated there can now be no question but that the plaque is on the wrong house". From July 1876 to March 1878 Thomas Hardy and his first wife, Emma, lived in the Riverside Villa which looks out westward over the River Stour from the ridge at the north end of the town's recreation ground (Ordnance Survey map reference ST 784 137).

The trouble arose because Riverside is a pair of mid-Victorian semi-detached brick houses. Millgate wrote in his 1982 work *Thomas Hardy: a Biography*: "In view of the erroneous tradition which has grown up in recent years it is necessary to insist that the Hardys lived in the more northerly of the two houses − the one further from the present recreation ground. When the Hardy Players visited Sturminster Newton in June 1921 they were entertained by William Ponting and his wife, occupants of the more northerly house; they were also photographed in front of the house. Hardy was present, with his [second] wife, and indicated that *The Return of the Native* had been written in the first-floor front room, overlooking the river; a photograph of the same house carries on the back a note in Hardy's hand, 'House in which *The Return of the Native* was written − 1877.'"

That you would think decisive but local writer Olive Knott insisted that the monkey-puzzle he had planted stood in front of the southern house: "Hardy lovers who visit the house often take away a piece of wood from the stump as a souvenir." She could not grasp the fact that Hardy, not being able to do things by halves, planted a pair of monkey-puzzles − one in front of each house. It was a dumb thing for an ex-architect to do as they would totally block out the view he had celebrated in his poem *Overlooking the River Stour*. Both trees, inevitably, were felled and it was the southern one, unfortunately, which left the relics that passed into Sturminster folklore.

It is a pity that the town has mismanaged its Hardy associations as *The Return of the Native* is Hardy at his greatest and it was the achievement of a time which, in a retrospective poem, he called *A Two-Years Idyll*. He looked upon Sturminster as "our happiest time".

STURMINSTER NEWTON

'Rabin Hill': dialect poet.

Robert Young [1811-1908], a friend of William Barnes who would follow the latter into print with dialect verse, lived at The Hive. This large three-storey house is midway along the ridge overlooking the River Stour from the western edge of Sturminster Newton (Ordnance Survey map reference ST 783 141).

His family also owned Riverside Villas at the south end of the hill; the northern half of which they rented to Thomas Hardy in 1876-78.

In middle life Young called himself "An Olde Dorset Songster" and penned verse under the pseudonym Rabin Hill.

In 1863-64 he published two Dorset dialect verses on *Rabin Hill's Visit to the Railway* which he followed in 1867 with *Rabin Hill's Excursion to Weston-super-Mare to See the Opening of the New Pier*.

Young died at Riverside, three years short of his century, a few months after completing the manuscript recollections of his *Early Days*. A posthumous collection of his *Poems in the Dorset Dialect* was issued in 1910.

STURMINSTER NEWTON

From *Rabin Hill's Visit to the* [former] *Railway*.

> The enjun gied another shriek,
> And Rabin Hill looked rather whitish.
> "Bother dthik screechèn thing" zed he;
> "Dthik naïse do always meäke I spitish".
>
> "My eye!" zed he, "now don't he gaw!
> Dthik hoss mus' be uncommon strong:
> Jis' hark how he do pank and blaw;
> He mus' gie out avore be long."
>
> "Odd bless the man, the brudge is crars'd,
> An' we be vleeèn pást King's Mill;
> In Sta'bridge Common we be now."
> "The deuce we be!" zed Rabin Hill.
>
> The enjun gied another scream,
> The speed began to zlackèn now.
> "'Tis strange to I," said Rabin Hill,
> "Thik hoss shood kick up sich a row."
>
> And now the train had zased to move;
> An' standen by the Sta'bridge Stashun,
> "A vew sich starts," zed Rabin Hill,
> "'Ud car us lap bang droo the nashun."
>
> The guard's shrill whissle then was hurd,
> The engine answer'd wi' a znoort;
> An' zoon the traïn wer in vull spád.
> "Goo on," zed Rabin; "That's yer zoort."

"An' if me life wurden ensured,
I dthink that I shood meet me doom."
"Don't tark sich stuff," said Varmer Styles,
"Why, here we be at Templecombe."

"At Templecombe!" zed Rabin Hill;
"I'm blow'd ef tidden like a dreäm."
Rabin begun to steare about,
Vor now he yeard another scream.

"An' now then, Rabin, we'll git out,
An' wait a bit for t'other traïn;
An' then, I dthink, be ha'f-past twalve
We'll git to Sturmi'ster again."

STURMINSTER NEWTON — see STALBRIDGE for R.L. Stevenson: *The Wrecker*

Sullivan — for SIR ARTHUR SULLIVAN [1842-1900] see HANFORD

SUTTON POYNTZ — see WEYMOUTH (SUTTON POYNTZ)

SWANAGE

Andrew Bell: absentee teacher.

Of all the clergymen who have entries in the *Dictionary of National Biography* I have yet to find one with a less appropriate quality than that attributed to Dr Andrew Bell [1753-1832] who was rector of Swanage from 1801 to 1809: "Perhaps the most marked feature in Bell's character was his love of money."

His other interest was education and he was a strident self-publicist. In India he had pioneered the teaching method of using the brighter eight-year-olds to teach the infants. It became known as "the Madras system".

Back in Britain, Bell was often an absentee rector, pushing pupil-teacher ideas rather than tending his flock, and claimed to be tyrannised by his wife, Agnes. His writings on his chosen subject began with *An Experiment in Education* [1797] and included *A Sermon on the Education of the Poor* [1807] and *A Sketch of a National Institution for Training up the Children of the Poor in the Principles of our Holy Religion and in Habits of Useful Industry* [1805].

SWANAGE

David Jardine: brilliant law writer.

The "Judge's seat" on Peveril Downs, Swanage, is inscribed "D.J. 1852". It was erected by David Jardine [1794-1860], the Recorder for Bath, who came from Weybridge and had adopted the Purbeck quarry town. As well as the Peveril stone seat he erected the "Rest and be thankful" one on Studland Hill and paid £120 towards providing the 1859 parish church clock — half its cost.

He was a brilliant writer on legal history, "very learned and ingenious" to quote Macaulay who used Jardine's work as the source for his own popularisations of English history. *A Reading on the use of Torture in the Criminal Law of England previously to the Commonweath* [1837] was followed by a study of the Gunpowder Plot and *Remarks on the Law and Expediency of requiring the presence of Accused Persons at Coroners' Inquisitions* [1846].

Jardine also provided Swanage with a policeman, John Cripps, who would come close to losing his life at the hands of the natives in a Christmas Eve riot.

SWANAGE
Sir Reginald Palgrave: *Appreciation of Cromwell.*

The cross on Church Hill at Swanage was erected in memory of Sir Reginald Palgrave [1829-1904], the brother of Francis Turner Palgrave [1824-97] of Lyme Regis. Sir Reginald was Clerk of the House of Commons [1886-90]. He had written a book about Parliament, *The House of Commons: Illustrations of its History and Practice* [1869] but was better known for *The Chairman's Handbook* [1877] which ran to many editions.

He felt the Victorian age had become hysterical, his own daughter Mary Palgrave being a prime example, in its pathological hatred for Oliver Cromwell. This he attempted to redress with *Oliver Cromwell, the Protector: An Appreciation based on Contemporary Evidence* [1890]. Sir Reginald lived at Hillside in Peveril Road.

SWANAGE and CORFE CASTLE
Mary Palgrave: *Brave Dame Mary.*

Mary Palgrave was one of the five daughters of Sir Reginald Palgrave, of Hillside, Peveril Road, Swanage. In *Brave Dame Mary*, published in 1873, she produced a classic and typical Victorian tale with plenty of moral force, describing the heroism of Lady Mary Bankes who defiantly held Corfe Castle against its first Civil War siege in 1643. There is no shortage of condemnation of the Parliamentarians and with this kind of book selling tens of thousands of copies and running to many editions, it is not surprising that we were all conditioned from birth in the righteousness of the king's cause.

In *Under the Blue Flag*, Mary Palgrave moved the action to Godlingston Manor, near Ulwell Gap in the Purbeck Hills, and extended the conflict to the Duke of Monmouth's rebellion of 1685.

SWANAGE
West End Cottage: Hardy's lodgings.

West End Cottage, then the home of "an invalid captain of smacks and ketches", provided Thomas Hardy [1840-1928] and his first wife Emma with lodgings for the autumn and winter of 1875-76.

This period widened his experience of tragedy with occasional bodies that came in naked with the sea. "The sea undresses them," ships' masters told him, about the victims of drownings that floated in with the tide from Portland and the west.

"He has read well who has learnt that there is more to read outside books than in them," Hardy wrote in his diary. That winter he finished *The Hand of Ethelberta*.

West End Cottage survives, in a cul-de-sac off Seymer Road, west of Peveril Downs open space (Ordnance Survey map reference SZ 034 785).

SWANAGE
Sir Charles Robinson: V&A art-tomes.
Charles Robinson: *Picturesque Rambles*.

Sir [John] Charles Robinson [1824-1913], Director of the Victoria and Albert Museum [1852-69] produced numerous art publications for the South Kensington Museum, as the institution was then known. He lived at Newton Manor, Swanage (Ordnance Survey map reference SZ 020 789) and embellished its seventeenth century rooms with Italian and other European fittings. These include doors, a staircase, shields, carved friezes dated to 1656-58, and a flying-fish weather vane which is said to have come from Billingsgate Market.

Sir Charles was a frequent contributor to the arts columns of The Times and the Nineteenth Century Review. His eldest son, Charles Robinson [1853-1913], published *Picturesque Rambles in the Isle of Purbeck* in 1882. He also wrote *The Cruise of the 'Widgeon'* [1876] and several collections of poems.

This Charles was a barrister. He adopted the Swanage house name to distinguish himself from his father and in later life was known as Charles Edmund Newton-Robinson. He collected engraved gems, was an accomplished yacht racer, and sword-fenced for Britain in the Athens Olympics of 1906.

SWANAGE
Enid Blyton's recommendation.

"She always spent her holidays at Swanage." From an obituary of the children's author Enid Blyton, who died in 1968.

Sydenham — for THOMAS SYDENHAM [1642-89]
see WYNFORD EAGLE

SYDLING ST. NICHOLAS
George Millar: reporter into war-hero.

George Millar [born 1910] will be remembered as Dorset's hero-author of the twentieth century. Like an earlier Dorset writer he started off as an architect but then moved through a series of Fleet Street offices as the storm gathered over Europe in the 1930s. He was the Daily Express man in Paris in 1939 when he volunteered for the Rifle Brigade and found himself back in France to fight for that country.

Things took a downturn with defeat and capture but Millar escaped from a German prisoner-of-war camp and made it back to England. Thereon his knowledge and experience of the continent was put to better use, and as an agent for the Special Operations Executive he serviced the Resistance in occupied France.

By the end of the conflict he had gathered the Distinguished Service Order, the Military Cross, Chevalier de la Légion d'Honneur and Croix de Guerre avec Palmes.

Back home, at Sydling Court, he expanded a 400 acre holding into a thousand acre farm. The journalist in him turned into something more substantial. He had the life to put an edge between the words and the *Maquis* [1945], *Horned Pigeon* [1946], *My Past was an Evil River* [1946], *Isabel and the Sea* [1948] were followed in 1950 by *Through the Unicorn Gates*. The latter was the hiccup in the proceedings and it unsettled the natives, with the local county set claiming to see themselves in the choice of characters that he had set to a backdrop of Sydling St Nicholas and the Dorset Downs.

His reputation with the fox-hunters was fully restored in 1970 with *Horseman*. The remaining later books were largely set in that other land where the world was still safely at war − *A White Boat from England* [1951], *Siesta* [1952], *Orellana* [1954], *Oyster River* [1963], *The Bruneval Raid* [1974], and *Road to Resistance* [1979].

Sometimes, between books, he escaped on a long-distance yacht cruise.

TALBOT WOODS − see BOURNEMOUTH (TALBOT WOODS)

TARRANT CRAWFORD
Bishop Poor: *Ancren Riwle* for Tarrant nuns.

Bishop Roger Poor may have been born at Tarrant Keyneston, and certainly he came to die at Tarrant Crawford, being buried in 1237 in the abbey church he had founded. This he established about 1230 as a small Cistercian house for three nuns and their helpers. Control of it, the establishment being a nunnery, he handed to Johanna, Queen of Scots and sister of Henry III of England, who was brought to rest at Tarrant Crawford in 1238, a year after Poor. Henceforth the abbey was described as "Locus Benedictus Reginae super Tarent".

Richard Poor was seen through his last illness by the Tarrant Crawford nuns and was buried "sicut vivens praeceperat". Excavations of the abbey chapel in about 1850 uncovered a stone coffin slab which was assumed to be that which probably covered the bishop and was subsequently mounted beside the altar of what is now the parish church. Likewise, flanking it, is what is believed to be Johanna's lid (Ordnance Survey map reference ST 923 035).

Poor was a notable cleric of the early mediaeval church in England. The Pope ordered him to investigate a series of anti-priest outrages and in 1236 he was Rome's man at the witnessing of Henry III's ratification of Magna Carta. He had been bishop of Chichester, Salisbury − to which his heart was sent in 1237 and given an urn-burial in the lady chapel at the Cathedral − and then Durham.

He has the credit for writing the *Ancren Riwle*, otherwise known as the *Regulae Inclusarum*, which was said to have been addressed to the sisters at Tarrant. Authorship was formerly ascribed to a later Salisbury bishop, Simon of Ghent, but its Victorian editor argued that the stylistics and grammar had to mean an early thirteenth century date.

It is now accepted, on the supporting evidence of Poor's surviving letters, to be his work. It sets out the duties of monastic life in crisp, concise language, and has been called "one of the most perfect models of simple natural eloquent prose in our language".

TARRANT GUNVILLE (EASTBURY)

Bubb Dodington: political poet of Eastbury House.

Eastbury House is large enough now, yet it is but one wing of the seat of George Bubb Dodington [1691-1762], who had it built to Sir John Vanbrugh's designs in 1724-38 (Ordnance Survey map reference ST 933 127). The cost was £140,000; astronomical in those days, and multi-millions in terms of late twentieth century values. Some idea of the palace-sized creation can be gained from the fact that it was top league of country house extravaganzas and that Blenheim Palace, at £250,000, was about the only project to top it.

Dodington was completing what had been his uncle's ambition and vision, having inherited the wealth and estate of George Dodington in 1720, though his natural habitat was in the corridors of power. He had six Parliamentary seats in his pocket – Weymouth and Melcombe Regis (four members), Winchelsea, and Bridgwater.

Something of a poet, he wrote verses to Horace Walpole: "In power a servant, out of power a friend." His wit was highly regarded, as was his patronage which went to many of the best writers of the day. Edward Young [1683-1765] addressed his third satire to Dodington in about 1726 and was sent verses in return. The Scottish poet James Thomson [1700-48] dedicated his *Summer* blank verse of 1727 to Dodington, in a collection that prepared nature for the attentions of the Romantic poets. Henry Fielding [1707-54] has an epistle to Dodington, entitled "True Greatness", in the *Miscellanies* [1743]. Similarly Richard Bentley [1708-82] published an epistle to him in 1763. Dodington also patronised satirist Paul Whitehead [1710-74] and was inevitably surrounded by sycophants of lesser worth.

He had a national reputation for corruption, as did his steward, William Doggett, locally. Dodington was incessantly absent and Doggett did little to cover his frauds. The sequel I recorded in *Mysterious Dorset*: "Then, according to the tale that was handed down in the Bugle Horn, the watering hole at the park gates, for generations to come, he had the unexpected news that Dodington was standing beside the Blandford road. He had just alighted from the London mail coach. With evidence of his fiddles all around, and only minutes in which to do anything, Doggett did the first decent thing of his life. He went into the library, closed the door, and shot himself."

Dodington was created Baron Melcombe, of Melcombe Regis, in 1761 and died the following year. He had no children and Eastbury passed to Lord Temple, who gave up trying to find a paying tenant and then in desperation offered £200 a year to anyone who would live in it! No one would. The house began to decay and Temple, who had been created Marquis of Buckingham in 1784, had all but the one wing pulled down in 1795.

The corrupt William Doggett had meanwhile passed into village folklore as one of the most sinister of Dorset ghosts, being said to haunt the stone-flanked park gates (Ordnance Survey map reference ST 927 127) and, being unworthy of burial in consecrated ground, to emerge from his tomb in Tarrant Gunville church at night as a vampire and drink the blood of sleeping villagers.

TARRANT GUNVILLE

Thomas Wedgwood: the first photographer.

Thomas Wedgwood [1771-1805] is commemorated by a marble tablet on the wall of Tarrant Gunville parish church. He died at Eastbury House with a reputation that would come only with hindsight. For he had been the first photographer.

Thomas was the son of the famous potter Josiah Wedgwood, and his elder sister would also make her contribution to science by giving birth to Charles Darwin. His circle of friends included Samuel Taylor Coleridge, William Wordsworth, Sir John Leslie, Sydney Smith, Thomas Campbell, Sir Humphry Davy and Thomas Poole.

It was known that silver nitrate blackened on exposure to sunlight but Thomas was the first to take this fact a stage further and demonstrate that it would produce an image. In 1802 he worked out "a method of copying paintings upon glass, and of making profiles by the agency of nitrate of silver". This was done by coating a sheet of white paper with salt of silver in solution, and then placing a silhouette on the sensitised paper, in strong sunlight. A fern leaf was chosen for the first of what became his "shadow graphs".

He wrote *An account of a Method of copying Paintings upon Glass, and of making Profiles by the agency of Light upon Nitrate of Silver*.

Disappointingly, Thomas knew nothing of the qualities of hyposulphite which could have fixed his pictures and made them permanent — instead he had to keep them out of the light, in a drawer. His attempt to take the idea a stage further, with a camera obscura, failed because it needed an impossibly lengthy exposure.

Wedgwood's other scientific achievement, at the age of twenty, was to put forward the concept that all bodies become red-hot at the same temperature. His papers on the *Production of Light from different Bodies by Heat and by Attrition* were read to the Royal Society [1791-92]. His was a productive life that would have discovered so much more if it had not been overwhelmed by a worsening battle against disease, which he lost at the age of thirty-four.

TARRANT HINTON, TARRANT GUNVILLE and TARRANT MONKTON

Great War huts: echoes of Rupert Brooke.

Among the last surviving contemporary buildings which Rupert Brooke would have seen — and perhaps actually used — at Blandford Camp is an ex-War Department hut which now serves as the village hall at Tarrant Hinton (Ordnance Survey map reference ST 937 112). It was in one of these huts that Brooke wrote his prophetic lines on "some corner of a foreign field".

The building dates from 1914-15 when it was among the two hundred erected for men of the Royal Naval Division who would take part in the Gallipoli landings.

There are similar village halls at Tarrant Gunville and Tarrant Monkton.

TARRANT KEYNESTON — see FONTMELL MAGNA for Sir Newman Flower: Brewery to Cassells

TARRANT MONKTON (BLANDFORD CAMP)

Rupert Brooke: 'some corner' where he wrote *The Soldier*.

The most famous, in retrospect, of those who passed through Blandford

Camp was Sub Lieutenant Rupert Brooke [1887-1915] who was to die of blood poisoning in the Middle East on 23 April 1915 and is buried on the Aegean island of Skyros as he would have wished:

> If I should die, think only this of me:
> That there's some corner of a foreign field
> That is for ever England . . .

These lines, from the sonnet, *The Soldier*, are thought to have been written in Blandford Camp, in C Lines on the east side beside Blackland Plantation (Ordnance Survey map reference ST 930 085), when he was with the Anson Battalion of the Royal Naval Division [1914].

Taylor — for SIR HENRY TAYLOR [1801-86]
see BOURNEMOUTH

Thomas — for HUGH SWYNNERTON THOMAS [born 1932], created BARON THOMAS,
see SHERBORNE

THORNCOMBE (FORDE) and WOOL (BINDON)

John of Forde: *Song of Songs.*

John of Forde [?1140-1214] entered the Cistercian monastery at Forde (Ordnance Survey map reference ST 360 052) as a young man. As a prior there he wrote the *Life of Wulfric of Haselbury* [1185]. Then he was appointed Abbot of Bindon [1186-91], which had in 1172 moved from the sea at West Lulworth to the banks of the River Frome at Wool (Ordnance Survey map reference SY 854 867).

He returned to Forde to be its Abbot [1191] and resumed his elegant Latin writing with *Sermons on the Final Verses of the Song of Songs*. These have not only survived as a manuscript but are available in a late twentieth century edition, having been translated and printed in three volumes by Cistercian Publications, Michigan [1977].

THORNCOMBE (FORDE)

Baldwin: his literary period.

Forde Abbey was one of the word factories of monastic Britain. In the mid-twelfth century it had a future Archbishop of Canterbury as its scribe. Baldwin [died 1190] had only been a Forde monk for a year when he was appointed Abbot [1175]. His *De Commendatione Fidei* and *De Sacramento Altaria*, together with sixteen sermons, represent the literary side of a life that would move on to political turmoil.

He had the stuff of legends. In 1184, as Bishop of Worcester, he heard that Gilbert of Plumpton was being executed for abducting an heiress. Baldwin rode up as the rope was literally in place around Gilbert's neck and told the assembled crowd that there would be no execution on a Sunday. A royal pardon was procured for Gilbert.

On promotion to Canterbury, Baldwin disappointed Pope Urban III who found he had an impetuous prelate, and the city's monks who tried to prevent his creation of what became Lambeth College. Henry II supported Baldwin whom Urban called "the most fervent monk, the zealous abbot, the lukewarm bishop, the careless archbishop".

THORNCOMBE (FORDE)

Jeremy Bentham: Forde's thinking tenant.

Jeremy Bentham [1748-1832], the exponent of the utilitarian philosophy of constitutional government, leased Forde Abbey in 1815-18. He lived there, as one would expect of the person and the place, in style — en grand seigneur, as Sir Samuel Romilly, the law reformer, put it on his visit in 1817.

"We found him," Romilly wrote, "passing his time, as he has always been passing it since I have known him, which is now more than thirty years, closely applying himself for six or eight hours a day in writing upon laws and legislation, and in composing his civil and criminal codes, and spending the remaining hours of every day in reading or taking exercise by way of fitting himself for his labours, or, to use his own strangely invented phraseology, taking his ante-jentacular and post-prandial walks to prepare himself for his task of codification."

It was at Forde that he wrote *Chrestomathia*, on extending systems of education, and loaned a piece of the grounds to Francis Place to start a school to put the ideas into practice. He also explored *The Church of England and its Catechism* and ventured deeper into religious controversy with *Not Paul but Christ*, which argued that Saint Paul had hijacked the basic primitive Christianity of Christ and given it an entirely different gloss. *Swear not at all* [1818] then denounced oath-takings on the Bible as anti-Christian. All were exercises in logic over bigotry.

TINCLETON

Clement Walker: stabbed his wife and died in the Tower for *History of the Independency*.

Clement Walker was born at Clyffe House on the ridge above Tincleton (Ordnance Survey map reference SY 782 922), probably in the 1570s, and was living there again in 1623-32. His notable act at home seems to have been an assault upon his wife, who was forbidden to speak with her friends unless he was present. The puritan William Whiteway recorded the incident, without embellishment, on 2 June 1629: "Mr Clement Walker stabbed his wife at dinner."

Mrs Walker may have found some pleasure with Sir Robert Willoughby of Turners Puddle who had been boasting of having lain with all the women of the parish from the vicar's wife down.

Walker's robust personality brought him to the heart of the nation's troubles in 1648 when as a Member of Parliament he voted for a compromise with Charles I. The justification of his actions in his *History of the Independency* led to his committal to the Tower of London on a charge of high treason. Meanwhile the king would lose his head and Walker was never brought to trial. He died in the Tower in October 1651 and is buried in All Hallows church, Barking.

Tolkien — for J.R.R. TOLKIEN [1892-1973]
see BOURNEMOUTH

TOLPUDDLE

George Loveless: *Victims of Whiggery.*

That the Tolpuddle Martyrs were brought home from Australia, where they had been transported in 1834 by the Assize court sitting in Shire Hall at High West Street, Dorchester, was in large measure due to the power of printed words. The most compelling of these, against the sentence for having administered "an unlawful oath" in connection with the Friendly Society of Agricultural Labourers that George Loveless [1797-1874] and brother James [1808-73] established in their home village of Tolpuddle, were George's own.

Supporters in London, calling themselves the London Dorchester Committee, published the crucial pamphlet by George Loveless in 1837. In it he asked: "Has not the working man as much right to preserve and protect his labour as the rich man has his capital?"

Victims of Whiggery, a Statement of the Persecution experienced by the Dorchester Labourers kept their case alive in national politics – as distinct from Dorset where it would remain virtually unmentionable for another century – and led to the six men receiving the royal pardon and coming home in 1838.

Tomlinson – for HENRY MAJOR TOMLINSON [1873-1958]
see ABBOTSBURY (WEST BEXINGTON)

TRENT

Thomas Gerard: Dorset's first book.

Thomas Gerard [1592-1634] of the Manor House at Trent, in the corner of Dorset to the north of Sherborne that was part of Somerset until boundary changes in 1896, wrote the first book to be devoted exclusively to the county. It was written in 1623-24 but when the manuscript eventually appeared in print as the *Survey of Dorsetshire* [1732] it was wrongly attributed to Rev John Coker [died about 1635] from Mappowder who was related to Gerard by marriage. Coker was the parish priest at Tincleton, near Dorchester.

Two impressions were printed of the 1732 edition, differing only in their title pages, and I reprinted the book in 1980 with an "Afterword" that explains its complicated pre-publication history and the clues to dating the work and finding its true authorship. Gerard was buried in the family chapel at Trent parish church. Its entrance, an arch in the nave wall, was painted by Thomas Gerard with laurel leaves entwining the forty armorial shields of the families to whom the aristocratic Gerards were related.

Treves – for SIR FREDERICK TREVES [1853-1923]
see DORCHESTER

Turberville – for GEORGE TURBERVILLE [?1540-1610]
see WINTERBORNE WHITECHURCH

TURNERS PUDDLE (CLOUDS HILL), WOOL (BOVINGTON CAMP), MORETON and WAREHAM

T.E. Lawrence: *Seven Pillars of Wisdom.*

Biographers of Colonel Thomas Edward Lawrence [1888-1935] continue to probe the legends that surround the most enigmatic hero of the twentieth century, my own contribution being *Lawrence of Arabia in Dorset* [1988]. He had brought glamour and excitement back into a world weary of its war, in a sideshow far from the impasse and the carnage of the Western Front, where posing on a camel as a Prince of Mecca he led the Bedouin in hit and run attacks against the Turks in the Desert Revolt [1917-18].

Lieutenant-Colonel Lawrence enjoyed his war as it rolled up through the Holy Land and took the road to Damascus. Then the final triumph was marred by greater tragedy, the death by typhoid of the brown-eyed Arab donkey-boy Salim Ahmed — nicknamed Dahoum, "The Dark One". He had been adopted by Lawrence long before the war, during the excavations at Carchemish [1911], and brought home to London and Oxford for a summer [1913]. The only exuberantly happy moment to be captured by the camera in Lawrence's life was when he swapped clothes with Dahoum.

His death left Lawrence devastated. He cut short his war and flew back to London. He was invited to Buckingham Palace to receive the Distinguished Service Order and Companionship of the Order of the Bath. These he curtly handed back to King George V with the comment that he did not accept honours from a government reneging on its promise of Arab independence.

For a time, however, he did indulge in diplomacy, attending the Paris Peace Conference [1919] and advising on Arab affairs at the Middle East department of the Colonial Office [1921-22]. Then, however, he chose what he called the "mind-suicide" of enlistment in the ranks, as Aircraftman John Hume Ross [1922].

Dismissed in a blaze of publicity, after the secret slipped out, he tried again for anonymity. This time it was in Dorset, enlisting as 7875698 Private Thomas Edward Shaw in the 1st (Depôt) Battalion of the Tank Corps at Bovington Camp, on the heathland north of Wool [12 March 1923].

His hut, in Tintown as it was then called, was F-12 in Marcelcave Road (Ordnance Survey map reference SY 834 892) which ceased to exist with the building of the Sandhurst Barrack Block [1938]; it lay beside its north-east wing.

A mile from the camp, on the magically named Clouds Hill in the parish of Turners Puddle (Ordnance Survey map reference SY 823 909), Lawrence found an empty gamekeeper's cottage "with Dorsetshire to look at", dating from 1805, which he rented from the Frampton family of Moreton [September 1923]. There, on its return from George Bernard Shaw, whom he had asked for advice, he reworked a massive manuscript that was destined to become a milestone in English literature. Dedicating it to Salim Ahmed, but with the "S.A." shrouded in enough ambiguity to create a riddle of the sands in the league of the "W.H." of Shakespeare's sonnets, he had written the ultimate account of their war.

He wove a saga around the Desert Revolt that extended beyond reportage, transcending where necessary any restraints of precise events, actual memory or literal truth, to achieve in *Seven Pillars of Wisdom* the higher objective of the creation of the Homeric prose epic of the twentieth century. The Lawrence part of his life then exorcised, he changed his surname by deed poll to Shaw [1927].

Clouds Hill was the refuge during his backstage military career, which returned to the Royal Air Force and had him on India's troubled North-West Frontier District [1928-29], translating the *Odyssey* of Homer, and then designing and building fast rescue launches in Southampton Water in the project he described in *Notes on Handling the 200 Class Seaplane Tender* [1931].

The cottage on its rhododendron-smothered knoll was intended for a "lifetime of Sundays" but when he went into very public retirement from RAF Bridlington [February 1935], on a bicycle rather than the Brough Superior motor-cycle with which he was almost synonymous, it was a deliberate deception. He was Director Designate of a proposed Intelligence Directorate that was intended to embrace the country's entire secret services.

That was not to be. The scheme fell with Lawrence as he crashed from his motor-cycle, 400 yards south-south-east from his Clouds Hill cottage (Ordnance Survey map reference SY 826 905), as he swerved on his return from Bovington Camp to avoid two boy cyclists and, according to the only independent witness, a black car [13 May 1935]. He was taken to Bovington Military Hospital (Ordnance Survey map reference SY 828 888) but died without regaining consciousness [19 May 1935].

Winston Churchill led the mourners from his funeral at St Nicholas church, Moreton, to the burial in the cemetery 200 yards out of the village (Ordnance Survey map reference SY 804 893) on the west side of the lane towards Wool [21 May 1935].

Clouds Hill and its impenetrable seven acres was given to the National Trust [1937]. His friend Eric Kennington [1888-1960], who had illustrated *Seven Pillars of Wisdom*, sculpted a life-size effigy of Lawrence but neither Moreton nor Turners Puddle churches were prepared to become shrines to the legend and the Bishop of Salisbury came up with a compromise [1939]. It was placed in St Martin's church on the Saxon north wall at Wareham (Ordnance Survey map reference SY 923 877). The other Lawrence memorial is an oak tree, in a small roadside car-park beside the spot where he was fatally injured, which was planted [1985] by armoured car machine-gunner Tom Beaumont. He had been outside the tent when Lawrence held the dead Salim Ahmed in his arms and wept. "I loved that boy," Beaumont heard him say.

Controversy on the circumstances of Lawrence's death-crash was renewed by my book. I have since heard that motor-cycle manufacturer George Brough noted black paint on the offside handlebar and petrol tank of Lawrence's machine. He would have said it had been in an impact with a black object, but was not asked to give evidence at the inquest.

Vachell — for HORACE ANNESLEY VACHELL [1861-1955]
see SHERBORNE

Verlaine — for PAUL VERLAINE [1844-96]
see BOURNEMOUTH

Walker — for CLEMENT WALKER [?1575-1651]
see TINCLETON

Warner — for SYLVIA TOWNSEND WARNER [1893-1978]
see CHALDON HERRING (EAST CHALDON)

Wallace — for ALFRED RUSSEL WALLACE [1823-1913]
see POOLE (BROADSTONE)

Wallace — for EDGAR WALLACE [1875-1932]
see POOLE (BRANKSOME PARK)

Walmsley — for HUGH MULLENEUX WALMSLEY [19th century]
see POOLE (BRANKSOME PARK)

Wanostrocht — for NICHOLAS WANOSTROCHT [1804-76], known as NICHOLAS FELIX, see WIMBORNE

WAREHAM and BRADFORD PEVERELL

John Hutchins: County Historian.

John Hutchins [1698-1773] was born at Bradford Peverell, two miles north-west of Dorchester, the son of its curate, Rev Richard Hutchins. After education at Dorchester Grammar School and Hart Hall, Oxford, John Hutchins followed his father into the cloth and became curate at Milton Abbas in 1723.

There Jacob Bancks arranged his advancement, to the Rectory at Swyre on the coast near Bridport, in 1729. Additionally he held the benefice of Melcombe Horsey on the central Dorset Downs from 1733-44. Then, Hutchins became the rector of Holy Trinity, beside the South Bridge at Wareham, though he retained Swyre as well until his death.

Anne Hutchins would risk her life in Wareham's disastrous fire of Sunday 25 July 1762 as she rescued her husband's manuscripts by the armful. The previous year he had transcribed masses of Dorset archives from the national records in the Tower of London. His patrons Jacob Bancks and Browne Willis had encouraged this interest in antiquarian topography which would culminate in *The History and Antiquities of the County of Dorset*. The dedication is dated 1 June 1773 but on 21 June Hutchins was dead, and is buried in the old chapel beneath the present south aisle of St Mary's church at Wareham. Publication progressed posthumously, in 1774, in two folio-sized volumes.

Others would expand the work into two very different four-volume editions. The rare one, and that which also has the most lavish quantities of plates, both in terms of number and their size, is the Second Edition of 1796-1815. It was edited by Richard Gough [1735-1809] and is an extreme rarity thanks to a calamitous fire that destroyed the Red Lion Passage printing works of John Nichols [1745-1826] in Fleet Street on 8 February 1808. Only 112 copies of the first two volumes of the set escaped the inferno, having already been sold, but most of them have subsequently been broken up by booksellers and gallery owners to provide prints to decorate our walls.

The common edition is the Third Edition of 1861-70, augmented almost out of all recognition from Hutchins's original by William Shipp [died 1873], who displays some impatience with the original author and lost his own helpmate, James Whitworth Hodson, midway through the project. It is a product of the age of mechanised printing and the paper is smooth and modern, unlike the characterful rough texture of the earlier editions.

Subsequent historians remain in Hutchins's debt, which can best be repaid by learning where to place his apostrophe — I see the name being mis-spelt nearly everywhere I look, often by those who, as did the master, hold the "M.A." degree.

WAREHAM and BERE REGIS

Orme Angus: Bere's whirlwind.

J.C. Higgenbotten, the author who wrote under the pen-name Orme Angus, lived for many years at Wareham. He was writing after the Great War and is best remembered for his character Sarah Tuldon, whom he puts in a sleepy village called Barleigh, which is a thinly disguised Bere Regis. There she rebels first against domestic chores and then everything. The novel has her creating havoc throughout the village; out of which arises the harmony of a new order.

WAREHAM

P.F. Westerman: gung-ho stuff.

Percy F. Westerman [1876-1959], a Boy's Own adventure writer, lived for most of his life at Eastcote, Bestwall, Wareham and died in the town. The Air Police were his creation, led by Captain Standish. He wrote well over a hundred and fifty such stories.

They were translated across Europe, from France to Hungary and Finland, with the exception of Germany — which is self-explanatory from his titles for 1940 alone. They were *At Grips with the Swastika*, *The War and Alan Carr*, *When the Allies Swept the Seas*, and *Sea Scouts at Dunkirk*.

And that was the year when we were losing! *A Lad of Grit*, to quote the title of his first book, appeared back in 1908.

WAREHAM — see TURNERS PUDDLE (CLOUDS HILL) for T.E. Lawrence: *Seven Pillars of Wisdom*

WARMWELL

John Richards: a prize bore.

"The Pepys of South Dorset", John Richards of Warmwell House (Ordnance Survey map reference SY 754 859) has been called. He lived at the end of the seventeenth century and kept a diary in which he recorded a character so bigoted and unpleasant that it is worthy of a satirist. It is now in Dorset Record Office.

The joke is that Mr Richards is given hoax honours by his fellow gentry.

But first, the exit of Hunibon the shepherd from Mr Richards's employ. On the night of 9 November 1697 "Hunibon brot home my flock from Knighton, consisting of 458 sheep, having lost two there in the autumn." Two was hardly a significant mortality considering the vast size of the flock, and if Hunibon was the only shepherd he must have been fully worked. The man was not slow to walk out on the job, as we read on 5 May 1698: "I fell out with Hunibon on Little Furzy, or rather he with me, and told me he would be gone."

Neither did Squire Richards get on with his wife. Having for two days kept himself "strange" — distant from her — on Friday 23 February 1700 "she said to me in the morning if I did not mend my manners in a short time, she declared etc. Upon which insolence, losing all patience I burnt my will before her eyes."

The following Monday morning, Alice Richards set off at five o'clock "with M.White to meet ye Dorchester coach for London at Puddle-Town or Blandford".

She does not seem to have stayed there long for he writes on 21 July "qta notte dormivo in cellar chamber p esser in riposa dal ecla", which roughly translated is: "This night I slept in the cellar to be at rest from her."

He must have been a hard man: "Sunday 10 ditto [October 1697], Tho. Symes came hither to borrow £20 of me, but he went away without it."

However, like a good Englishman, the squire did love his pets. On 18 April 1699, "This day my cat Titty kittened on my bed." Other entries include "I gave away the megpy and black-bird" and "this evening Gamr. Bound took home one of my starlings, and another of em was brot into my chamber". On 15 July 1697 he records a bird-of-prey incident:

"Yesterday I by chance rescued one of my chicken in court, from the kite."

Trespassing for game provides the sort of encounter that brings out the best in the squire's writings. On 13 October 1731 he came back from Dorchester via Knighton field and "espyed a pack of hounds with a man on horseback in my green lewell, abt my chalk hills, shortly after we espyed the hare (which they pursued) in Knighton field; yt ran into my Brots adjoining mead hedge. I waited awile to speak with ye huntsman whome I met as he was rideing after the hounds in a wheat land, asking him by what authority he presumed to enter upon my ground, disturb my sheep; and break down my fences. He told me they were Dorchr dogs and he a gentleman's servt, and at last after I pressed to know his name and place of abode, he told me he was Counsellr Loder's servt.

"I scolded him very passionately, whipt off his dogs, and forbade him coming any more in yt circuit, on pain of having all his dogs killd and himself soundly banged. Whereupon he packt away in hast, and promised not to come yt way no more."

It would be disappointing if someone living as well as Squire Richards did not at times have to retreat into his perfumed chamber to suffer the gout. Typically, he did: "Last night the gout came into my left foot, and all this day it was very troublesome, but much worse on Tuesday the 27th ditto [June 1699] abt noon this day I applyd 5 leaches to it, next day ye 28, was very severe and all yt night much worse not permitting a moment's sleep."

He enjoyed a wager as only a true gentleman can. On 24 July 1679: "Mr Penny layd me 2 bottles of Claret that Barcelona was taken by the French, and this day in their possession, and 6 bottles more that the Duke of Saxony remained not King of Poland."

When the news finally seeped through to the Dorset countryside, Mr Penny would have won his two bottles, but the Duke of Saxony was still king, so the squire had the best of the bet. He took on another on 22 February 1701: "This afternoon, at the Club at Meatman, I layd a wager of a guinea with Captn. Trenchard, that 5 new regiments were raised by his maj King William by this day 12 months."

As we have already noticed, Squire Richards was not universally liked, as this entry for 9 August 1697 seems to prove: "At a County Court held this day in Dorchester my Bro. James and I were nominated for coroners, but it being opposed by Mr Byles, Mr Gillingham &c, the election fell on Mr. Arnold and Mr. Gerard Wood."

It is not quite clear what happened on 29 December 1698: "This afternoon about 4 0'clock came two Sherborn Trumpeters to salute me as high Sheriffe &c. An hour after 2 other from Captn. Coker, on the same errand." There must have been a mistake about Squire Richards receiving the honour as we are told on 19 January 1699: "Last Munday's Gazet wch came by this day's post mentioned Wm. Okedens being sheriffe for Dorset."

On 7 January 1702 the same thing happened: "Yesterday the trumpeters came from Mr. Eastment to salute me Sherriffe." Again, it was false assumption.

Confirmation of social rejection came later in the month: "This afternoon I recd. the news of my being taken off from ye Shrievalty. Mr Hardy of Woolcomb, being put in my place."

The squire was left only with his grip on parish affairs, and these were mundane. For instance: "Thursday 25 May 1697, I went with Mr Bound and other parishioners in procession, about the bounds of Warmwell."

Even the swans in the Frome belonged to Richards: "Mr. Jno. Wms. of Lewell sent me 4 young swans whc I marked with I.R. on the right side of their bills, and sent ym down by Richard Stephens into my river." That was on 10 July 1697 but on 1 August there was an accident: "This day Benjn. Stephens brot up one of my young swans killed as he suppposed by my miller's dog."

He mentions hare coursing more than he does eating, and minor blood sports do seem to be the squire's major pleasure in life. Cockfighting he specially liked: "This morning I sent 4 of my shakebag cock-chicken to Tho. Symes, by Pymer, also my dog Paint, to be made a good started of."

He prepared his birds:

"This evening I cut my young black cock's comb, and markt my other young cocks as well as that wth a punch in ye outer claw of the right foot." There was a tragedy for Richards in the ring on 12 March 1700:

"My great shakebag cock given me by Col.Trench'd was mortally wounded with a pike prong by Mr Bound's man, and dyed threof the same night."

Unsurprisingly, he had a taste for alcohol: "This evening [31 March 1701] 8 quarts of Mr Hill's brandy were put to ye black cherrys in my old wicker bottle."

Occasionally he underwent a little abstinence: "I began to leave off snuff, tobacco, having taken none all this day [11 December 1699]."

There was labour trouble on 4 May 1699: "This day my dairyman Chappell fell out wth my servt maid Joan." And in the afternoon of the same day: "I turned Jhn. Andrews out of doors for giving me the Ly in my chamber, and was angre with him for having endeavoured to."

John Richards, a great bore of his day, lived for another twenty years but we are spared any diaries surviving after 1702.

Webster – for AUGUSTA DAVIES [1837-94], known as AUGUSTA WEBSTER,
see POOLE

Wedgwood – for THOMAS WEDGWOOD [1771-1805]
see TARRANT GUNVILLE

Weekes – for HENRY WEEKES [1807-77]
see CHRISTCHURCH

Wells – for HERBERT GEORGE WELLS [1866-1946]
see STUDLAND

Wesley – for SAMUEL WESLEY [1662-1735]
see WINTERBORNE WHITECHURCH

West – for JOHN WEST [1778-1845]
see CHETTLE

WESTBOURNE – see BOURNEMOUTH (WESTBOURNE)

Westerman – for PERCY F. WESTERMAN [1876-1959]
see WAREHAM

WEST LULWORTH – see LULWORTH, WEST

WEST STAFFORD

Talbothays Lodge: T. Hardy, architect.

A villa that is the work of Thomas Hardy the architect, a virtual copy of his own 1885-dated Dorchester home, Max Gate, stands on land at West Stafford that his brother Henry inherited from their father. It is known as Talbothays Lodge, and was designed in 1893. Taking its name from Hardy's fictional placename for Lower Lewell Farm, a little further along the road, it stands half a mile east of the village (Ordnance Survey map reference SY 734 896).

Henry would live there along with Mary and Kate Hardy, sisters of Henry and Thomas, and it was their home for the rest of their lives.

They had moved from the thatched "Birthplace" of the author at Higher Bockhampton. Talbothays has five bedrooms, a stable yard and outbuildings — the farthest out being the two summerhouses that were built by Henry. Here on 2 June each year, a flag was hoisted in honour of the birthday of the member of the family who had brought it into the middle classes, a flag for Thomas.

WEST STAFFORD — see MELCOMBE HORSEY
for Reginald Bosworth Smith: birds and Allah

WEYMOUTH

'One of the idlest haunts in the kingdom.'
— Jane Austen
[1775-1817]

WEYMOUTH

Thomas Love Peacock: sentimental satirist.

The Peacock family seemed to have lived close to what has become 2 Charlotte Street, Weymouth, where they had a bookshop, but Thomas Love Peacock [1785-1866] had a father who was a London glass-seller and though the satirist is known to have been born in Weymouth the connection with Dorset is otherwise vague. His mother was from the Love family, which had branches along the coastal belt westwards to the Exe estuary. Father died when Thomas was only three.

Young Thomas would fall desperately in love at twenty-two, but the girl's parents disapproved and she was married off elsewhere, to die within the twelve-month. They had met in the ruins of Newark Abbey and Thomas would wear a locket containing her hair for the rest of his life. It would be of her that he would dream on his deathbed six decades later.

The protest against society was incorporated into his comedy *Nightmare Abbey* [1818]. His other early works include *Maid Marian, The Misfortunes of Elphin, Headlong Hall,* and *Melincourt.* They were followed by *Crotchet Castle* at middle age and *Gryll Grange* as the final reckoning from a seventy-five-year-old.

Daily life was as an administrator at India House, where his was the vision and drive that re-launched the top fleet of the British Empire — the Eastindiamen, the ships of the East India Company — into an age of steam and steel to replace sail and wood. *A Memorandum respecting the Application of Steam Navigation to the Internal and External Communications of India* was Peacock's most influential piece of writing. It hatched "my iron chicken" as he called his ships. He found more stimulation from them than in contact with his colleagues at Britain's overseas civil service, whose day he lampooned:

> From ten to eleven ate a breakfast for seven;
> From eleven to noon, to begin was too soon;
> From twelve to one, asked "What's to be done?"
> From one to two found nothing to do;
> From two to three began to foresee
> That from three to four would be a damned bore.

At twenty-seven, in 1812, he met Shelley and began by ridiculing the poet's inadequate diet. He would share with Byron the honour of being Shelley's executor and receive the compliment that "his sharp wit makes such a wound the knife is lost in it".

WEYMOUTH
James Silk Buckingham: Weymouth guidebook.

A Summer Trip to Weymouth and Dorchester, published in 1842, runs to 206 pages and is ascribed to "an Old Traveller". He was James Silk Buckingham [1786-1855] who was not that old but could claim to be as well travelled as any early nineteenth century politician. He had just returned from four years in North America and had a total of five volumes in print on *America . . . the Northern or Free States* [1841] and *The Slave States of America* [1842].

He had also written volumes on his travels in Europe, the Middle East, and India. His political milestone was the *Parliamentary Report on the Extent, Causes and Consequences of the Prevailing Vice of Intoxication* [1834] and he became the first president of the London Temperance League in 1851.

WEYMOUTH (RADIPOLE)
Cameron: explorer who couldn't find Livingstone.

Verney Lovett Cameron [1844-94], who was born at Radipole near Weymouth, was selected by the Royal Geographical Society in 1872 to lead the expedition in search of David Livingstone, whose whereabouts had been unknown since he ventured into the interior of Africa. In the event, however, it was Henry Morton Stanley who found him, with one of the best lines in history: "Dr Livingstone, I presume?" Cameron's fame came in 1875, when he made history as the first European to cross the continent of equatorial Africa from east to west.

Across Africa described his journey [1877], and *Our Future Highway* [1880] detailed all the quirks of fate that prevented his attendance at the Zululand disasters and somehow had him return to England instead, from Karachi, after a misunderstanding. He also wrote a number of adventure stories for boys and his last interview was given to the magazine Chums.

WEYMOUTH
Hardy's lodgings: 3 Wooperton Street.

Whilst working as a church architect, for G.R. Crickmay in Weymouth, the author Thomas Hardy lodged at 3 Wooperton Street, which is the second from the left of a terrace of four three-storey brick houses with bow-fronted first-floor windows that project over the pavement on to what is now a municipal car-park. He arrived in midsummer 1869, after Crickmay had taken over the Dorchester practice of Hardy's previous employer who had died, and left in February 1870 to work on *Desperate Remedies* at Higher Bockhampton, Stinsford.

A week later he had an urgent request from Crickmay to go to Cornwall where, at St Juliot Rectory, he met Emma Lavinia Gifford, who would become the first Mrs Thomas Hardy.

Thomas returned to Weymouth on 4 April 1870, and replied to a letter from Macmillans rejecting *Desperate Remedies,* and then went to London to push it into print. On 30 March 1871 he was back in Weymouth, still helping Crickmay to redesign churches. There was the prospect of another Cornish trip as the reward.

"Gothic drawings" were still the order of the day in June and July 1871 and then, after returning to the peace of the Bockhampton cottage to complete *Under the Greenwood Tree,* he was once more back with architecture at Weymouth for the winter of 1871-72.

WEYMOUTH

George Alfred Henty: *Out in the Pampas.*

Crimean veteran and war correspondent George Alfred Henty [1832-1902] died at Weymouth. He had written a dozen novels and some seventy adventure stories for boys. The best known were *Out in the Pampas* [1868], *The Young Franc-Tireurs* [1872], *The Cat of Bubastes* [1889], *Redskin and Cowboy* [1892], and *With Frederick the Great* [1898]. His final book, published just before he died, was on the most recent of the world's wars, *With Roberts to Pretoria.* Henty came to Weymouth to yacht.

WEYMOUTH and STUDLAND

Virginia Woolf: 'The Dreadnought Hoax'.

William Horace de Vere Cole [1881-1936], alias the man from the Foreign Office, and Miss Virgina Stephen — known to us as the writer Virginia Woolf [1882-1941] — carried out one of the greatest practical jokes of all time at Weymouth in 1910. Fitted out by Clarkson's in suitable oriental costume were alleged members of the Abyssinian royal family, who for the convenience of their interpreter spoke a mix of Swahili and Latin pronounced backwards.

They telegrammed HMS *Dreadnought,* lying off Portland, on 10 February. Or rather, sent the message in the name of Sir Charles Hardinge [1858-1944], the Permanent Under Secretary for Foreign Affairs, who would later in the year be created first Baron Hardinge of Penshurst:

"COMMANDER-IN-CHIEF HOME FLEET PORTLAND STOP PRINCE MAKALEN OF ABYSSINIA AND SUITE ARRIVE FOUR-TWENTY TODAY WEYMOUTH STOP HE WISHES TO SEE DREADNOUGHT STOP KINDLY ARRANGE MEET THEM ON ARRIVAL STOP REGRET SHORT NOTICE STOP FORGOT WIRE BEFORE STOP INTERPRETER ACCOMPANIES STOP HARDINGE FOREIGN OFFICE STOP"

It was received by Admiral Sir William May [1849-1930], Commander-in-Chief of the Home Fleet, at anchor in Portland Harbour, aboard his flagship

HMS *Dreadnought*. The time was 3.45 in the afternoon and there was only half an hour in which to put on full dress, arrange for a guard of honour to be mounted on board, and send a launch to the jetty to meet the royal party.

Meanwhile, they were being met off the London train by the town's civic dignitaries, the Mayor and Corporation of Weymouth, and ushered into "a four-wheeler" and a taxicab for the short drive to the harbourside. Willie Clarkson had fitted them out magnificently the Daily Mirror reported:

"All the princes wore vari-coloured silk sashes as turbans, set off with diamond aigrettes, white gibbah tunics, over which were cast rich flowing robes, and round their necks were suspended gold chains and jewelled necklaces.

"Their faces were coloured a deep brown with a specially-prepared powder, and half-hidden under dark false beards and moustaches, while, except in the case of the lady, their hair was dyed black and crisply curled.

"The young lady's make up — she is described as very good looking, with classical features — was precisely the same as that of the other princes, save that her long hair was bound up tightly on the top of her head, and she also wore a black curly wig.

"They also all wore patent leather boots which, Oriental fashion, tapered to a point, the ends projecting fully six inches beyond the toes.

"White gloves covered the princes' hands, and over the gloved fingers they wore gold wedding-rings — heavy plain circlets, which looked very impressive.

"Prince Makalen, as chief of the royal party, had an additional ornament. This was the real Imperial Order of Ethiopia — a star-shaped jewel, in the centre of which was a sapphire-like piece of glass. It was suspended from a red, gold and blue ribbon, and was pinned on — with a safety-pin — to a gold chain worn round the neck. The metal was of Abbysinian silver plated with gold. The total value of the jewellery worn by the princes was at least £500."

Stepping out of the Admiral's launch and climbing the gangplank of the battleship they were piped aboard and welcomed to the strains of the Zanzibar national anthem, which was the closest tune the band could attempt, "not knowing that of Abyssinia, if such a thing exists".

First up the gangway was Horace de Vere Cole, purporting to be Herbert Cholmondely, the Foreign Office Attaché. He shook hands with Admiral May. Then came the princes — Prince Makalen, Prince Sanganya, Prince Mandok and Prince Mikael Golen. Prince Sanganya was in fact a young lady, known to us as Virginia Woolf. The others were Duncan Grant, Anthony Buxton and Guy Ridley. They were formally introduced to Admiral May and then to Captain Herbert W. Richmond, the chief officer of the *Dreadnought*.

The princes then inspected the guard of honour of the Royal Marines. Prince Makalen was talking gibberish. "Yembo inscara milu berrango scutala bonga asterma el crashbi shemal," was an approximation of one of his utterances.

Herr George Kauffmann had come with the party and was, said Cholmondely, a German who was acting as the official interpreter. He was Adrian Stephen, Virginia's brother, disguised by beard and bowler. "The Prince wishes to know," said Kauffman, "the difference between the red and blue marines."

The explanation was provided and duly translated by Kauffman into gibberish for the benefit of Prince Makalen.

173

"ONCE BITTEN, TWICE SHY."

THE ABYSSINIAN PRINCES HOAX

WHAT WILL HAPPEN NEXT TIME SOME GENUINE EASTERN PRINCES VISIT A BRITISH MAN-O'-WAR

DAILY MIRROR via GERALD NORRIS

From the Daily Mirror of 17 February 1910:
'Everybody has been talking of the practical joke
played by some funny people who dressed up as Abyssinian
princes and, in this disguise, were received with royal
honours on HMS Dreadnought a few days ago. Our cartoonist
imagines that the next time Oriental personages, however
genuine, visit a man-o'-war, their reception will be
rather warm, and something of the sort shown here.'

The question of a salute was raised. Eighteen guns was suggested but naval officers were embarrassed that they had no Abyssinian flag to hoist as it was fired. Kauffman relayed the British regret to the princes who gracefully accepted the apology and said they would waive any claim to a salute.

As they proceeded around the entire ship, with everything being shown to them and explained via Herr Kauffman, the princes "alternately beamed with pleasure and glared ferociously".

Cholmondely, the man from the Foreign Office, went below with a group of officers to take tea. He explained the family's relationship with the chief. Next day, he added, the princes intended going to Eton to make arrangements for sending their sons and nephews to school in England.

He was taken to task about the short notice that was given of the impending visit. "We ourselves had only a matter of hours in which to arrange things," Cholmondely explained. "The party was visiting France but had to be rushed away suddenly from Paris in order to escape the floods. The Seine is still rising, apparently."

Admiral May then came down to ask Mr Cholmondely if he could be of further service. He was thanked for his courtesy and kindness and told that the princes, Mr Cholmondely was sure, would excuse him from further ceremony. The Admiral departed to disrobe and put on mufti to go ashore.

The royal party had then to make their excuses, saying they had already eaten far too much that day, in order to avoid drinking tea — being "afraid that the least moisture would remove the powder from their skin".

They were now making their goodbyes but the Flag Officer insisted on accompanying the party to the jetty at Weymouth Harbour. As they left the *Dreadnought*, walking down the gangway, the long pointed boots nearly caused the downfall of one of the princes and the exposure of the sham: "He slipped on a step and would have fallen into the sea had not one of his royal confreres caught him by the arm and saved him from an untimely ducking, to say nothing of the exposure of the hoax that would have followed."

The band had again struck up the Zanzibar national anthem. Two official motor cars were waiting for the party at the harbour. Here the chief Prince of Abyssinia, Prince Makalen, was so overwhelmed with the warmth of their reception that he conveyed to the Flag-Lieutenant his wish to present to him the Imperial Order of Ethiopia.

The young officer declined, saying that he would not accept or wear a foreign order without special permission, but that he was deeply touched by the kind thought.

On the return train, the masquerade was maintained, with Cholmondely telling Great Western Railway officials that the princes could not eat any meals that had been served with the naked hand, Miss Stephen told the Daily Mirror. "There were no spare gloves on the train, and the officials subsequently had to buy a few pairs, grey kid gloves. We gave them princely tips."

Prince Sanganya's story appeared in the Daily Mirror of 15 February 1910. Virginia Stephen was asked how difficult it had been to pose as a man.

"I spoke as little as possible in case my voice, which I made as gruff as I could, should fail me. I found I could easily laugh like a man, but it was difficult to disguise the speaking voice.

"As a matter of fact the only really trying time I had was when I had to shake hands with my first cousin, who is an officer on the *Dreadnought*, and who saluted me as I went on deck. I thought I should burst out laughing, but happily, I managed to preserve my Oriental stolidity of countenance."

Her cousin was Captain Willy Fisher, who became Admiral Sir William Wordsworth Fisher [1875-1937]. "He took it to heart a great deal," in Virginia's words, and for the rest of his life avoided seeing her again. Unlike the two Herberts in the story.

Herbert would meet Herbert again in the days that followed the hoax. On the Sunday afternoon, in the West End, Captain Herbert Richmond of HMS *Dreadnought* came face to face with Horace de Vere Cole, alias Herbert Cholmondely of the Foreign Office. They smiled and shook hands, and the captain was also reunited with Herr Kauffman, the German interpreter, now sans fiery moustache and whiskers.

"It was very cleverly done," Captain Richmond said, admitting that the audacious trick had deceived them completely. The officers had no idea at the time that a practical joke was being played on them and later, when they learned they had been hoaxed, they laughed heartily.

Press interest had now become insatiable and Admiral May sensibly took the *Dreadnought* to sea and waited for the joke to die down. "Bunga-bunga" had become the local form of address for her sailors, and Pavilion music-hall comedian Medley Barrett opened his act with a doggerel verse to the tune of *The Girl I Left Behind Me*:

> *When I went on board a* Dreadnought *ship,*
> *Though I looked just like a costermonger*
> *They said I was an Abyssinian prince,*
> *Because I shouted "Bunga-bunga".*

Miss Stephen, as herself, was already a frequent visitor to the Dorset coast. She had holidayed with Clive and Vanessa Bell and Walter Lamb in rented cottages at Studland in the second half of September 1909. They returned to Harbour View, Studland, on 26 March 1910, after the *Dreadnought* hoax, and she did not return to 29 Fitzroy Square until 16 April 1910.

The Bells had helped her through a nervous breakdown and the first two weeks were described as "splendid". The "third was pretty good" but back in London, Virginia said she "stupidly" made her "head bad again and have been doing nothing".

From 19 to 27 September 1911 her Studland lodgings were at 2 Harmony Cottages. Lytton Strachey was also there, as were Roger Fry and family.

Years later, as successful author and the wife of Leonard Woolf [married 1912] − she had written *The Voyage Out* [1915], *Night and Day* [1919], *Monday or Tuesday* [1921], *Jacob's Room* [1922], *The Common Reader* and *Mrs Dalloway* [1925] − Virginia Woolf called at Max Gate, Dorchester, to meet the ageing Thomas Hardy. The brief encounter is recorded in *A Writer's Diary* for Sunday 25 July 1926:

"At first I thought it was Hardy, and it was the parlour-maid, a small, thin girl, wearing a proper cap. She came in with silver cake stands and so on. Mrs Hardy talked to us about her dog. How long ought we to stay? Can Mr Hardy walk much etc. I asked, making conversation, as I knew one would have to.

"She had the large sad lack-lustre eyes of a childless woman; great docility and readiness, as if she had learnt her part; not great alacrity, but resignation, in welcoming more visitors; wears a sprigged ooile dress, black shoes and a necklace."

The Hardys walked each day, but not far as Wessex, the dog, was unable to go any distance.

"He bites, she told us. She became more natural and animated about the dog, who is evidently the real centre of her thoughts − then the maid came in.

"Then again the door opened, more sprucely, and in trotted a little puffy-cheeked cheerful old man, with an atmosphere cheerful and business-like in addressing us, rather like and old doctor's or solicitor's, saying 'Well, now ...' or words like that as he shook hands. He was dressed in rough grey with a striped tie. His nose had a joint in it and the end curves down. A round whitish face, the eyes now faded and rather watery, but the whole aspect cheerful and vigorous."

Hardy sat in a three-cornered chair at a round table, on which were the cake-stands and the chocolate roll — "what is called a good tea" — but he drank only one cup. He was "extremely affable and aware of his duties" and recalled that he had seen Virginia, or perhaps her sister, in her cradle, when he called at her father's home. That was at 22 Hyde Park Gate; he was Sir Leslie Stephen [1832-1904], the editor of the Cornhill Magazine and author of *Essays on Freethinking and Plain Speaking* [1879], *The Science of Ethics* [1882] and *An Agnostic's Apology* [1893].

"Your father took my novel — *Far from the Madding Crowd*", Hardy continued. "We stood shoulder to shoulder against the British public about certain matters dealt with in that novel. You may have heard."

It slipped into the Cornhill Magazine after "some other novel had fallen through" with its package being lost in transit from France, and against "all the Cornhill laws" Leslie Stephen never saw the complete Hardy story until it had virtually appeared in print: "I sent it chapter by chapter and was never late. Wonderful what youth is! I had it in my head doubtless, but I never thought twice about it. It came out every month.

"They were nervous because of Miss Thackeray, I think. She said she became paralysed and could not write a word directly she heard the press begin. I daresay it is bad for a novel to appear like that. One begins to think what is good for the magazine, not what is good for the novel."

The discussion continued on the subject of manuscripts with Hardy saying that after the original of *Far from the Madding Crowd* had been found in a drawer during the Great War and sold for the Red Cross he now ensured that they were returned. He was disappointed that "the printer rubs out all the marks". These should be left as they prove the manuscript is genuine.

Then, "with his head down like some old pouter pigeon", Hardy talked of the Strand, which he last saw six years ago, and his old haunts in London. "He has a very long head; and quizzical bright eyes, for in talk they grow bright."

The revelations were rather inconsequential, about buying secondhand books in Wyck Street and wondering why Great James Street should be so narrow but Bedford Row so broad. "I have often wondered about that," he mused. London was changing fast and would soon be unrecognisable. "But I shall never go there again."

Mrs Hardy tried to persuade him that it was still a possibility, being "an easy drive — six hours or so", and that though she knew everyone in Dorchester the people in London were more interesting.

Virginia asked if it was true that Mr Hardy had gone up to London during the First World War to see an air-raid. "What things they say!" he replied. Mrs Hardy pointed out that it was she who was in London at the time, staying with Sir James Barrie. "We just heard a little pop in the distance. The searchlights were beautiful. I thought, if a bomb were to fall on this flat, how many writers would be lost."

Hardy smiled in his "queer way" — fresh, sarcastic, shrewd and without a trace "of the simple peasant". He was aware, undoubting, uninterested in novels — his or anyone's.

They then talked about poetry as Wessex, the rough brown and white mongrel, intervened. Poetry did win through, but Hardy would only say that he did not write the poems at the same time as the novels, sending them about, "but they were always returned" and, he added with a chuckle, "in those days you believed in editors. Many of the fair copies were lost. He was still finding the notes for them. "I found one the other day; but I don't think I shall find any more."

Hardy's ease with the writing of the novels was compared with E.M. Forster taking a long time to produce anything. "Seven years," said Hardy with his characteristic chuckle. As for his own work, he refused to be drawn on which of his books he was most pleased with, or on which might be given to a young lady as a wedding present. "None of my books are fitted to be wedding presents," he said.

Friends had urged him not to give up poetry. "I am afraid poetry is giving up me," he had replied. Now he was sometimes seeing sixteen people in a day, and though that might not preclude writing there was the question of physical strength. Among the visitors had been T.E. Lawrence, bicycling with a broken arm "held like that" from Lincoln to Dorchester, and listening at the door to hear if there was anyone there.

"I hope he won't commit suicide," said Mrs Hardy, pensive and despondent as she leaned over the tea cups. "He often says things like it, though he has never said quite that perhaps. But he has blue lines around his eyes. He calls himself Shaw in the army. No one is to know where he is. But it got into the papers."

Hardy remarked: "He promised me not to go into the air."

"My husband doesn't like anything to do with the air," Mrs Hardy explained.

Eyes began to shift to the grandfather clock. Virginia started to make her excuses. Leonard had been offered a whisky and water. They got up and signed the visitors' book. Hardy duly signed Virginia's copy of *Life's Little Ironies*, misspelling Woolf "Wolf" − it could hardly have been either the first or last time it would happen − "which I daresay had given him some anxiety".

Wessex returned, as acknowledged master of the house, "weezing away". Hardy's "ordinary, smallish, curled-up hands" had swept in a gesture suited to a "very great Victorian" and Mrs Hardy thrust an old grey hat into his fingers, "and he trotted us out on to the road".

He mentioned the night-time lights of Weymouth, reflected by the clouds and visible above the downs, and Mrs Hardy asked if Virginia knew Aldous Huxley. She did. They had been reading his "very clever" book, with her having to read aloud for Thomas whose eyes were now so bad, but he could not remember it. This drew the final comment of substance: "They've changed everything now. We used to think there was a beginning and a middle and an end. We believed in the Aristotelian theory. Now one of those stories comes to an end with a woman going out of the room."

If he was still writing, he implied, it was now restricted to minor matters of duty, such as replying to small boys who had written from places like New Zealand.

WEYMOUTH (SUTTON POYNTZ)

Albert Bailey: the bard at The Laurels.

Albert Charles Bailey [1860-1916] came at the age of seven from Osmington to the cottage at Sutton Poyntz that is now known as The Laurels. It was formerly the village poor house. In later life he retired from market gardening after a heart attack and composed more than two hundred poems and sonnets. "Son of the soil," he called himself but the Daily Mail changed this to the "Ploughman Poet" when in 1911 they printed nine verses of the thirty that comprised the *Passing thoughts of a Village Bard:*

> When earth at times sweet call resounds
> For summer dost prepare,
> Bell-echoes hill and vale rebounds
> Their music pleased to share.

> The grateful bosom of the earth
> Will heave to hear its voice
> Great nature — bursting into birth —
> Her offspring will rejoice.

> 'Twas on a wild November morn
> The winds did huffle loud,
> The trees of half their beauty shorn
> Were by the tempest bowed.

> The rain in floods came pouring down
> Fierce driven by the wind,
> Methought it look'd like fortune's frown
> When beating on the wind.

> Upon my tree a little bird
> Sat shivering wet and cold,
> Its song were hush'd, its voice unheard
> But still a tale is told.

> The dreary morn, that artless sight,
> My spirits all depressed,
> I watched until its laboured flight
> Poor thing it had no nest.

> The sheep, that from the open field
> Had gathered 'neath the trees,
> Now one by one from shelter steal
> And shake their sodden fleece.

> Behold, 'twixt yonder opening skies
> The radiant sun breaks through,
> The rain where 'ere each arrow flies
> Seems to turn to crystal dew.

> But soon its full resplendent light
> O'er hill and vale doth break,
> Sweet robin hopped to see the light
> And rubbed his little beak.

Albert Bailey was a national poet, if only for a day. Thomas Hardy found himself asked for an opinion. Yes, he said, he knew of Mr Bailey. "In any other country he would be a prodigy."

WEYMOUTH (PRESTON) — see WINTERBORNE WHITECHURCH for John Wesley's father: attacked poets' morals

WEYMOUTH (SUTTON POYNTZ) — see DORCHESTER for the print behind *The Trumpet Major*

Whas — for JOHN WHAS [flourished around 1400] see SHERBORNE

Wheeler — for MAURICE WHEELER [?1648-1727]
see WIMBORNE ST. GILES

WHITCHURCH CANONICORUM — see LYME REGIS for Silvester
Jourdain: inspired Shakespeare to *The Tempest*

White — for GLEESON WHITE [1851-98]
see CHRISTCHURCH

Wightman — for RALPH WIGHTMAN [1901-71]
see PUDDLETOWN

Willis — for BROWNE WILLIS [1682-1760]
see BLANDFORD ST. MARY

Willis — for JOHN WILLIS [?1570-1628]
see IWERNE MINSTER

WIMBORNE
Matthew Prior of Eastbrook: poet-diplomat.

Matthew Prior [1664-1721] was born at Eastbrook, Wimborne — that's the tradition and it is now generally accepted. He was always said to have been the young scholar who fell asleep over the copy of Sir Walter Raleigh's *History of the World* in the chained library at Wimborne Minster and caused it to be perforated by the dripping wax from a guttering candle. G.A. Aitken spoiled that story in the *Contemporary Review* of May 1890 by showing that the book wasn't in the library until long after Prior's youth.

By the late 1670s he was in Westminster School with Lord Dorset as his patron and after an Oxford scholarship he entered diplomatic service as secretary to Lord Dursley, who was William III's ambassador to the Hague. In 1697 he was rewarded with a two hundred guinea gratuity for negotiating the peace treaty of Ryswick. By 1711 he was famous as a poet as well as a diplomat, and managed to combine the professions in a couplet:

> *In the vile Utrecht Treaty too,*
> *Poor man! he found enough to do.*

Prior was too involved in national and literary affairs for a return to Dorset and his own vanities could be indulged with the £4,200 proceeds of *Solomon on the Vanity of the World* to which Lord Harley had added a similar sum so that Down Hall, Essex, came to fulfil his ambition:

> *Great Mother, let me once be able*
> *To have a garden, house and stable*
> *That I may read, and ride, and plant,*
> *Superior to desire or want;*
> *And as health fails, and years increase,*
> *Sit down, and think, and die in peace.*

WIMBORNE
Felix the Bat: lived at 23 Julians Road.

Nicholas Wanostrocht is buried in Wimborne cemetery but there is no mention beneath his Maltese cross headstone of the name for which he is remembered.

To the Loved memory
of Nicholas Wanostrocht
Born October 5 1804
Died September 3 1876.

He was Nicholas Felix to a multitude of admirers: having in 1845 been the author of *Felix On the Bat: being a scientific inquiry into the use of the Cricket Bat, together with the History and use of the Catapulta*.

His own illustrations provided humorous vignettes including a frontispiece of himself wielding a bat on the back of a bat (the mammal sort) flying over a village cricket match. This first great manual to the skills of the game brought instant fame and a match was played in his honour in 1846. He then toured the country as the President of the All England XI. In 1872 he retired from Brighton to Wimborne and spent his last four years in No 1 Julians Villas, which is now 23 Julians Road — the Dorchester road — on the south side, near the east end.

WIMBORNE
Llanherne: Hardy's home, 16 Avenue Road.

Thomas Hardy lived with his first wife, Emma, at Llanherne in The Avenue, Wimborne, from June 1881 to June 1883. The Avenue had a gravel surface at this time and the land between it and Grove Road was a grass field. The Osborne Road development was for the future. "Llanherne" was how Hardy spelt it but later versions have tended to lose the second 'l' and the final 'e' — and the house is now 16 Avenue Road.

These were Hardy's 42nd and 43rd years. A younger friend, George Pike, lived in Grove Road from 1877-94. Hardy also befriended his physician, Dr George Batterbury and allowed the town's Shakespearean Society to meet at Llanherne. George Lock was his hairdresser. Hardy went for country walks with a local architect, Walter John Fletcher, who designed St John's church, consecrated in 1876.

As for literary output, Wimborne can only claim that *Two on a Tower*, the Drax tower at Charborough Park, was written at Llanherne. It is hardly among Hardy's most inspired works and neither is the author's name for his adopted town — "Warborne".

His nostalgic tribute would come in later life, recalling the young limes of The Avenue:

> They are great trees, no doubt, by now
> That were so thin in bough —
> That row of limes —
> When we housed there, I'm loth to reckon when.
> The world has turned so many times,
> So many, since then.

WIMBORNE
Montague James Druitt: Jack the Ripper?

The headstone to the young barrister and cricketer Montague James Druitt stands among the Victorian graves in Wimborne cemetery. He would lie there in near-total obscurity, of note only in that he carried a local family name which still produces solicitors at Christchurch, but for the timing and method of his death. The significance of the date is that the five Whitechapel prostitutes who were cut up in a variety of ways – possibly by different hands but attributed by the newspapers to one Jack the Ripper – met their knifeman between 31 August and 9 November 1888. "Jack the Ripper" was the "trade name" (also his expression) that the killer, or one of the killers, gave himself in a red-ink letter to the "Central News Office, London City" on 25 September 1888.

Contemporary police investigators also considered the deaths of two other women, Fairy Fay in December 1887 and Martha Tabram in August 1888, to have been part of the same Ripper sequence. The tendency to attribute the killings to a single madman is reinforced by the "fact" that they started and stopped so abruptly. But did they?

Conveniently for modern Ripperologists, Druitt drowned shortly after the spate of gruesome killings that I have listed – but there would be other similar murders, of Alice McKenzie and Frances Coles, whose mutilations seem to be dismissed as copy-cat butchery. Accepting that, however, brings its own problems as it opens the possibility that some of the earlier seven deaths were also the work of Ripper-imitators.

These points are not satisfactorily answered either in Tom Cullin's *Autumn of Terror*, the 1967 book which put forward Druitt as the Ripper, or in *The Ripper Legacy* by Martin Howells and Keith Skinner which repeated the claim in 1987.

In Victorian times, as now, several thousand depressed people committed suicide each year. Only a statistically insignificant proportion of them had murdered anyone. A Wimborne grave-hand has poked into Druitt's plot with a bar and tapped on what he found to be an iron coffin. That is unusual, but then so too was Druitt's death. His waterlogged body had to be sent from London to Wimborne for the funeral and it strikes me as perfectly logical that the undertakers would have decided upon a leak-proof metal box.

John Carey summed up the so-called evidence in his Sunday Times review of the crop of books for 1988, one per "official" Ripper murder: "Who actually did the killings remains mysterious. All these books are good at discrediting other people's suspects, but hopeless at promoting their own."

Bill Waddell, the curator of the Black Museum at Scotland Yard, has monitored the endless crop of books on Jack the Ripper and has custody of the surviving police files. His prime suspect – Montague Druitt.

With a major television series starring Michael Caine, the emergence of twentieth century rippers, and the tourist interest in Whitechapel, the great unsolved Victorian crimes have lost none of their fatal attraction with the passage of time. Apart from his notorious letter writing, the Ripper was not a literary figure but in death he is at the centre of a whole publishing industry that puts the academic gloss on ghoulish fascination. Druitt's home, at the north end of Redcotts Lane, Wimborne, has been redeveloped and is now Westfield Court.

WIMBORNE

Le Fleming, father and son: doctor and musician.

Eminent doctor Sir Kaye Le Fleming [1872-1946] of St Margaret's, Rowlands Hill, Wimborne, was the chairman of the British Medical Association. He was knighted in 1937. A regular contributor to the Lancet and British Medical Journal, he also wrote *An Introduction to General Practice*, and chaired committees that reported on nutrition and physical education. It was to the relief of those who knew him that he did not have to agonise over the painful birth of the National Health Service.

His son Christopher le Fleming [1908-85], who preferred a lower case 'l' in the middle of his name, came under the wing of composer Ralph Vaughan Williams. The result was a succession of choral works, including the *Five Psalms* [1947] and *Valley of Arun* [1962], and songs which drew on poetry of Thomas Hardy, Walter de la Mare and Hillaire Belloc. Christopher had something of his father's talent for organisation, which he threw into educational initiatives with the Composers' Guild of Great Britain, and the equally innovative Rural Music Schools Association.

Journey into Music, his autobiography, was published in 1982. He died at Woodbury, Devon, on 19 June 1985.

WIMBORNE — see PAMPHILL (KINGSTON LACY) for Henry Bankes: *History of Rome*

WIMBORNE ST. GILES
Sir Anthony Ashley: first English sea-charts.

The originator of the Admiralty charts, with which the British would, to quote Tennyson, "sail wherever a ship may sail, and found many a mighty state", was Sir Anthony Ashley [1551-1628] of St Giles's House (Ordnance Survey map reference SU 033 117). He has a magnificent tomb in Wimborne St Giles church.

As Clerk of the Privy Council, he had been shown the first known collection of maritime charts, which were produced in Holland in 1584, and his English versions came out in the Armada year of 1588, replete with tributes to Charles Howard, second Baron Howard of Effingham, for his achievements in smashing the Spanish fleet, and not forgetting Sir Francis Drake for his pre-emptive attack on Cadiz: *The Marriners Mirrour ... of Navigation. First made and set forth in divers exact Sea Charts by that famous Navigator Luke Wagenar of Enchusien, and now fitted with necessarie additions for the use of Englishmen by Anthony Ashley. Heerin also may be understood the exploits lately atchived by the right Honorable L. Admiral of England with her Maties Navie, and some former services done by that worthy knight Sr. Fra. Drake.*

WIMBORNE ST. GILES
John Locke: Shaftesbury's secretary.

The "Shaftesbury Papers" of Anthony Ashley Cooper [1621-83], first Baron Ashley and first Earl of Shaftesbury, of St Giles's House, show the extent to which he had one of the greatest philosophers of the age acting as his secretary, speech adviser, and prompter. John Locke [1632-1704] became his master's voice in 1672, the year Ashley was created Earl of Shaftesbury in April and then, in November, Lord Chancellor of England.

Much of the work, however, would pass through his London residence, Exeter House, and other offices in the capital. They shared intellectual stimulation, as is shown by the list of books Shaftesbury took back with him to St Giles House in 1774, out of which Locke published in 1690 two of the great milestones in the development of libertarian dogma-free thought, *An Essay Concerning Humane Understanding* and *Two Treatises of Civil Government*.

WIMBORNE ST. GILES
Maurice Wheeler: *The Oxford Almanac.*

Almanac compiler Maurice Wheeler [?1648-1727] was born at Wimborne St. Giles. He became rector of St Ebbe's, Oxford, in 1670, and began preparing the statistics and listings for what would be the much celebrated *Oxford Almanac* for 1673.

Wheeler also translated Plutarch, contributing the section "Of Curiosity" to the English printing of the *Moralia* [1684]. The same year he was experimenting with an automatic "domestic timepiece" in what was to be the last century before a clock appeared in most homes.

WIMBORNE ST. GILES
Third Earl: *Inquiry concerning Virtue.*

"A celebrated author" say the largest words, in capitals, on the memorial to Anthony Ashley Cooper [1671-1713], third Earl of Shaftesbury, in Wimborne St. Giles church. He had the philosopher John Locke as his tutor and featured as the "shapeless lump" in John Dryden's satire on the first Earl.

Anthony Ashley Cooper, then Lord Ashley, was elected to Parliament for Poole in 1695 and made his maiden speech in support of prisoners at treason trials being allowed representation by lawyers. He fluffed his words but brilliantly capitalised upon the error: "If I am so confounded by a first speech that I cannot express my thoughts, what must be the condition of a man pleading for his life without assistance."

He wrote a study on ethics entitled an *Inquiry concerning Virtue* in which he coined the phrase "moral sense". This had considerable influence among European writers generally but, says *The Dictionary of National Biography*, his style — "always laboured, often bombastic" — led to the inevitable neglect of his writings, to the extent that his "former vogue has become scarcely intelligible".

WINTERBORNE CAME
William Barnes: much more than a folksy poet.

Second only to Thomas Hardy is Reverend William Barnes [1801-86], English poet, philologist, and clergyman. Master of a Dorchester boys' school, executed woodcuts, D.D. St John's Cambridge [1850]. Author of *Hwomely Rhymes* [1859] and *Poems of Rural Life,* both in Dorset dialect, *Philological Grammar* [1854]; *Outline of English Speechcraft* [1878]. Plus much more . . .

For the visitor there is a surfeit of reminders, including the statue by the porch of St Peter's church in the centre of Dorchester, and Came Rectory a mile out of Dorchester, on the A352 Wareham road (Ordnance Survey map reference SY 709 894).

Here the Dorset poet, William Barnes, spent his last twenty-four years.

The great grief of Barnes's life descended on 21 June 1852: "Oh, day of overwhelming woe! That which I greatly dreaded has come upon me. God has withdrawn from me his choicest worldly gift. Who can measure the greatness, the vastness of my loss? I am undone. Lord, have mercy upon me. My dearest Julia left me at 11.30 in the morning."

For a year his diary entries would be punctuated with the word "Sorrow" or a longer sigh: "Sad for my dearest wife." He wrote verses to her memory. For the remainder of his life he would say a prayer for her each day and write "Giulia" at the end of each diary entry. Thirty-five years later he would still have occasional bouts of sadness about what might have been: "The young that died in beauty."

Former Barnes pupil Sir Frederick Treves describes Came Rectory as "a solitary house by the roadside, as homely as a cottage, but with a garden worthy of a manor".

Today it is unchanged from when Barnes's biographer wrote of "a thatched cottage with wide eaves and wider verandah, on whose rustic pillars roses, clematis and honeysuckle entwine".

Barnes lies under a Celtic cross in the shadow of Winterborne Came church, in the grounds of Came House (Ordnance Survey map reference SY 705 884). His other church was Whitcombe, in the middle of a field on the A352 Wareham road two miles out of Dorchester (Ordnance Survey map reference SY 717 883), surrounded by the grassed mounds and dips of a deserted mediaeval village.

Barnes memorabilia is on display in the Dorset County Museum, next to St Peter's church, Dorchester. His fame currently rests on his Dorset dialect rhymes, particularly *Linden Lea*, which Ralph Vaughan Williams [1872-1958] set to music, but ultimately, the poems of William Barnes will not matter. They were a diversion and plaything that developed into something more serious.

The legacy of his teaching years was *Se Gefylsta: an Anglo-Saxon delectus* [1849], which W.G. Locket would describe in 1893 as "the first practical school primer in the language".

The great and lasting achievement of William Barnes lies in the mountain of ideas that were the most fertile outpourings of the age in philology and linguistics. These, spread evenly through a lifetime's output of a hundred highly original books and papers, amount to the monolith standing above the rest. Barnes never stopped his development of a progressive doctrine of linguistic thought. He discussed words to the last, with Thomas Hardy sitting at his deathbed. From his researches into sixty of the world's languages he had put together a whole explanation of pattern and origin which, in the words of Willis D. Jacobs, places Barnes "at the forefront of language theorists". The doctrine may fail in some of its details, but overall it still stands.

Jacobs, in a study carried out in the University of New Mexico at Albuquerque, produced *William Barnes Linguist* which is the most stimulating and forceful book to be written on the real passion of Barnes's life.

He particularly praises *An Outline of English Speech-Craft* [1878]: "Few books are more interesting in the Anglo-Saxon tradition, and none more important. All that William Barnes had thought about purity of speech, all he had learned, all he employed came to fruition here. It is a full blossoming. The book can lay just claim to the label 'monumental' ... the climax of Barnes's achievement." Lucy Baxter, Barnes's daughter, described the book as "one of William Barnes's favourite mind children ... He boldly puts away all derived or foreignised words, and substitutes Saxon ones, or words formed by himself from Saxon roots, in their place."

For *A Philological Grammar* of 1854 there is wider acclaim. "His handsome volume is such a contribution to English literature as is not made above once in a generation" the Phonetic Journal commented. Agreed Aneirin Talfan

Davies: "*Philological Grammar* is now acknowledged as a pioneering effort of some importance in the field of comparative grammar. That it was compiled by a man who hardly moved from the quiet Dorset countryside, adds to our admiration for the work."

It is a verdict endorsed by Trevor Hearl in *William Barnes the Schoolmaster*: "If he had written nothing else in his life, students of language would still marvel at its ingenuity as a miraculous piece of scholarship."

Barnes must one day be recognised, even in Dorset, as more than a folksy poet. He published a massive "declared program of purification of word regimes, connections, and neologising based on Anglo-Saxon models and concepts. A goodly number of these have already entered normal usage, without proper credit to Barnes; many more are meritorious."

Much of this disregard comes about because F.J. Furnivall, creator of the Oxford English Dictionary, resented Barnes's prolific coining of words, and ignored him completely. One of the hundreds of Barnes words made it to the news-stands. Bird-lore was on general monthly sale for years, as a mass-circulation international magazine covering ornithology. Its title was one of Barnes's alternative words — introduced by him in a contribution made to the Gentleman's Magazine for June 1830 under his pen-name "Dilettante".

Yet, says the Oxford English Dictionary, the "suggestion was never adopted". How can a word be dismissed as a failure when it travelled the world as the official name of the magazine of the Audubon Society from 1899 to 1940?

The basic Barnes philosophy was simple and logical. The purpose of language is to communicate thought. But the introduction of alien words would not only destroy its theoretical purity but harm its flexibility. Such borrowed words also became socially divisive, and their adoption and use was restricted by barriers of class and wealth.

Barnes felt it was not pride but folly to use a word that others might fail to understand, as it perverted the whole attempt at communication: "It may be said that the borrowed words are understood by well-educated people, which I allow to some extent; but they are critically understood by those only who know the languages from which they are borrowed; and it is no commendation to the English tongue, to say that one must learn three or four others to understand it." Barnes, then, was enlightened and before his time.

His sideways excursion into the Dorset dialect fulfilled two objectives. It proved to him that the roots and purity of the language could be traced better in its conservative backwaters than in the refined speech of the drawing room.

Dialect also enabled Barnes to bring poems about the countryside into the hands of some of those whose language it was — a validity they had then but have since lost. The speech of the deeper country may preserve its accent and inflexions but its word-forms as presented by Barnes are fossils.

It is the fact that the mind of William Barnes went beyond this, into wordwide linguistics, that marks him out as a contributor to modern thought. Mr Barnes is out there and waiting for a scholar to bring him back to earth. A proper analysis of his mountain of work may also explain why he failed as a schoolmaster. For, as Giles Wordsworth has pointed out, "the one reason people in Dorset pay to send their offspring to private schools is to have them taught to speak so that they do not sound as if they have come from Dorset. They would never hand their children over to an expert in dialect!"

WINTERBORNE CAME

Barnes on class: then retreat from Darwinism.

Lectures and writing continued as a diversion for William Barnes the pastor. In the new County Museum in Dorchester he took his educational crusade to the middle classes with a talk on "Light and Heat" which was followed by an exposition of his views on "Gold and Social Wealth". That, to Barnes, was an extrapolation of logic, but to most of his listeners it must have seemed uncomfortably close to what the twentieth century has known as socialism.

It would not be the kind of topic for a lecture in the museum today. As with his Saxons in his own hometown — he had told them that they and their speech were the living legacy of the age of King Alfred — the diversion into economics had to be worked out of his system with a book.

I have only once come across William Barnes's principal work on economics, his 1859 *Views of Labour and Gold*. That was in 1978 at Sotheby's, and I had to pay £104 for it.

Barnes recognises that "cunning and selfishness, and unrighteousness of several kinds, may bring in more ready money than goodness and truth".

His attack on monopoly capitalism may be quaintly expressed but it is nonetheless damning: "The kindness which is done by capital when it affords employment to people from whom, by a monopoly, it has taken their little business, is such as one might do a cock by adorning his head with a plume made of feathers pulled out of his own tail."

Barnes shows that iron is more valuable in real terms than gold, because it can be used to make tools and create wealth. Iron was the substance of Victorian expansionism — and it made an empire — so Barnes is on strong ground when he explains that gold reversed the fortunes of another nation: "Spain is none the more wealthy for the silver and gold she drew from America, and the wealth of England in all kinds of life-gear and handywork might be no less with less bullion than is the store we now hold."

He sees the home and local community as the basis of stability: "For what is England, that she should be dear to me, but that she is the land that owns my county? Why should I love my county, but that it contains the village of my birth? Why should that village be hallowed in my mind, but that it holds the house of my childhood?" Barnes defends the values and class system of the countryside of his birth, saying the squire and his lady can bring social graces and sober influence: "Nay, it is good to expose to the eyes of the poor toilers for the bare animal man, the clean gravel path, the shrub-adorned lawn, the bright windows and the amenities of a good house." What he resents are the new rich.

"But on the other hand the increase of a truly idle class, a class who may do nothing for the bodily man, and cannot work any good to the intellectual one, is a social evil."

Describing those who live off capital investments he reaches into language that one would expect more from Engels than Barnes, warning that "in a community of many richer idlers, care should be taken of the working classes, or else they will become degraded and dangerous".

He points out that "all the necessaries of life consumed by the idle are produced by the labours of the workers". Detailed figures from Dorset census returns are analysed to calculate, after four pages of complicated mathematics, that in the countryside there should be a labourer's cottage for every 130 acres of land.

William Barnes then urges drastic reform of the rating system, that was to come about with the Local Government Act at the end of the century. His concern is "that the intentional destruction or unrestrained decay of cottages should not leave dwellings enough on the lands of a parish for the labourer employed on them, but that any of its labourers should be driven into houses in a neighbouring parish, which is burdened with them as soon as they become unproductive from sickness or years, or a lazy depravity of mind, is not fair to the place of their abode . . . it is an evil for which, as our poor law now stands, it is hard to find a remedy.

"The best may be a national, or county, or district rating, instead of a parochial one."

Another improvement in the quality of life, urged by Barnes, is now universally accepted and expected. He demanded the basic right to a weekly rest, and on economic as well as compassionate grounds: "For the health of our bodies and minds it is to be feared that some classes of Englishmen are overworked, and a weekly half-holiday would be a boon for the health and happiness of a degenerating class of labourers, and we believe no less an one to others. If there be such a thing as overwork, then it is clear that the man under its effects will be sooner worn out of labour, and in England sooner thrown on the poor's-rate."

Barnes speaks of the dignity that comes from work, not because he believes in exploiting people, but from a simple belief that abilities exist in order to be used: "Man gains swiftness of foot by running, strength of arms by wielding them, power of body by work, and skill by art."

By 8 January 1857, Barnes had moved far from his old talks about comparative languages and was at the Corfe Castle Mutual Improvement Society, in the British School Room in the village, to deliver "A Lecture on the Atmosphere". In it he explained the "Composition of the Air, Its Elasticity, Weight, and Offices, Rain-Bearing, Trade Winds, Land, and Sea Breezes, Mechanical Action, Breathing, &c. &c.''.

Then the schoolmaster-pastor came up against the immovable obstacle of his own maxim: "Logic is the right use of exact reasoning."

That logic, in the minds of thinking people, was now playing a new tune at the hands of Charles Darwin and science and religion were in open conflict. The publication by Charles Darwin and Alfred Russel Wallace of their joint paper *On the Tendency of Species to form Varieties* [1858] was followed by the much more widely circulated great green tome by Darwin alone, *On the Origin of Species by means of Natural Selection* [1859].

William Barnes could no longer reconcile the serving of two masters. Science was winning but his loyalty was to the cloth. The arguments he had once used, back in 1849, in defence of the Biblical account of the creation, were now yesterday's logic. Previously Barnes had absorbed new knowledge and discoveries into his lectures but now they came as irreconcilable broadsides against all he had accepted as faith. He no longer had the answers.

Barnes the lecturer packed away his scientific instruments and retreated from the frontiers of solar and natural history into cosy talks on colour, form, law, scripture and obscure metaphysics. Barnes the schoolmaster, ever more mystifying to his pupils, was also a person of the past and the Academy closed in 1862.

WINTERBORNE CAME
Francis Kilvert's visit.

Rev Francis Kilvert [1840-79], the curate at Clyro, Radnorshire, visited Dorchester on 30 April 1874 and walked with Rev Henry Moule to visit William Barnes — "the great idyllic Poet of England" — at Came Rectory. This, with the exception of the chalky road, was much as it is now:

"The house lies a little back from the glaring white high road and stands on a lawn fringed with trees. It is thatched and a thatched verandah runs along its front. The thatched roof give the Rectory house the appearance of a large lofty cottage."

Kilvert found his favourite poet to be "a self-taught man, distinguished philologist . . . said to understand seventeen languages".

WINTERBORNE WHITECHURCH
George Turberville: poems from Ivan the Terrible.

"My pen doth praise thee dead, thine graced me living," poet Sir John Harrington wrote of "learned gentleman" George Turberville [?1540-1610] of Winterborne Whitechurch. Turberville was secretary to Thomas Randolph, Queen Elizabeth's ambassador to the court of Ivan the Terrible in Moscow in 1567-68, where he wrote *Poems describing the Places and Manners of the Country and People of Russia*. Some were reprinted in *Tragical Tales* [1587].

Turberville also enjoyed the true sport of kings and compiled *The Booke of Faulconrie, or Hawking* [1575] for "the only delight and pleasure of all noblemen and gentlemen"; he was ever the diplomat and for the second edition a woodcut of James I was substituted for that of Queen Elizabeth.

WINTERBORNE WHITECHURCH and WEYMOUTH (PRESTON)
John Wesley's father: attacked poets' morals.

Samuel Wesley [1662-1735] was born at Winterborne Whitechurch vicarage. He became the rector of Epworth, Lincolnshire, achieved some notoriety in 1716-17 as a result of poltergeist activity, and published a number of elegies and sermons including an attack on the morality of poets.

He would be remembered, however, as the father of the famous Methodist leader, John Wesley [1703-91]. Samuel did not stay long enough to have memories of Whitechurch; his father (another John) was ejected from the vicarage in 1663 for refusing to use the Book of Common Prayer; he had already been imprisoned.

The family moved to Manor Cottage, close to the school on the A353 at Preston, two miles east of Weymouth. They stayed there until the ousted clergyman's death, in 1678, and then moved to London.

WINTERBORNE WHITECHURCH
Mansel-Pleydell: county wildlife lists.

John Clavell Mansel-Pleydell [1817-1902] of Whatcombe House, half a mile up the valley from Winterborne Whitechurch (Ordnance Survey map reference

ST 837 013) set about the publication of the first collected natural history records for the county of Dorset. Plant specimens, including the first recorded piece of the Argentinian cord grass that now covers more than a thousand acres of salt-marsh in Poole Harbour, were collected at the Whatcombe Herbarium.

The Flora of Dorsetshire [1874, expanded 1895] is the starting point for the county lists, together with his 1888 works on *The Birds of Dorsetshire*, *The Mollusca of Dorsetshire*, and *The Fossil Reptiles of Dorsetshire*.

Mansel-Pleydell owned 9,000 acres but was never mean with either hospitality or copies of his books. Many, if not most, were given away to encourage the interest of others. He was president of the Dorset Natural History and Antiquarian Field Club, which evolved into the Dorset Natural History and Archaeological Society, and he contributed to its annual Proceedings which have been published since 1877.

Wolff — for SIR HENRY DRUMMOND WOLFF [1830-1908]
see BOURNEMOUTH (BOSCOMBE)

Woolf — for VIRGINIA STEPHEN [1882-1941], known as VIRGINIA WOOLF
see WEYMOUTH

WOOL (BINDON) — see THORNCOMBE (FÓRDE) for John of Forde: *Song of Songs*

WOOL (BOVINGTON CAMP) — see TURNERS PUDDLE (CLOUDS HILL) for T.E. Lawrence: *Seven Pillars of Wisdom*

Wordsworth — for JOHN WORDSWORTH [1772-1805]
see PORTLAND

Wordsworth — for WILLIAM WORDSWORTH [1770-1850]
see BROADWINDSOR (RACEDOWN) and PORTLAND for *Abergavenny* wreck: claims a Wordsworth, inspires the *Happy Warrior*.

WORTH MATRAVERS

Eric Benfield: *Southern English*.

Benfield is a name associated with Purbeck quarrying, and Eric Benfield served his apprenticeship underground, but he came up to work with words and the local society never forgave him.

Bachelor's Knap [1935] is a novel set in those workings, as is *Saul's Sons* [1938], and both are robust regional writing, with descriptions of the mediaeval craft customs men who "think in stone" mixed with an insight into their private lives.

In *Purbeck Shop* [1940], Benfield moved from documentary fiction into a factual account of mining. He never lost the pride in his trade, describing the cleaving with wedges and the process through to finished sinks, troughs, staddles, curb-stones, steps, hearths, setts for street paving or whatever else was a product still within current demand or human memory when the world last went to war.

Southern English [1942] is an unusual product of that time. It has no sub-title inside but the dust-jacket was given one, perhaps as an afterthought: "Reminiscences of Purbeck country and people." This book, its subjects found, was highly individualistic, both in selection of persons and their portrayal for wider attention. It presents the "Dorset mentality" of real-life characters who have "a little magic" in their lives. Some are hermits, one of whom could count his days of married life on his fingers. "Such things will out" they tend to sigh. Benfield had come through his own "quiet time" when he sat and thought, or just sat, and the resulting reflections lashed at the hypocrisy he saw all around.

It is as dispassionate an appraisal, warts included, as *England Your England*, the essay by George Orwell that analysed the inherent contradictions of our Englishness, and was also the product of those anxious months before the war had turned. Both show the same mistrust for authority.

Those who were branded the scum of the earth when they appeared before Wareham magistrates in the 1930s were now the saviours of the nation. Ditto the irresponsible mothers who used to be condemned for uncontrolled breeding, who were now to be complimented on having such fine sets of sons.

"Workmen out of work" had been seen as the epitome of "moral disintegration" but, Benfield wryly observed, the denouncement usually came from those who themselves enjoyed abundant leisure time:

"Often I have heard women whose sole sum of work was perhaps arranging the flowers in some church, explain that a man was bound to slip downhill unless all his days were occupied with useful labour. Such women should be ignored, as it is not feasible to take them aside and quietly knock them over the head; but there are many men with no first-hand knowledge of what the worker feels, yet who have held and expounded the same ideas."

It is a Hardyesque but also a dangerous added ingredient, a pinch of socialism. Benfield saw his roots in the *Town of Maiden Castle* [1947], "glad to know that I should be entirely at home watching an Iron Age pot simmering amongst the embers in the cosy bottom of a pit in the chalk. Undoubtedly it was a good life for those who could stick it, and we of today are the proof that they could."

Dorset, he wrote in the blurb for the cover of the volume of that title, in the "County Book" series of 1950, "is a county where men appear to have little fear of themselves — a fact which has given rise to easy criticism that some Dorset literature is unreal. Dorset is not shy of being an emotion as well as a charming bit of England."

Benfield's exposition of the "Dorset touch" was out of tune with his host community, and ultimately with himself. He was ostracised as the prophet in his own land though his philosophy was a general offensive against not merely "the Party" but attitudes as a whole — for that reason it was insidious and resented all the more.

I have met several of his contemporaries but none who claimed friendship. The mediaeval craft closed ranks to disown their self-appointed spokesman, and a quarryman told me that although Benfield had been buried at Worth Matravers the body had been sent back from London:

"There was nothing special about him, just that he was different. He wrote about us, but it was in London that he belonged, in that kind of living. He ended up killing himself. He wasn't one of us."

It is fortunately given to few men to see themselves.

WRAXALL

William Lawrence: a problem with Martha.

Lawyer William Lawrence [?1611-81] was born at Wraxall, near Maiden Newton. He was an MP for the Isle of Wight and a vigorous pamphleteer. His publications include arguments for the Duke of Monmouth becoming king and the Protestant case on *The Heavenly Divorce: or, our Saviour divorced from the Church of Rome his Spouse* [1679].

More fun surrounded the attempted publication of *Marriage by the Morall Law of God vindicated against all Ceremonial Laws of Popes and Bishops destructive to Filiation, Aliment, and Succession, and the Government of Familys and Kingdomes* [1680]. Its genesis was a row with his wife, the former Miss Martha Sydenham from Wynford Eagle, whom Lawrence denounced as dishonest. Printing was abandoned amid "disturbances at the press".

Among Lawrence's poetical oddities is his own epitaph, in the church at Lower Wraxall (Ordnance Survey map reference ST 576 008).

Wren – for PERCIVAL CHRISTOPHER WREN [1885-1941]
see BOURNEMOUTH (TALBOT WOODS)

WYNFORD EAGLE

Thomas Sydenham: *Observationes Medicae.*

Dr Thomas Sydenham [1624-89] of Wynford Eagle Manor (Ordnance Survey map reference SY 585 960) was the world's first epidemiologist. His *Methodus Curandi Febres* [1666] was expanded into *Observationes Medicae* [1676] which was favourably reviewed by the influential Philosophical Transactions in London, reprinted in Amsterdam, and spread his fame to doctors across Europe.

Sydenham's work had brought about a new epoch in medical science. His work contained, for the first time, adequate descriptions of chronic bronchitis, influenza, chorea, scarlet fever, measles and hysteria. His account of the gout, from which he had suffered since 1649, would be the best ever written. He noted the periodic and varying occurrences of epidemic diseases, and popularised the cooling method of relieving smallpox, and introduced the use of bark in shivering fevers.

His youth had been traumatic. He enlisted with the Parliamentary army early in the Civil War, in Dorset in 1642, and was wounded and imprisoned at Exeter. Mary Sydenham, the mother of Thomas and a whole household of Cromwellian soldiers at Wynford Eagle, was murdered at their home in July 1644 by a Royalist officer, Major Williams.

The circumstances were not reported but the killing would be avenged in 1645 when Colonel William Sydenham [1615-61], one of Thomas's brothers, received the surrender of the King's army in Dorset from Sir Lewis Dyve. Colonel Sydenham summarily and personally put Major Williams to death.

Young – for ROBERT YOUNG [1811-1908], known as RABIN HILL,
see STURMINSTER NEWTON

Younghusband – for LIEUTENANT-COLONEL SIR FRANCIS YOUNGHUSBAND [1863-1942]
see LYTCHETT MINSTER

Max Gate, Alington Avenue, Dorchester. Thomas Hardy was the only major English novelist to design his own house [1884-85] and he died here [11 January 1928]. It is now owned by the National Trust and the present writer is campaigning for it to become the Hardy museum. When this photograph was taken, Hardy was an octogenarian. See pages 91-92

MAX GATE,
DORCHESTER.

Thomas Hardy at fifty [1890].

Thomas Hardy with Florence Dugdale, staring wistfully into
the North Sea from Aldeburgh beach, Suffolk, on 16 August 1909.
Robert Gittings and Jo Manton also use this poignant picture,
in 'The Second Mrs Hardy' where it is described as being by
'an amateur photographer'. Its composition is superb and our
copy looks even more pensive as a sepia-tone — it would have been nice
to have credited the unknown person behind the camera, who was so
professional in terms of quality. As for the subjects, the Hardys
were staying at Strafford House, Aldeburgh, with rationalist and
pro-evolution theory pundit Edward Clodd [1840-1930]. Later that
day a boatman cut a corner and managed to strand the couple
on a mud bank. Hardy would marry Miss Dugdale at Enfield,
Middlesex, on 10 February 1914. See page 88

Thomas Hardy's study from Max Gate as it has been recreated
in the Dorset County Museum, High West Street, Dorchester.
It is the present writer's aim that it will eventually
return to Max Gate, which is National Trust owned and
should be opened to the public, where it could still be
managed by the Dorset Natural History and Archaeological
Society while freeing space in the museum for more ancient
exhibits. See pages 91-92

Thomas Hardy at about eighty-six [1926].

OPPOSITE
Thomas Hardy at about sixty-seven [1907].

"HIS HEART IN WESSEX"

Eric Kennington [1888-1960] sculpted the bronze of Thomas Hardy that was erected at the top end of The Grove, Dorchester [1931]. He did not please all of Hardy's friends, failing totally with artist Augustus John who called it a 'depressing object'. Being an incorrigible admirer of the female form he had suggested a statue of Tess of the d'Urbervilles instead. Hardy's literary editor, Sydney Cockerell [1867-1962], had pressed for a tall tower beside Hardy's Cottage birthplace at Higher Bockhampton. See page 93

OPPOSITE
'His heart in Wessex' was the contemporary caption for this drawing by Leonard Patten in 1928. St Michael's church, Stinsford, is glimpsed behind the spreading yew. Hardy's relatives were appalled that he was not laid to rest beneath it in the manner that he had wished.
See pages 148-149

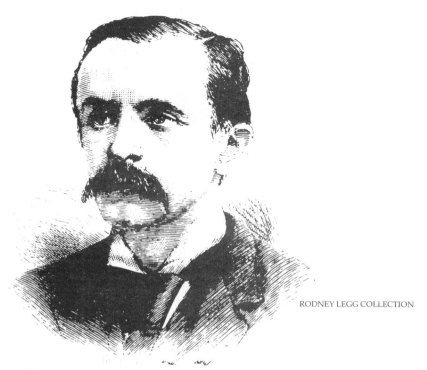

Sir James Barrie [1860-1937] unveiled Thomas Hardy's statue
at Top-o'-Town, Dorchester, in 1931 — to murmurs of disapproval.
Publisher Sir Newman Flower [1879-1964] recalled the reason:
'Barrie began his speech with a piece of futile humour that had
none of the real Barrie in it. He waited for smiles — possibly
for laughs — but he looked over a sea of stony faces. I thanked
God for those stony faces of my own people, for my heart was in
rebellion at humour in this hour.' See pages 93-94

Effigies
Nathanaelis Highmory
in Medicina Doctoris
ætatis suæ 63. ano Dom:1677

A:Blooteling f.

Nathaniel Highmore [1613-85], born and buried at Purse Caundle,
wrote 'Corporis Humani' and discovered and described what is
now known as the 'antrum of Highmore' — an air pocket in the cheek bone.
See pages 132-133

Thomas Hollis [1720-74] of Corscombe was the rich book editor who endowed Harvard Library and named the farms and fields of his Dorset estate for North American places and the catchwords and epithets of libertarian thought. See page 84

OPPOSITE
John Hutchins [1698-1773] of Bradford Peverell and Wareham died twenty days after completing 'The History and Antiquities of the County of Dorset'. The book that he never saw [two volumes, 1774] was expanded by subsequent editors into a rare four volume second edition [1796-1815] and a common third edition [1861-70]. See page 166

Cantle Beslland pinx.   *In. Vellemore Sculp.*

John Hutchins, A. M.

Rector of WAREHAM & SWYRE, & Author of the HIST.Y & ANTIQ.S of Dorset

CECIL
DAY LEWIS
1904-1972
Poet Laureate

Shall I be gone long?
For ever and a day.
To whom there belongs?
Ask the stone to say.
Ask my song.

COLIN GRAHAM

**Poet Laureate Cecil Day Lewis [1904-72] lying in 'Mellstock'
churchyard, to fulfill John Betjeman's prediction that
other literary greats would come to rest among the
Hardy graves beside Stinsford church. See page 149**

Henry Moule [1801-80], vicar of Fordington, Dorchester's artisan quarter, was the champion of its cholera-ridden poor. He was the model for the title character in Thomas Hardy's story 'A Changed Man' [1900] and appeared with wife Mary, as Angel Clare's parents in 'Tess of the d'Urbervilles' [1891]. See pages 87-88

Th. L. Peacock.

**Thomas Love Peacock [1785-1866] was born in Weymouth.
As a sentimental satirist his best known protest was
the comedy 'Nightmare Abbey' [1818] but his contribution
to world history was made at India House from where his
'Memorandum respecting the Application of Steam Navigation'
re-launched the top fleet of the British Empire with 'my
iron chicken' as he called the new ships. See pages 170-171**

John Cowper Powys [1872-1964], who wrote 'not of heroes or even of men, but men beside nature' in the shipwreck scene in his novel 'Weymouth Sands', wanted his ashes cast upon Dorset's cruel sea. That was duly done from the Chesil Beach at Abbotsbury. See page 51

Llewelyn Powys [1884-1939], the Dorset essayist, suffered
constant ill health but that made him all the more appreciative
of life: 'To be alive, only to be alive, may I never forget
the privilege of that.' See page 78

OPPOSITE
Letter from essayist Llewelyn Powys, writing from his
home on the Dorset cliffs, 'Chydyock, East Chaldon, Saturday'
in the early 1930s, to Yeovil librarian Clifford Musgrave.
See page 78

Chydyock
East Chaldon
Saturday

My dear Mr Musgrave,

I thank you for your letter and for the two lovely fragments of glass which we intend presently to have set in the diamond frames of our parlour window of slates. How did you get hold of such treasures? Did you make your way through like a cat burglar at midnight and bring them back in your famous knapsack? You certainly have a gift for seeing gifts — and how excellent your letter is about these fragments.

— I liked very much the quotation from Carlyle and also the cenotaph with the picture of the bewildered lover. I am longing to read the Pearl but we are still very occupied with the small house and its adjustments and are likely to be so for a long time.

Below here discovered by a restless death — yet there is a certain ... I think in losing your life in so immemorial a contest — Everything is in order here & I think we will find it far more harmonious the ... Still None more friendly and ... half suspicion of ...

Yours Llewelyn Powys

Chydyock, the home of Llewelyn Powys, beside a flinty track that winds over the coastal downland from East Chaldon to the chalk cliffs at Bat's Head (often spelt 'Chideock' but not to be confused with Chideock the village). See Page 78

Beth Car was 'the house of the pasture' in the words
of its owner, Francis Theodore Powys who wrote 'Mr Weston's
Good Wine' here in what he called Folly Down. Like much
of chalkland Dorset this field at Chaldon Herring has
since gone under the plough. Village people were portrayed,
according to a contemporary reviewer, as 'queer, blind,
half-dumb, earthy folk, lusting and fumbling in the endless
preoccupation of sex'. See pages 77-78

OPPOSITE
'Llewelyn Powys, 13 August 1884. 2 December 1939.
The living, the living, he shall praise thee.'
Sculptor Elizabeth Muntz [1894-1977] carved the
block of Portland stone and put it above the ashes
of the Dorset essayist, on the windswept downs at
Chaldon Herring, on 3 October 1947. The spot
overlooks Weymouth Bay. See page 78

**Theodore Francis Powys [1875-1953] moved from Chaldon Herring
on the Dorset coast to Mappowder in the Blackmore Vale
when a German invasion seemed imminent in the summer of 1940.
See pages 117 and 118**

The lodge next to the church at Mappowder, in the Blackmore Vale,
was the last home of Theodore Francis Powys, from 1940, and where
he 'went searching for God'. The problem was reconciling
the earthly humanity of his books with the divinity that
co-exists with life. See page 118

Stone pages of an open book in Mappowder churchyard. T.F. Powys
went into the church of Saint Peter and Paul for weekday contemplation
and to ring the bell, but he never attended services: 'In loving
memory of Theodore Francis Powys, at rest 27th November 1953,
aged 77 years. Also of Violet Rosalie, his wife, died 22nd
November 1953, aged 79 years.' See page 118

St Nicholas's churchyard beside the beeches at East Chaldon
missed out on having one of the literary Powys brothers
but makes up for it with lesbian lovers Valentine Ackland
and Sylvia Townsend Warner, David Garnett, author of
'The Sailor's Return', the sculptor Elizabeth Muntz,
who carved Llewelyn Powys's gravestone, and her sister,
'The Golden Warrior' of saga writers, Isabelle Hope Muntz.
See pages 78-80

Sir Walter Raleigh [1552-1618] or 'Ralegh' as he consistently
spelled his name, built the 'New' Sherborne Castle. He was stripped
of his Dorset lands on the death of Queen Elizabeth [1603], on a
charge of conspiring against James I. He was sentenced to death
but lived with his wife and son in the Tower of London, writing his
'Historie of the World' which in elegant Elizabethan prose protested
the Stuart absolutism that was to claim his head. The mariner was
a friend of the poet Spenser, and composed his own poems, but only
about thirty fragments of these survive, including 'Cynthia, the Lady
of the Sea' and 'Methought I saw the Grave where Laura Lay'.
See pages 73-75

TO THE MEMORY OF
PERCY BYSSHE SHELLEY,
POET,
BORN AT FIELD PLACE, IN THE COUNTY OF SUSSEX, AUGUST 4. 1792.
DROWNED BY THE UPSETTING OF HIS BOAT IN THE GULF OF SPEZZIA JULY... 1822;
HIS ASHES ARE INTERRED IN THE PROTESTANT BURIAL GROUND AT ROME.

ALSO TO THE MEMORY OF
MARY WOLLSTONECRAFT SHELLEY, HIS WIFE.
BORN AUGUST 30. 1797, DIED FEBRUARY 1. 1851,
HER REMAINS ARE INTERRED, TOGETHER WITH THOSE OF HER FATHER WILLIAM GODWIN,
AND HER MOTHER MARY WOLLSTONECRAFT GODWIN,
IN THE CHURCHYARD AT BOURNEMOUTH.

"HE HAS OUT-SOARED THE SHADOW OF OUR NIGHT;
ENVY AND CALUMNY, AND HATE AND PAIN,
AND THAT UNREST WHICH MEN MISCALL DELIGHT,
CAN TOUCH HIM NOT AND TORTURE NOT AGAIN;
FROM THE CONTAGION OF THE WORLD'S SLOW STAIN
HE IS SECURE, AND NOW CAN NEVER MOURN

Bournemouth got the poet Shelley's heart but turned down
his spectacular memorial by sculptor Henry Weekes [1807-77]
which went instead to Christchurch Priory. More than
a century later, Bournemouth received from Italy the
Shelley Museum. Neither town had any earthly connection
with the great poet Percy Bysshe Shelley [1792-1822] —
the memorabilia came later, after 1849 when his son
Sir Percy Florence Shelley [1819-89] built Boscombe Manor.
In 1851, Sir Percy did great things to launch the Victorian
new town of Bournemouth with a literary flying start.
He brought, to St Peter's churchyard, Hinton Road, the
exhumed remains of his grandmother, 'Rights of Women'
free-thinker Mary Wollstonecraft Godwin [1759-97], plus
those of his anarchist grandfather William Godwin [1756-1836], author
of 'Caleb Williams', and his mother Mary Wollstonecraft Shelley
[1797-1851], creator of 'Frankenstein', who had just died
in London. See pages 58-60 and 82

Robert Louis Stevenson's grudging acknowledgement for £2.12s.6d
written in Bournemouth on 28 November 1884 with the protest
that Cassell and Company had been discourteous in neglecting
to provide a penny stamp across which he would have signed
to validate a lawful receipt: 'No stamp sent in contradiction
with the habits of all English publishers. R.L.S.'
See page 63

Robert Louis Stevenson [1850-94] lived at Skerryvore,
in Alum Chine Road, Westbourne, Bournemouth, from 1884
until his departure for New York and the Pacific in 1887.
He was one of the first distinguished guests of Thomas
and Emma Hardy at their new Max Gate home in Dorchester [1885].
While at Bournemouth, Stevenson completed 'Kidnapped' and
'The Strange Case of Dr Jekyll and Mr Hyde'. A visit to
Stalbridge produced the setting for 'The Wrecker'.
See pages 63, 92-93 and 144

Skerryvore as the R.L. Stevenson memorial garden at
61 Alum Chine Road, Bournemouth. The house was damaged
by a German bomb on 15 November 1940 and never repaired.
In 1954 its ruins were demolished. Paths and low walls
preserve the floor-plan of the building in an attractive
glade between the houses at the head of Alum Chine.
See page 63

TIMOTHY EDEN

Sydenha

**Dr Thomas Sydenham [1624-89] of Wynford Eagle, near
Maiden Newton, was the world's first epidemiologist.
'Observationes Medicae' [1676] opened a new epoch in medical science
as he gave the first detailed descriptions of several infectious
diseases and noted their periodic occurrences. See page 192**

Sir Frederick Treves [1853-1923] of Dorchester carried out the appendicectomy that delayed the coronation of King Edward VII. The royal surgeon wrote the county's best-loved guidebook, 'Highways and Byways in Dorset' [1906], and the touching story of 'The Elephant Man' which would become a successful film six decades after its author's death. See pages 94-95

Alfred R Wallace

OPPOSITE
Alfred Russel Wallace [1823-1913] of Broadstone was the man who could have been Darwin. For he had been thinking along the same evolutionary lines and it was as their joint paper that the pamphlet 'On the Tendency of Species to form Varieties' appeared in 1858. See pages 125-126

RODNEY LEGG COLLECTION

Browne Willis [1689-1760] of Blandford St Mary used his inheritance to produce 'Notitia Parliamentaria' [1715] and to act as a benefactor, informant and catalyst for other local historians — notably, in Dorset, John Hutchins of Wareham. See page 57

OPPOSITE
The Old Orchard at Broadstone. The villa was built by Alfred Russel Wallace in 1902. He had lived at Parkstone since 1889 and had been visited by the distinguished French geographer Elisée Reclus, the pair of them spending the afternoon discussing anarchism. The move to Broadstone was forced upon Wallace by the spread of suburbia: 'Building had been going on all around us and what had been open country when we came there had become streets of villas, and in every direction we had to walk a mile or more to get into any open country.' See pages 125-126

The Daily Mirror

THE MORNING JOURNAL WITH THE SECOND LARGEST NET SALE.

No. 1964   Registered at the G. P. O. as a Newspaper   WEDNESDAY, FEBRUARY 16, 1910   One Halfpenny

HOW THE OFFICERS OF H.M.S. DREADNOUGHT WERE HOAXED: PHOTOGRAPH OF THE "ABYSSINIAN PRINCES" WHO HAVE MADE ALL ENGLAND LAUGH.

Virginia Stephen, better known as Virginia Woolf [1882-1941] successfully passing herself off as Prince Sanganya (left) of the Abyssinian royal family, for a state visit to HMS Dreadnought, flagship of Admiral Sir William May and the Royal Navy's Home Fleet, on 10 February 1910. Her other Dorset connections were several holidays at Studland and an eminent father, Sir Leslie Stephen [1832-1904] who had skilfully edited Thomas Hardy's novel 'Far from the Madding Crowd' for serialisation in the Cornhill Magazine. Virginia discussed literary matters with Hardy at Max Gate on 25 July 1926. See pages 172 to 178